I, CYBORG

I, Cyborg

Professor Kevin Warwick

First published by Century in 2002

Copyright © Kevin Warwick 2002

Kevin Warwick has asserted his right under the Copyright,
Designs and Patents Act, 1988, to be identified as the author of this work

First published in the United Kingdom in 2002 by
Century, 20 Vauxhall Bridge Road, London SW1V 2SA

Random House Australia (Pty) Limited
20 Alfred Street, Milsons Point, Sydney,
New South Wales 2061, Australia

Random House New Zealand Limited
18 Poland Road, Glenfield
Auckland 10, New Zealand

Random House South Africa (Pty) Limited
Endulini, 5A Jubilee Road,
Parktown 2193, South Africa

The Random House Group Limited Reg. No. 954009

A CIP catalogue record for this book
is available from the British Library

Papers used by Random House are natural, recyclable
products made from wood grown in sustainable forests.
The manufacturing processes conform to the environmental
regulations of the country of origin.

ISBN 0 7126 6988 4 – hardback

Typeset in Garamond by MATS, Southend-on-Sea, Essex
Printed and bound in Great Britain by
Clays Ltd, St Ives Plc

ACKNOWLEDGEMENTS

MANY PEOPLE AND robots helped me make this book possible. As with any sort of autobiography the first folk who need to be included are one's parents. I would like to thank mine for going to Bournemouth for their Witsun holiday in 1953. Second, I would like to thank the English weather for being so awful as to make them stay in most of the time. As a result I was born nine months later in February 1954.

From my school days I wish to single out Eggy Lay, who showed me how maths could be useful as well as fun. Subsequently Frank O'Farrell deserves a mention for not signing me on, when, as manager of Leicester City Football Club, he had the chance.

In more recent times my agent, Robert Kirby, was brilliant in winning an extortionate deal for me as far as this book is concerned. However, those at Random House who have been lucky enough to land up with it have done fantastically well in turning my vague meanderings into what I hope is a readable bestseller. As such, my gratitude goes to Mark Booth, Anna Cherrett, Cassie Chadderton and Jonathan Sissons in turn.

For the heart of the research work that has made this book possible, I need look no further than the Cybernetics Department at Reading

University. I will never be able to give enough thanks to Iain Goodhew, Mark Gasson and Ben Hutt for their research input, knowledge, criticism and, on many occasions, companionship. Others who deserve a mention are Rak Patel, Justin Gan and Darren Wenn, and several more whose help has been invaluable. Particular faculty members whose input I have much appreciated are Dave Keating, William Harwin, Peter Kyberd and Mark Bishop. However, there is a happy, family atmosphere in the department that makes it a real pleasure to belong to. I think everyone has been helpful in some way, including many of our students.

With regards to the cyborg work, George Boulos and Jacqui Saunders deserve enormous thanks for taking a chance on me with the first implant. In more recent times, Peter Teddy and Amjad Shad at the Radcliffe Infirmary in Oxford provided a brilliant surgical team, while Ali Jamous and Brian Gardner at Stoke Mandeville in Aylesbury helped make the second implant a reality. David Tolkien also contributed much with his advice and support. But above all I wish to express my sincere gratitude to Brian Andrews, as without his joint project leadership, the second implant operation would not have happened. Thanks Brian.

Kate Darby has been particularly helpful in giving me a hand obtaining the financial support necessary for the projects involved, Carole Leppard has been wonderful at organising my working life and Anna Bradbrook has helped throughout with the book. Thanks to all of you. My kids, who are kids no longer, Maddi and James have been their usual supportive selves, I love you both.

But in thanking people for their help with this book, there is one person who stands out well above all others – my wife, Irena. Not only did she listen to initial, way-off-target project ideas ad nauseum, but she cheered me up when it wasn't going well and shared in the wine for the remaining 99.9% of the time. Most of all though, she decided to become part of the cyborg project, and in doing so put her body at medical risk. There is no way I can thank her sufficiently; my undivided love will have to do.

Kevin Warwick
August 2002

PREFACE

THIS BOOK IS all about me.

One problem, when writing about oneself, is that it is extremely difficult to be objective. We tend to think we are in the right even when it is obvious we are in the wrong. When we win, well it was obvious, we were better than the other fellow. When we lose, then there was an obvious mistake, the referee was biased, or, failing that, we may have lost, but how we performed in doing so was in a much better way than the other guy.

When looking at a situation from a human standpoint, it is just as difficult for us all to be objective. If we look at our abilities in comparison with other creatures it can be impossible for us to concede defeat on any point. At length we may concede that some creatures are faster or stronger, but at least we can fall back on the undeniable fact that we are obviously more intelligent than they are.

Unfortunately, since the advent of machine intelligence, even this stalwart reasoning has come into question. When we can clearly witness a computer performing feats that we consider important aspects of intelligence – such as mathematical equations or fact retrieval – and easily outperforming humans in doing so, we try to find some excuse.

We say, well, it's not really an intelligent act. Or, it's not doing it in the right way. Or, it's not conscious like we are. Or, worst of all, it's not conscious at all – how can it be, it's a machine.

What matters is performance. Whether we like it or not, we know that machines can perform aspects of intelligence with a performance that outshines those of humans. The question we can then ask ourselves is, okay, rather than admit defeat, can we join forces? After all, partnerships and alliances are often the most powerful combinations of all. In this instance, can we upgrade the human form, directly linking with technology to become cyborgs?

This is the story of my own attempt to push someway in that direction. Why should I want to do that? What led me to it? Why is it important to me? Most of all though, why do I think it is the most important topic facing the human race at this time? In reading these pages I hope that you will find answers to these questions and more. But please forgive me if you I feel that I am only indicating my own point of view. Although I am writing this as a cyborg, I still suffer from that human frailty of a lack of objectivity, particularly when it is myself in the dock.

Kevin Warwick
August 2002

CHAPTER 1

I WAS BORN human.

This was merely due to the hand of fate acting at a particular place and time. But while fate made me human, it also gave me the power to do something about it. The ability to change myself, to upgrade my human form with the aid of technology. To link my body directly with silicon. To become a cyborg – part human, part machine. This is the extraordinary story of my adventure as the first human entering into a Cyber World; a world which will, most likely, become the next evolutionary step for humankind.

Humans are pretty good at doing one thing – being humans. In our present form as *Homo sapiens* we have been on this planet for around 100,000 years, not a particularly long time in comparison with the Earth or many of its other creatures. One thing is clear: evolution keeps on going and things change. Over time, creatures adapt, becoming more successful and possibly surviving or, on the other hand, dying out. Some may feel that evolution stops here, that humans are as good as it gets. I do not think this way.

When comparing human abilities, and in particular our intelligence, with other creatures on Earth, by and large we come out with a favourable report. As a result, humans have enjoyed a halcyon period of relative dominance, treating many other creatures with contempt. Their lives have been at our disposal. For some creatures, humans merely destroy their habitat, others we keep captive, and the most 'fortunate' we farm, killing them for food, sometimes just for political reasons, or even for fun.

Although humans have, until now, been fairly successful in evolutionary terms, we are restricted in what we can do. We have distinct physical limitations. However, technology has been employed to help us out – to lift heavy loads, to carry out tasks repetitively and accurately, to fly. With only five basic senses at our disposal, we are also very limited in how we sense the world. Again, technology has helped us, providing us with information in the ultraviolet, infrared and X-ray spectra.

But two factors far more important than these directly indicate humankind's restricted capabilities. Firstly, our brains have evolved to perceive and understand the world around us only in terms of three dimensions, suffocating our thinking and severely restricting our beliefs in what is possible and what is not. Meanwhile, technology has the ability to process multi-dimensional data, thereby having the potential to perceive the world in many dimensions. In fact, we have enormous problems attempting to field the plethora of information that technology throws at us. Second – and we have to be honest here – when we compare ourselves with technology, the way humans currently communicate is so poor as to be embarrassing. Human speech is serial, error-prone and an incredibly slow way of communicating with others. Our coding procedures, called languages, severely restrict our intellect, as all our thoughts and ideas have to be transformed into signals that do not always accurately represent the original concept.

But humans *have* brought about a technological world. This is the 'age of machine enlightenment'. Intelligent computers can learn, adapt and think for themselves. They are becoming commonplace. We are not only happy for machines to do many physical things for us, but because they can outperform humans, we are also generally willing for them to undertake our thinking and decision-making. But inevitably, this will lead us into trouble – because technology can think faster and more accurately than we can, questions will soon arise as to who is controlling whom. How can humankind hope to stay in control of a technology that is far more intelligent than ourselves?

Is there an alternative way ahead? Can we conceive of a creature with technological capabilities? Could it be possible for this creature to sense the world in a multitude of ways? Could they understand the world in many dimensions and have physical abilities much greater than any human? How would the world appear when perceived in eight dimensions? Is it possible for us to upgrade humans to take on such characteristics directly? This is what I want to find out.

I believe we will be able to add to the five basic human senses. The possibilities for our brains to receive direct information from infrared and X-ray sensors are being realized. These signals will not come through our normal senses, like Ray Milland in the film *The Man with X-Ray Eyes*, but when received directly, they will allow us to comprehend the world on a broader scale.

Similarly, I believe that we are about to see the biggest change of all. Human communication is on the verge of a complete overhaul. We will shortly make much more use of the technology that can send and receive millions of messages, in parallel, with zero error. We will interface with machines through thought signals. We will become nodes on a techno-network. We will be able to communicate with other humans merely by thinking to each other. Speech, as we know it, may well become obsolete.

How will we achieve this? Quite simply with silicon-chip technology implanted into the human body. One or two very small devices will connect directly with the human nervous system and brain. Electronic signals in silicon will become electro-chemical signals in the human body and vice versa. Ultimately, the connecting devices will be put in place by a swift and simple injection.

Humans will need to be educated in the ways to use this technology, to maximize its efficiency; this is true of any new technology. But in the fullness of time our children's children will look back with wonder at how their ancestors could have been so primitive as to communicate by means of silly little noises called speech.

With our brains linked to technology, we will not need to learn basic mathematics. Why should we when computers can do the job so much better? We will not need to remember anything as computers have much better storage facilities. When we need to recall something, we will merely download the required piece of information. We will even be able to relive memories that we didn't have in the first place.

In this way humans will be able to evolve by harnessing the super-intelligence and extra abilities offered by the machines of the future, by joining with them. All this points to the development of a new techno-human species, known in the science-fiction world as 'cyborgs'.

Of course it doesn't mean everyone has to become a cyborg. If you are happy with your state as a human then so be it, you can remain as you are. But be warned – just as we humans split from our chimpanzee cousins years ago, so cyborgs will split from humans. Those who remain as mere humans are likely to become a sub-species. They will, effectively, be the chimpanzees of the future.

With extra-sensory capabilities, a high-performance means of com-munication and the best of human and machine brains, I know what my choice is. My goal is to become a cyborg.

It is now 1 January 2001 and I am on the threshold of the most incredible scientific project imaginable, one that is sure to change, incalculably, humankind and the future. But the project is also very dangerous, and hence I feel like someone waiting to take a ride on a roller coaster. I am both extremely excited and very scared. If it all goes wrong then I will not be able to finish writing this book myself. I will probably be a mental vegetable.

As I embark upon this adventure, I am not thinking of negatives. As a scientist, I want to find out what is possible and what is not. In the pages that follow you will join me in taking the first amazing steps along the way.

But why should I have a desire to step off the security of the solid cliffs of life into the darkness of the unknown? Is it purely scientific curiosity, or is there something of the explorer in me? It may be that the answer lies somewhere in my childhood. In fact, there seemed to be some clear pointers from the moment I was born.

CHAPTER 2

MY MOTHER IS English, but my father, who died at Christmas 1990, was Welsh. There was much of the frugal spirit about him. He was from Pontllanfraith, the son of a miner, who, like many Welshmen, came to England as a teacher. In his case he was sent to Coventry, where I was born on 9 February 1954.

We lived on Poitiers Road, in a prefab built during the Second World War. Pathways snaked between the prefabs on our road, forming a warren through which I would drive my little red pedal car for what seemed like miles. It was always my aim to investigate new places and see how much further I could travel each day. Sometimes, when it got dark, my mother would come looking for me, worrying that I might be lost, but I never was. I may have been somewhere that I hadn't been before, and may not have known where I was, but I saw that as a positive. I was just somewhere else.

When I was three and a half years old, we moved a few miles down the A45 to a semi-detached house in Ryton-on-Dunsmore, just outside the Coventry boundary. The house was new and my parents' pride and joy. They put all they had into it, so we did have a house, but not much else – not even a television, just a radio. Whenever I wanted to watch *The Lone Ranger* on TV I had to go next door.

Before I started school in Ryton at the age of four and a half, I had a good time, as it was around this age that I fell in love with football. I sometimes played football with my toys including Little Ted, Sandy, a rubber Big Ears and Wilfred, a bendy toy. There were four teams, although different players seemed to appear in several teams and a Kelly Man often made up the numbers. I studiously wrote down all the scores and soon a league table appeared, filled with mathematical intricacies such as addition, subtraction, multiplication and division. I had begun to learn maths because of football, even before I started school.

Once at school I soon began to learn about things other than football. When I was about seven, I had a crush on a girl called Sue Kenney. I had liked her for some time, but didn't know how to break the ice. However, my father had a BSA 70cc Scooterette, and this proved to be the winning ticket. Associated with the Scooterette were a pair of goggles that I used to borrow from time to time to wear when hurtling about on my push-along scooter. On one occasion, while wearing my goggles, I suggested to Sue that she might like to look closely into them to see some strange optical effects that couldn't be seen from a distance. Naturally she came close and looked, and was startled when I kissed her fully on the lips – wow! Despite its success, I can't say that it's a technique that I have ever tried again since.

Our family life was perfectly pleasant until I was eight years old, when my father rapidly developed agoraphobia, the fear of open spaces. At first he had problems getting to the school at which he taught, but very soon he couldn't even step outside the house, and had to take leave of absence from his job. Despite rest and tranquillity, rather than getting better, his fear became much worse. Very soon it was decided that a neural operation should be carried out.

The operation was, potentially, highly dangerous, but fortunately it was a major success. As my father loved to recount, the surgeon drilled a couple of holes in the top of his head through which he was able to snip out quite a few neural connections. In other words, the surgeon cut out some of Dad's brain cells. At first there was no certainty that he would be okay – in fact, he remained in hospital for several months.

However, eventually he came home and his agoraphobia was gone. At first he had a bit of a sharp temper, though not a violent one, but that dissolved before long. During his recuperation period he also developed into quite a respectable snooker player, something he wasn't at all good at before the operation. For some time afterwards I was sure that this meant good snooker players had fewer brain cells than the rest of us.

It was father's illness and subsequent cure that first prompted me to think objectively about how the human brain operates and what exactly our mental processes are all about. I regarded the brain in a physical way rather than in a spiritual way, seeing it as a bunch of cells connected together to operate along the lines of a machine. I likened it to a Lego building, made up of lots of small bricks, and even to the television set, which we now had. Just a few small changes to the workings of a TV set can make it operate in a different way, and this was the case with my father's brain. Perhaps it was that experience, at a relatively early age, that allowed me to think about things in a more analytical, more emotionally distant way than otherwise might have been the case.

When my father came home, a certain semblance of normality began to return, so much so that a couple of years later my parents decided to adopt a baby daughter, named Joanne. From the start, and despite almost ten years difference in age, Joanne, my only sister, and I got on very well.

I attended the school in Ryton until the age of eleven. In my year at school there were only seven others – three boys and four girls. As a result, the school football team contained children ageing from seven to eleven. We used to win some games, but often lost to the bigger schools. I was fiercely competitive, and didn't like losing or being beaten in any way, so playing football against some of these schools was a difficult lesson for me. It taught me that you might not win *all* the time, but it also taught me not to judge by appearances. No matter how tall, smart, strong and confident the other team looks, I realized that it was quite possible to score goals against them – they will certainly have some weak points, and there is always a chance that you will win.

Because the school was relatively small and a wide range of abilities were taught together, it meant that finishing top of the class in a test wasn't anything special for me. In fact, I came to expect it. It wasn't much of an achievement to win a running race. I expected that too. So, by the time I reached my last year at Ryton-on-Dunsmore school I was cocky, confident, brash and very big-headed. I took the eleven-plus examination in English, General Knowledge and Maths, and passed with flying colours, going on to Lawrence Sheriff School, Rugby, in 1965. I felt as if the world should be quaking in its shoes.

Lawrence Sheriff School was quite different from my junior school. It was a boys-only school and we were told that we were the cream of the cream. Everyone had done well at the eleven-plus. Most of the other boys came from bigger schools and all seemed to know each other. But it doesn't take me long to make friends, and I soon mucked in. In some ways the Sheriff was fine – I got on well with the other boys and was very much part of any action going. The problem was that I lived just outside Coventry and had to travel ten miles by bus every day to school. By contrast, my social life, friends and connections were all in Coventry. My father worked (at school again) in Coventry. I had belonged to a Cub group, and now a Scout group, attached to Coventry. I was familiar with Coventry. I even went to church regularly in Coventry.

As far as going to church was concerned, I did not really have a choice as I was dragged along by my parents. Usually we went to the Methodist church in the town centre. At the start of the service I would be in the main hall, and then would head off, with the other children, to Sunday School. I got to know the Bible stories really well, and I suppose at times like Christmas and Easter it was quite a special place to be. But I always seemed to have questions about what I was being taught. How do we know that God exists? and, Do we believe everything in the Bible?

I converged on the belief that Jesus Christ actually existed. He certainly was quite a storyteller, talking in ways that people could understand, and that's not a bad talent to have. He also seems to have been a good person and most of the concepts of morality he raised I agree with wholeheartedly. However, even at the age of eleven I realized that there was only one way that I could ever believe in God, and that was if I had some proof. I never got any. In reality, God seemed to be what people conjured up to fill the gap in their knowledge. Who created

8

the earth? Don't know. Let's say it was God. Who made Mary pregnant? Don't know. It must have been God again. Where did my money go this week? God knows.

But Sunday School had its uses. Girls went to Sunday School. Girls didn't go to Lawrence Sheriff. I think I spent most Sunday mornings smiling and winking at girls. To go further than that was quite difficult. After all, you can't really wear goggles in Sunday School, can you?

Overall, I didn't find my time at Lawrence Sheriff particularly enjoyable. It was an academic grammar school, with a clear emphasis on examination results, and every night we were supposed to do homework in three subjects. But I had a life outside school, so how was I regularly supposed to do homework? Most subjects were presented to us in a very factual way: here it is, learn it, regurgitate it. The general ideology seemed to be: if it was in a book, it was correct. I hated it, particularly science. I wanted to know *why*. I wanted to find out if what I was being told was correct. Some of it I didn't believe, and I switched off very quickly.

But it was really only science that I felt so strongly about. I enjoyed finding out things for myself. I enjoyed watching science programmes on television, and The Royal Institution Christmas Lectures I usually found absolutely enthralling. Unlike at school, you didn't get equations thrown at you. I also enjoyed reading about how scientists had made their discoveries – people like Faraday, Davy and Barnes-Wallace.

I also loved reading adventure books and science fiction. Robert Louis Stevenson's *Dr Jekyll and Mr Hyde* made me think about how you could actually change the way a brain works and an individual's personality, albeit to a lesser extent, in real life. Oscar Wilde's *The Picture of Dorian Grey* had a similar effect on me. Meanwhile, watching the film of Scott's rush to the South Pole spurred me into reading *The Worst Journey in the World* by Apsley Cherry-Gerrard. At the same time I inherited my father's BSA, and gleaned a lot of physics from taking it apart. School physics didn't seem to relate to this at all.

I remember doing a physics experiment in which we heated iron rivets in water, trying to show that they expand. There are hundreds of other experiments you can carry out to show that metal expands, and all of them are a lot more exciting than heating iron rivets in water. I spent most of my time in classes at Lawrence Sheriff messing around, looking out of the window, daydreaming about football and girls.

School just wasn't where I wanted to be, and, by about the age of fourteen, I had totally lost interest. I felt that life was passing me by. I wanted to get on with other things. I wanted long hair, which, in the 1960s, was very much the fashion, while my parents wanted me to look like something from a 1930s film, with short back and sides and a generous dollop of Brylcream. At school I was generally getting up to everything I shouldn't, so much so that my parents were called in at the end of my third year. They were told that I was a nice enough person, and that, possibly, I had ability, but if I didn't pull my socks up then the writing was on the wall. My socks stayed down.

In the school there were four houses, each with a different coloured tie. Each pupil was responsible to the prefects in his house, and we were often roped into doing all sorts of things, such as sporting events, to earn our house points. I therefore purchased a range of house ties from the Lost Property office at one old penny a shot and, by a judicious choice of tie at the right moment, I was able to avoid much volunteering and numerous detentions.

One thing I found completely abhorrent about school was the plethora of stupid rules. See what you think of this actual selection:

Ballpoint pens are not allowed

At the weekend if any article of school uniform is worn, then the whole uniform must be worn

Each boy should spend not less than two hours each evening on homework

No boy should be out after dark

Parents should not take their sons or allow them to go to the cinema during the week in term time

And so the list went on. By the end of my fourth year I was really rebelling. I started wearing brown shoes, instead of regulation black, and red socks instead of the regulation grey. I used only a ballpoint pen, was constantly chewing gum, and went frequently to the cinema. At school I could only play rugby, so I started playing soccer with the Rowan

Athletic team in Coventry at the weekend. Because the rules did not permit me to take a bicycle to school, as soon as I was sixteen I purchased a motorcycle.

But I always had my dreams. Watching TV programmes such as *Dr Who and the Daleks* made me think about what might be possible with machine-like creatures, robots even, in the future. It appeared to be an extremely exciting area of science that had not yet opened up. My father's operation and then other things such as *Dr Jekyll and Mr Hyde* made me think more about how brains work and what the brain of a Dalek might be like. On TV the Daleks had a different set of values. Well of course they did, I felt, their brains were different from those of humans.

I was always certain that I would achieve something in my life. At the time my ambitions mixed the pioneering single-mindedness of Scott of the Antarctic, who gave his life for what he believed in, with a little bit of Dr Jekyll, who experimented on himself, a sprinkling of Christian Barnard, who carried out the first heart transplant, and my own love of, and respect for, machines. I felt that science presented a challenge, and it was clear to me that actually achieving a significant scientific advance was the direction in which I wanted to head. Unfortunately, how I would get there was not so easy to envisage, particularly in the short term.

At the age of fifteen or sixteen, one major problem I was experiencing was a lack of money. To go to the cinema, to watch a football match (Coventry were by this time in the top division), to buy a motorcycle, to play football: they all needed money. I therefore took up a regular collection for cancer research around Ryton. Ten per cent of the income went to the collector (me), the remainder was passed on. I extended the round and made quite a lot of money for myself. It did mean, however, that, contrary to school rules, I was out after dark. I also worked doing odd jobs in a butcher's shop.

At the age of sixteen, apart from having to go to school, life wasn't too bad. I was bringing in a reasonable income. I had wheels and could quickly flick in and out of Coventry, or often go down to Bournemouth on my BSA. I started to get into pop music and bought quite a variety of records, from Dave Dee, Dozy, Beaky, Mick and Tich, to the Jimi Hendrix Experience; from Edison Lighthouse to the Tremeloes.

Although I had some good friends at school, my best friend by far at this time was Derek Chant, who lived in Coventry. We would meet up on a Friday night and go to places that you shouldn't go to until you're eighteen, and buy drinks you shouldn't buy. Derek and I remained good friends for a long time, and eventually reciprocated as each other's best man. Derek's father used to brew his own beer, and was pretty good at it. Occasionally he would have too much of it lying around, so Derek and I, and a couple of others, would help him get rid of it by locking ourselves in the garage with as many bottles as we could, only to crawl out some time later when the last bottle was empty.

At the weekend, football started to play an ever-increasing role. On Saturdays, I would work at the butcher's shop when I could, but I also enjoyed watching Coventry City or Bournemouth. One Saturday afternoon I was privileged to see a certain George Best turn out, and score, for Manchester United. It is difficult to imagine there ever being a more exciting football player to watch. On Sundays, attending church had given way to a regular commitment to playing football, which I loved.

As a result of all my extra-curricular activities, I had become rather disconnected from school by this time. I therefore decided to leave and get a job. I had a look around at a number of possibilities, but when a friend of my father showed me inside a telephone exchange, it really caught my imagination. He spent a couple of hours describing it all to me and explaining how it worked. I understood all the words he was using, but the sentences he finished up with didn't make sense. It was all extremely complicated. The telephone exchange itself was a mass of switches and noises, and I saw it as a real challenge. I took tests in maths and physics, and got enough marks for the GPO (General Post Office, now British Telecom) to offer me a job as a Trainee Technician Apprentice, starting when I finished school in the summer of 1970.

But before that I had to sit my O-levels. From Easter through to the exams in May and June I did get my act together enough to gain six passes, including maths and English, but nothing in science other than engineering drawing. Looking back, I think I was lucky to get what I did.

On my first day at the GPO I travelled to the Mason Road Depot in Coventry where I began my three-year apprenticeship under Dickie Downs, who installed telephones. First we went to a café, then to his house, then a few shops, and then we installed a phone or two. We followed the same procedure most days. I tried to do as much as possible when it came to putting the phones in, and quickly discovered that I had to overcome my fear of heights when it came to ascending telegraph poles. Although I managed to do that, when I was asked to climb a sixty-foot pole in the centre of Coventry – no way.

My apprenticeship comprised having a go at, and learning about, a variety of technical jobs, from planning and subscriber (telephone) maintenance to exchange maintenance and jointing (digging holes). It was great fun. Every day seemed a little bit different, and I would only be in one job for two or three weeks at the most before moving on to the next one.

Subscriber maintenance was one of the most enjoyable jobs. If someone, whether an individual or a company, reported a fault, then you had to go and fix it. I never knew what to expect. In those days there was something called a party line, which two telephones shared. This needed a common earth – a piece of copper wire at both of the houses – going down from the telephone to earth outside. For the earth connection a metal stake was hammered into the ground, and the wire connected to this. However, the link relied on moisture in the soil, so in hot weather, a party line telephone would sometimes stop working simply because the ground was too dry and the connection had been lost. The technical cure was to pour a bucket of water on to the stake. On one occasion we were called out to one such likely fault straight after a lunchtime session in the pub. The technician I was with at the time relieved himself on the stake before we rang the doorbell. Quite amazingly, the telephone had started working again only moments before.

After two years, I had to select the job in which I wished to settle. My choice was telephone exchange maintenance and I was assigned to

Coventry's central exchange in Little Park Street. The main purpose of the job was to try and stop the switches failing by keeping them well maintained. It also involved tracing calls for emergency purposes as well as trying to trace nuisance calls. If someone had been receiving nuisance calls, their telephone was then connected to the loudspeaker in the exchange. This way, if a nuisance call occurred, we would become aware of it immediately, and be able to trace the call back quickly to find out where it had originated from.

On one occasion nuisance calls were being received by a woman belonging to the oldest profession of all. The colourful discussions that emanated from the loudspeaker at that time made me realize just how limited my education had been. As a young boy I had naively felt that Smarties were merely chocolate sweets for children to eat. I discovered, in one phone call in particular, that in fact they have a variety of uses.

Although the job was a Monday to Friday one, there was, from time to time, the possibility of Saturday morning overtime. In particular, this opportunity arose when there were more than the usual number of complaints about problems with telephone calls. If complaints occurred earlier in the week they could probably be looked into in our normal working hours, but if Friday saw an increase in complaints then overtime was clearly on the cards. It was surprising how many switches accidentally got knocked out of position on a Friday afternoon. Today when I am making a call on a Friday afternoon and the line suddenly goes dead, I immediately grin and think of someone in the exchange trying his or her best to do some Saturday overtime.

One other trick we had was to patch together ten completely separate telephone conversations, making them into one single connection. Occasionally one of the callers would shout to the others to get off 'their' line, and sometimes an argument would ensue. The most usual case, however, was for nine pairs of callers to remain completely silent while one call continued as though nothing was amiss. When we patched the lines back to their normal state, every conversation of each of the nine pairs would be centred on a discussion about the call they had just been listening to!

When I was eighteen or nineteen, Friday nights became a night on the town with Derek and other friends. Usually we would try to do something different each week, but we did have some rituals. We started frequenting a pretty run-down pub, The Hare and Squirrel, and eventually began a darts team there. Derek and I both became reasonably good players, and although the team didn't win too many matches, we did win some and never lost by much.

I was very much into motorcycles at this time, and wore a leather jacket. The 'uniform' also consisted of a sleeveless denim, which was worn over the top of the leather. On my denim I had a collection of metal badges, and on the back, in silver studs, were the words 'Coventry Kev'. In the jargon of the time, I was a Greaser. I sold my BSA Bantam, and bought a brand new BSA 250 Gold Star, in turn selling that to buy a Triumph 500 Trophy with dual chrome pipes down the side. I loved my bikes, and would often spend Saturday mornings taking my latest bike apart, tuning it up, repairing it and cleaning it, while listening to music at the same time.

My football career never amounted to a great deal. I played fairly regularly, but wasn't interested in training. I was essentially a parks player, but was pretty good at that level. I first got a mention in the local newspaper, the *Coventry Evening Telegraph*, when I scored my third hat trick in three weeks, and then again when I scored eight goals in an 11-2 win. The headline read, 'Highlight of the 11-2 victory was the performance of . . .' yours truly! In fact, at one time I was regularly notching up quite a few goals, so much so that one day someone from Leicester City turned up on our front door step asking if I was interested in a career with them. I was out at the time, so in my absence my father dealt firmly with the situation himself. He told the man that I had a perfectly good job already and that no, I certainly wouldn't be interested in taking up their offer. A short time later a chap called Gary Lineker started knocking in goals for Leicester on a regular basis, and went on to be England's centre forward. You never know, if I had signed up for them . . . My highest level in football actually came a few years later, when I was paid 'expenses' while playing for Moor Green, a team in Birmingham.

My job as an apprentice, and then a technician, with British Telecom was a good one. I thoroughly enjoyed it, learned a lot, and am extremely grateful to them. In the end, I was with BT for a total of six years. I always put in maximum effort, trying to do the best I possibly could, working hard for whatever hours were necessary to achieve my goals. If any of my friends were to ask me what I had done in a week, I was able to hold my head high and give them an answer with which they would be satisfied. It meant that I pushed myself to do more, something I didn't really do at school.

I used some of my spare time to read. One day I read, and was enthralled by, a book called *The Terminal Man*, by Michael Crichton. In it a crazy mass murderer is experimented on by surgeons carrying out pioneering neurosurgery whereby an attempt is made to change his behaviour electronically. Electrodes are inserted into his brain and stimulated to see what reactions occur, the basic idea being that his murderous feelings will be overwhelmed by pleasant ones every time he gets the urge to kill. Unfortunately things go horribly wrong and he begins to experience more and more murderous impulses in order to get high on pleasure. Reading this story made me wonder if, in the future, we would be able to send electronic signals into the brain to stimulate thoughts, feelings and emotions. After all, what is the brain, apart from a lot of cells? It made me think of my father and how a whole set of behaviours in his life were changed by a single operation.

The Terminal Man was an extremely stimulating book for me and looking back, it was one of the key factors in setting my mind to making a link between machine and human thinking. Could I, in the future, actually achieve anything like the events in Crichton's writing? Would there be, as a result, horrible consequences, as happened to Dr Jekyll? Answers to these questions would appear in due course when I actually became a Terminal Man myself, although I didn't know it at the time.

By the time I was nineteen I had not had a really serious relationship with a girl. I didn't regret this though, as I was too busy with other things. Then, one Friday night, a week before my twentieth birthday, everything changed. Our darts opponents didn't show, so we claimed a walkover. Derek, who was then working as a biochemist in Birmingham, and myself headed off to a dance, organized in aid of the local hospitals. It was while I was dancing to Mud's 'Tiger Feet' that I met Sylvia. I think my first words to her were 'Oh well', when asking her to dance. But whatever I said, it worked, and for the rest of the evening we were inseparable.

We met up again one week later on my birthday, although I didn't tell Sylvia about that beforehand. When she asked me when I was going to be twenty, I said I wasn't. So she asked me when I had been twenty, and I said I hadn't. She therefore realized it was my birthday. We went to Rebecca's, a nightclub in Birmingham, and had a great time, and the next week I sent her a Valentine's card. Our romance was instantly serious. Within three weeks I had left home and was living with Sylvia at her parents' house in Small Heath, not far from St Andrew's football ground – the home of Birmingham City. Our whirlwind romance continued, and in September we got married. It was 1974, I was twenty, Sylvia was twenty-one. We bought our own semi-detached house in Cranes Park Road, Sheldon, Birmingham, for the princely sum of £8,500.

Staying with British Telecom, I was able to move my job to Sheldon, where I continued working in telephone exchange maintenance. Sylvia worked as a secretary in the physiotherapy department of East Birmingham Hospital, but she soon transferred across to Marston Green Hospital, which was a lot nearer. I sold my Triumph Trophy and we bought a car. We were very much the happy young couple. We even inherited a crazy female cat that we called Archie Pelago, after Solzhenitsyn's book of a similar name.

During my time working with BT I had continued to study, attending Coventry Technical College to follow a City and Guilds course in Telecommunications and Electronics, which finished in 1974. In my spare time I had also taken further O-levels in sociology, history, additional maths and physics. I now understood physics, having learned it on my own terms, mostly by pulling motorcycles apart and finding out how they worked in practice. So generally, since leaving school, studying had been going very well.

In the summer of 1975, with married bliss very much in the air, I realized I had gone about as far as I was going to go in my job with BT.

Now I understood a lot more about science, I wanted to take things further. I therefore continued with my City and Guilds course, obtaining a Full Technological Certificate, and also signed up to do A-level exams in the summer of 1976. There were three universities near us: Birmingham, Aston and Warwick. Birmingham wanted three A-levels for entry to a degree course, and I felt that with working, football, and so on, that was going to be a bit much. Luckily, both Aston and Warwick offered me a place based on A-level passes in maths and physics. I had a look at both, and picked the BSc Honours course in Electrical and Electronic Engineering at Aston, as it seemed much more up my street. But I still needed to get the results.

As I didn't have the time to enrol for a course, I borrowed a maths book and a physics book from the local library and spent my coffee breaks and some lunchtimes reading and problem-solving. I set myself a rigorous regime to work to, and generally managed to stick to it. Sylvia was very helpful and supportive, and started working towards some subjects herself. While we still went out from time to time for a drink or a meal, studying had become an important element of my spare time.

In June 1976 I took both my City and Guilds Full Tech. Certificate exams and my A-levels in maths and physics. I needed a grade D in both subjects in order to take up my place on the BSc. Overall, the exams didn't go as well as I would have liked. The City and Guilds exams were fine, but I thought I had blown my maths A-level, and had to endure the agonizing wait for my results throughout the following couple of months. First my City and Guilds results arrived – I had passed with Distinction. Then came the A-level results. I was almost too nervous to open the envelope, but when I did, I discovered I had got a C in physics and a D in maths. At the age of twenty-two, I was off to university.

All of this points to an important part of my character. If I want to achieve something, I get on with it and do it myself. I don't look for, or want, handouts or gifts, but I'm happy to do whatever it takes to earn something. I have no airs and graces, no jobs would be beneath me. I feel that things happen when someone gets on with the task in hand. As soon as a committee or working group is formed to discuss an issue, lots of reasons tend to be found as to why things shouldn't happen, and often a compromise situation arises that no one really wants. A good idea can therefore disappear into a committee mulch, a good example of which is the Millennium Dome. So I tend to get on with things, which can upset some people from time to time. Why didn't I ask permission? is something that is often spouted at me.

While we're on the subject of character, I don't suffer fools gladly. I respect someone for what they do and who they are as a person. I don't respect someone because they have a title or a particular qualification. Qualifications open doors for you, but it's what you do when you go through the door that matters. Trevor Bayliss, the clockwork-radio inventor, once said something that I feel holds for me, too. There are those people who like to look down on me and that's up to them. But they shouldn't expect me to be looking back up at them because I won't be. I haven't got time for that sort of thing. I'm too busy getting on with my life.

CHAPTER 3

UNIVERSITY WAS A revelation. I was highly motivated, I wanted to achieve, and I couldn't get enough of it. There was no way I was going to let this opportunity slip through my fingers. I was surprised to find that, like me, quite a few of the students had not come straight from school. The eighteen year olds on my course seemed to be quite naive in comparison – not only with regard to life, but particularly in terms of the subject we were studying, and what it actually meant. Their approach seemed to rely upon what they encountered in textbooks, rather than the ability to relate the subject to the real world. I know it's not everything, but when you've held down a job for six years, been married for two, have a wife, a mortgage and a crazy cat, you're a bit more worldly-wise than the average eighteen year old.

Our car had to go, as did a few of our other possessions, to raise the money to get through university, but financially we weren't too badly off, as I was entitled to a grant from the local education authority and could sign on the dole in the holidays. In my first year Sylvia was working, although when she saw how much fun I was having she decided to go for it too and was successful in her application for a place at Aston, to begin one year later. As well as the grant, having worked for six years for BT paid off when I received an award from them. In addition, we had been able to put by a few savings over the years.

I cruised through my studies at school, but really worked at them at university. This mainly involved answering question sheets full of example problems and writing up laboratory experiments, which in turn got me into reading all around my subject as I wanted to discover what other possibilities existed. It was all a bit new to me, but I quickly became addicted to it, rapidly getting to grips with the subject. It was soon pretty clear that I was one of the top students. I teamed up with a couple of my fellow students, Pete Ulett and Tony Davis, and we would work on problems together, talking about the important issues, which was extremely helpful.

For a while I continued to play soccer with my old pre-university friends at the weekend. My colleagues had given me a good send-off from the telephone exchange when I left, and I had promised to pop back and see them from time to time. Most people say that, and maybe you do go back once or even twice. But, then there are some new faces on the scene who wonder who you are, they've got a job to do, and you've got a different life to lead. So you don't go any more. I stopped playing soccer with my old friends after a while.

In my first year at university we had to take a complementary course of one lecture period every week, a topic quite different from our main subject. I chose space exploration, which included contemplating the possibility of life on other planets. At one point we discussed what to look for when searching for evidence of extraterrestrial life, first considering how we define life on earth, and how beings from another planet would decide that life existed here. Inevitably, the regular, old-hat, biological definitions were churned out – growth, nutrition, irritability, etc. – until I piped up that a telephone exchange met all the criteria we had come up with, and that therefore an alien body could easily believe that telephone exchanges were the main lifeforms on earth, with other smaller parasites (humans) living off them.

This observation didn't go down too well with our lecturer, and certainly didn't meet with an enormous body of support. How stupid could I possibly be to think that aliens would consider a telephone network alive? Yet it confirmed my ideas about how dangerously blinkered people's views can be, and how some need to stick to well-defined, boxed definitions. On earth we have a biological definition of life that has served us reasonably well to include animals, insects and plants. But numerous machines that now exist on earth also exhibit a number, and in some cases all, of the defining characteristics we use. They have even become known as Artificial Life forms. Importantly, such machines may not look or act like animals – they might in fact be a complex network, possibly even a telephone exchange – but back in 1976 such views were considered disruptive. However, I certainly would not claim to be the only person with such thoughts – quite a few science-fiction writers were also developing ideas in this direction at the time, along with a number of senior scientists such as MIT's Marvin Minsky who, in the 1970s, was one of the founding fathers of the whole field of Artificial Intelligence.

Irrespective of what others on the course might have said, the discussion about aliens started focusing my own ideas so they grew from teenage speculation into a scientific treatise. Just how alive and how intelligent could machines be? Could they ever be more intelligent than humans? And if so, what would that mean for humankind? These ideas later culminated in my book on the subject, *In the Mind of the Machine*.

Overall, life at Aston meant a lot of hard work, a lot of studying and thinking, and not much play. Sylvia and I did go to see the occasional film, sometimes went out for a drink, and even had a Chinese takeaway once in a while, but we didn't have much cash, and saw our time at university as something of an investment. We made some good friends from many countries, and it was fascinating to see how students from different cultural backgrounds seemed to have different ideas about work ethics and what they wanted to get out of life. The students from Singapore, for example, had had to find a large sum of money to get as far as university, which they would have to pay back over many years. They viewed the degree course as a disciplined job of work, which they took on full time and were wholly dedicated to, although they ignored lectures for a couple of days when they first saw snow!

When Sylvia started university in 1977, she took a course in

Philosophy and Psychology. Through the discussions we used to have, and reading books I borrowed from her, I became interested in the classics of Descartes, Russell, Pavlov and Piaget. But the one to completely blow my mind was George Berkeley. Look at the person next to you. Now close your eyes and ears, no touching, no sensing at all – how do you know the person is still there? I was blown away by this idea and soon realized that his philosophy applied just as much to machines as it did to humans. Any individual's view and understanding of the world depends completely on how they sense the world and what they sense, and I will be forever grateful to Sylvia for injecting Berkeley into my life.

With the cyborg experiments of 2002, one of the big questions for me was would I, as a cyborg, actually value and perceive the world in a different way? If so, how might that differ from the way a human or a machine, a robot, perceives the world? These questions can actually be traced back to my introduction to Berkeley by Sylvia, and the answers surprised even me.

My three years at Aston went by like a flash. Everything I studied about electrical and electronic engineering was interesting, but I was particularly captivated by telecommunications – which I could relate directly to my time at BT – and control systems, which was a completely new area to me. I was more into the subject-matter and the quest to find out more than doing typical university 'things', such as going to the student bars, gigs, etc. I wanted to go deeper into the issues that I encountered, and ask *why*. I decided to stay on at Aston and do a PhD with Tony Barker, Professor of Control Systems, as long as I got a good enough degree.

I got a First! Over the summer of 1979 I worked as a playgroup leader in Sparkbrook, Birmingham, to earn some money. Working with inner-city kids from all sorts of ethnic backgrounds was great fun but quite a different test from that of university. I became very aware of the racial hatred between different communities, which I hadn't really en-countered before. Some children seemed ostracized by the other children altogether, just because they were different. The kids preferred to belong to and be part of a group, even if that meant going along with the general tide in every way, with no individual thought, and no question. I wondered at the time how this was generally true in life.

I was awarded a grant by the Engineering and Physical Sciences Research Council to undertake a three-year PhD. But then Tony Barker announced he was leaving for Swansea. What was I to do? There was no one else in Aston with whom I was happy to work, so Tony suggested I try Imperial College, London. First of all I contacted Abe Mamdani at Queen Mary in London. Mamdani was into fuzzy logic, which later became very popular, but the lure of Imperial, with its location in South Kensington and fine scientific tradition and reputation, was too great, so, in October 1979, off I went to digs in Chiswick. One weekend I would return to Birmingham for a couple of nights, and the next weekend Sylvia would join me in London.

I was working with a Greek supervisor called Panos Antsaklis, who had done his PhD in the US at Brown University, Rhode Island. He was a fantastic motivator and I quickly got into the whole research ethos of looking for something different – looking for a new angle.

During the week I studied hard in my room at Chiswick. Every Friday we took research lectures and the rest of the week we followed research leads, reading journal articles, and generally getting deeper into the subject. The research being conducted at Imperial College was more theoretically oriented than I was used to, and I had to do a lot of catching up, particularly in pure maths. I was studying computer control, and my research was technically based, but concerned with getting a computer to control all sorts of things, for example, the water level in a tank, the speed of a motor, or even financial systems. The key concept is not so much how the individual components behave, but how the system performs as a whole. The same is true when a human is part of the overall system.

When Sylvia came down to London we would go up to the West End and take in a show or a film. We also enjoyed visiting the museums, and to investigate some of the off-the-beaten-track parts of central London we followed the Jubilee walk, which mapped out a route using silver pavement discs, many of which can still be seen. The history and culture to be found in London was simply astounding, and we decided to move there. We put our Birmingham house up for sale and I found us a room in an Imperial College student house in Queensbury Place, just off the Cromwell Road. After Christmas 1979 we moved down to London, lock, stock and crazy cat. Sylvia had a student room in one of the Aston tower blocks for the remainder of the academic year, until July 1980, so was in London from Thursday night to Monday morning, and in Aston the rest of the time.

It was exciting to have 'Queensbury Place, South Kensington' as my abode. When I was younger, living in Ryton-on-Dunsmore, all the famous London addresses, the names on a Monopoly board, were just as fictional as film stars or sporting heroes, yet here we were, living right amongst them. Not only could we visit the theatre regularly but, with Harrods, Knightsbridge, and Mayfair nearby, the big names of the time would often suddenly appear out of a shop doorway. Sophia Loren was very short, Karl Malden very tall, Susannah York very attractive, and George Best, who we bumped into in Hyde Park, should have been playing football in Scotland at the time! It was in the summer of 1980 that the Iranian embassy siege took place. Only a few streets away at the time, we heard the blast and wondered what it was.

Sylvia graduated from Aston and got a job in London working for a recruitment agency. Renting student accommodation wasn't getting us anywhere financially – in fact we were losing out, so we decided to buy a place of our own. Unfortunately, the price of a Birmingham semi-detached doesn't get you very much in London, and in the early part of 1981, we bought a one-bedroom, ground-floor flat in Devonshire Road, Colliers Wood, SW19.

My PhD research involved looking at different systems, particularly industrial systems in manufacturing and production, and seeing how their characteristics change over time, due to, for example, ageing or modifications. If their performance needs to be tightly controlled, in order to make a profit perhaps, then a computer can continually monitor the system and adapt the control applied, in order to retain the performance even with the changes going on. In this way, the overall system, computer included, tunes itself – it is said to be 'self-tuning'. Essentially, the computer has to learn what the latest characteristics are and to respond automatically accordingly. I realized new ways of achieving this.

The first year of my studies was extremely fruitful. I worked very hard and was fortunate to discover a nice little niche area in the relatively theoretical studies I was doing. During the early part of the summer of 1980 I wrote my first academic paper, mainly while lying on the grass in the gardens of the Natural History Museum. If I needed a break I would stroll around the museum, dinosaurs and all, and then get back to work on the grass.

By September of that year the paper, which was to form a central focus for my PhD thesis, was completed and soon accepted for publication in the *International Journal of Control*, a respected academic journal. The paper, entitled 'Self-Tuning Regulators – A State-Space Approach', appeared in print in May 1981. It was the first time such an approach had been used in this field, and the paper was therefore something of a mini-landmark and was subsequently cited by many authors. It was incredibly exciting to see my name in print for the first time.

My studies continued to progress well, my research was turning up good results, and I was producing more papers that were quickly accepted for publication. Panos Antsaklis moved to Notre Dame University near Chicago, so I transferred to John Westcott who took over. He was a really good supervisor, who steered me rather than pushed me. It was around this time that I took on the supervision of some MSc students and started to co-supervise a junior PhD student, Frank Omani. Research and coming up with new results seemed easy and fun. It still does.

At that point my research was more concerned with computer control systems, now it is very much cyborg experimentation. Nevertheless, the research principles are the same – a good understanding of the present field of play, coupled with some new ideas on profitable lines to investigate. For the cyborg experimentation, which you will read about later, this meant trying things like adding an extra sense to a human, namely me, even though we weren't at all sure what might happen.

In the summer of 1981 we found out Sylvia was pregnant. I was thrilled, but I'm not so sure how Sylvia felt about it. Our marriage had been going through a rocky period, but the baby on the way certainly brought us together. But how could we possibly afford it?

I was not yet two years through my PhD studies, which normally last three years at least, but for many people takes a lot longer. However, I was fortunate in two respects: firstly I already had several papers either published or accepted for publication, and second, John Wescott offered me a Research Assistant position starting on 1 January 1982. I jumped at the chance, particularly as it involved using microprocessors to apply the type of computer controllers I had already been investigating.

In October and November of 1981 I concentrated on writing up my thesis. Having a number of papers already written was useful, as it meant I could sew them into an overall volume for the thesis. Apart from the occasional trip into college to obtain a few final results, or because of some formal event, I spent most of the time writing in our Colliers Wood flat.

In December my thesis was typed up. I had to spend time checking over and correcting my work, as well as getting on with my research, further paper writing, and preparing for my job in January. I submitted a paper for a big conference to be held in Washington in July 1982 with absolutely no idea where I would find the money to enable me to make the trip. To finish my thesis, plus the Washington paper, which had to be sent off by the end of 1981, much of Christmas 1981 was spent in the college, operating the computer while wearing gloves and a scarf because of the lack of heating. I succeeded in completing both, submitting my thesis in just under two years and three months from the start of my research.

March 1982 was very special. At the London Women's Hospital, just by Clapham South tube station, on the morning of the 3rd our daughter, Madeline, was born. Being present at the birth was one of the most wonderful experiences of my life. Not only was I there to help Sylvia through it, but I could also see when the squawking, wriggling, bloody, wrinkled mess that was our daughter appeared. She was, and still is, fantastic, even though she didn't stop squawking for over two years, especially at night.

Two weeks later I had my PhD viva. Derek Atherton from Sussex University was my external examiner. It lasted two hours, went very well, and I was pleased, although it had been very nerve wracking. Afterwards, while the examiners made up their minds, I went back to the laboratory where I was working. I thought they would call me in about ten minutes' time, but no message came. After an hour I went to see what had happened. It transpired that Derek and John Westcott had been talking and Derek had then left. They totally forgot to tell me the result: I had passed.

During the summer of 1982, I felt good. With a daughter, a cat and a one-bedroom flat, Sylvia and I had a family. But the research position I had at Imperial was only for a year, and we wanted some stability. We thought about a move to the US so, with the trip to the Washington conference coming up, I applied to a few American universities to see what would happen. I got offers from Iowa and Carnegie Mellon in Pittsburgh, so decided that when I went to Washington in July I would have a look at them.

My position at Imperial involved writing some computer software to get a microprocessor to control a heating system. The idea was that the controller could adapt itself to different circumstances – for example, if a draught appeared or the power supply changed – so the aim was to keep the overall temperature at exactly the same level. It actually worked. I was to present this aspect of my work at the Washington conference and, for practice, I gave a presentation at Imperial just before I left. After I had finished talking, David Mayne, one of the professors at the time, suggested that I remove a lot of the mathematics from my presentations, something I immediately responded to and have always remembered. I now try to keep equations out of conference presentations altogether. Interestingly, I went to one of David Mayne's presentations a couple of years later, only to find that it was jam-packed with mathematics – but I didn't say anything.

The Washington conference was quite an eye-opener to the games played by academics around the world. Some are fashionable, flavour of the month, and get younger, 'groupie' academics following them around, hanging on every word. Others are working in a field in which no one else is interested, and will give a presentation to maybe three or four people, including the session chairman and other presenters. But their publication appears in the proceedings, which is what matters.

When the time came for my own presentation I was scared I would be asked all sorts of questions I wouldn't be able to answer. However, I think I worried more that not many people would show up to listen. I need not have fretted: the room was full and quite a few of the big names of the time were present. Once I was up there in front of them the adrenaline flowed and I 'performed' my paper well, and the audience even laughed at my jokes! I was asked a couple of straightforward questions that I fielded without a hitch. There was, though, quite a pause at the end of my lecture when the chairman asked 'Any questions?' before the first person spoke. I realized then that it was better to be asked some questions, no matter how difficult, rather than to have no questions at all.

The speaker at the conference dinner was Judith Resnick, one of the first women astronauts. She was about to be launched into space on the shuttle. She was hugely excited about what she was doing and enthused me in the same way that John F. Kennedy had done around twenty years earlier with his challenge of landing a man on the moon. It was only a short time after this that the space shuttle on which Judith was travelling exploded soon after take off. There were no survivors.

Washington is a strange, almost manufactured, city. It was as though it had been specifically laid out as a tourist venue, with numerous monuments and landmarks spaced out with a short drive or a long walk between each one. A visit to the Arlington Cemetery and John F. Kennedy's grave was moving in the extreme. The Lincoln Memorial moved me in a different way: it got me thinking about what freedom of speech and liberty mean, and how important it is that there are opportunities for everyone. I have been a staunch Republican from that moment on. But the most moving thing of all was a visit to the National Aeronautical and Space Museum. In there I saw 'The Spirit of St Louis', the little plane Charles Lindbergh flew single-handedly from New York to Paris. What courage it must take to do something that has never been done before, especially when others have already died trying. I had flown over the Atlantic in a big jumbo jet and watched *On Golden Pond* at the same time (I didn't listen because I couldn't afford to rent the earphones), yet Lindbergh had made the trip in a small metal box.

As for the jobs I had been offered, Iowa City was among the corn fields, miles from anywhere. Pittsburgh was a really exciting town, and I quite liked the idea of the university because of its nice environment and excellent reputation. But the job there was only a one-year appointment and we were looking for something more permanent. So, when I got back to London, Sylvia and I decided I should look for a position in the UK. It didn't take us long to find something suitable.

I was offered a lectureship in the Department of Electrical and Electronic Engineering at the University of Newcastle-upon-Tyne. It was the department that Rowan Atkinson (Mr Bean) had graduated from only a short time before. I didn't know the Tyneside area at all, but it was from there that Sylvia's father had come. In November 1982 we sold our flat in Colliers Wood, loaded up the removal van, and caught the train from King's Cross with an eight-month-old baby and an eight-year-old cat.

We had obtained a university flat in which to start our new life in Newcastle, but on the first night we had booked into the County Hotel for one night's stay, so we could pick up the keys to the flat the next morning. We didn't actually know where the County Hotel was though, and didn't have a map, so when we arrived at Newcastle railway station, we piled all our luggage, our baby, our cat, and ourselves into a taxi and asked to be taken straight to the hotel. It was then that I had my first experience of an irate Geordie who has clearly been pushed beyond his limit. The County Hotel was directly opposite the station. So we took everything out of the taxi again and walked across the road. I didn't take a taxi in Newcastle for several months afterwards just in case it was the same taxi driver and he remembered me.

My research continued to go well. Not only did I expand on my previous theoretical results, arriving at some sound mathematical proofs, but I also successfully applied the controllers on small-scale laboratory prototypes. I soon took on two PhD research students, Mohammed Farsi and Karam Karam. Along with some undergraduate project students we got an active group going and produced some good work on adaptive computer control, controlling a variety of things, from water tanks to motors and even robots. At the same time I started work on an undergraduate textbook, and wrote the first chapter for an edited compilation on self-tuning control. At the end of my first year, although there were eighteen lecturing staff, including professors, I was personally responsible for almost half the department's published output.

After six months we bought a brand-new three-bedroom detached house at Kenton Bank Foot, not far from the Bank Foot metro station. Conveniently, the Metro went right to the centre of Newcastle, and therefore to the university. Bank Foot was also close by Newcastle airport, which was very useful, as I often had to make day trips down to London, either for university research or some committee meeting. Spurred on by my Washington experience, international conference attendance also featured in my schedule.

At the late summer of 1983, before we had lived in Newcastle for a year, Sylvia became pregnant again. Our son, James, was born on St George's day, 23 April 1984, in Gosforth, north Newcastle-upon-Tyne.

At the university, publications flowed and my research flourished. I went on conference trips to a wide variety of places, from San Francisco and Boston, to Athens and Toulouse, as well as many in the UK. Then an opportunity came within a European Community programme called ESPRIT. Myself, Charles Allen, and Costas Goutis, who were also lecturers at the university, put together a proposal which included two German companies – KUKA (a large German robot manufacturer) and Robert Bosch – and a research group in Athens. The project was concerned with getting an industrial robot arm to check visually and select different objects as they came past rapidly on a conveyor belt. We were successful, and the total project was worth more than £4 million over a three-year period. For the university it meant almost two-thirds of a million pounds would appear on the books during that time. Up until then, the department did not have much going in the robotics fields, but suddenly it was a major player. During the contract negotiations I had ensured that a large KUKA robot, worth around £100,000, was to appear in the university. Despite the other partners in the consortium finding all sorts of reasons as to why they should actually receive the robot instead, I got my way, and it duly appeared at Newcastle. The project meant a lot for the research group, which now had an important role, and therefore considerable power, in departmental decisions. My career was therefore going well, but the fruits of my labours were not to be enjoyed in Newcastle.

Although both my research and lecturing at the university were successful, Sylvia and I were not overly enthusiastic about our life there. A lot of the people we knew on Tyneside had their roots and links there and we felt like outsiders. Another problem was that the weather didn't particularly suit us. We were, by that time, soft Southerners, and in Newcastle there always seemed to be a cold wind blowing. Then one day the wind completely blew Maddi off her feet, and that was probably the final straw. I applied for, and got, a three-year research lectureship at Oxford University, my key role being the Engineering tutor at Somerville College, which was still an all-women's college at the time.

Although we had time to prepare for the move, it wasn't easy to sell our house in Newcastle. Although there was nothing wrong with it, the market was so slow that nobody came to view it. At one stage, although all our savings and previous moneys from earlier properties were sunk into the house, we actually thought about just walking away and leaving it to the building society that had lent us the money to buy it. Then we bought a house in Witney, about ten miles from Oxford. It was in the process of being built, so, for my first few months in Oxford, I lived in Somerville College, going up to Newcastle at the weekends. Apart from college porters, I was only the second man to live officially in college, the first being the author Andrew Wilson, whose wife was a college don. I was made to feel very welcome by the principal, Daphne Park, and was assigned the task of getting more female students studying engineering science at Somerville. Up until then they only had one student every three years or so.

I was given an absolutely idyllic room in Somerville in which to tutor students and use as an office. It looked out over a quiet garden and was absolutely perfect for my needs. One of the first things I did was finish the undergraduate textbook I had started writing in Newcastle, and it was soon sent off to the publisher.

Oxford was, and is, full of strange, old traditions. Although I had a BSc degree and PhD, neither was from Oxford or Cambridge. For some reason that probably dates back to the thirteenth century, to teach at Oxford you need to have an MA from either Oxford or Cambridge. As a result, one of the first things that happened on my arrival at Oxford was that I was awarded MA status. However, I wasn't made a Fellow of Somerville College because I was a man, and at that time it was only possible for a woman to hold that position. It has always struck me as strange how European laws involving equal rights seem to completely bypass Oxford University. A key problem that arose as a result of this policy was that to tutor in Somerville I needed to be a Fellow. So, in exceptional circumstances, I was made a Fellow of the Department of Engineering Science – whatever that meant.

Because of the college system, the government pays more per student to Oxford and Cambridge than to any other university. To me, this isn't right at all, especially as it means that there is money slopping around in some parts of the university, some of which seems to be spent on free lunches and dinners for the Fellows, and frequent dinners to which important people are invited, such as politicians and managing directors. In this way it is ensured that the government continues to pay more per student.

However, having my lunch provided in the dining hall at Somerville every day was something I quickly got used to, even if I felt guilty when eating it – my father wouldn't have approved at all. Oxford dinners were also very special, although they have strange rules. In some of the colleges only certain topics of conversation are acceptable – talking about students or politics, for example, is not permitted. In Somerville, like many others, the one person you cannot sit next to is your dinner partner. So, if you go with your spouse to an Oxford dinner, you will be seated as far away as possible from each other. It means you do get to meet people in different disciplines, but you can be poles apart in interests. If you're not someone who gets on well with others you can be left out in the cold, eating your dinner silently. That has never been my problem though. While I found my interests in football and pop music didn't seem to elicit much of a response, my literary preferences for

H.G. Wells and P.G. Wodehouse generally went down very well, particularly on the night I found myself sitting next to H.G. Wells's granddaughter. Sylvia was somewhat shy though, and she did tend to find these evenings quite difficult.

As the GEC Fellow at Oxford, I was very much a free agent, and hence could largely do the research I wanted to do. With Dave Clarke, who had been at Oxford since leaving school, I was able to continue working in computer control and computer systems that adapt. I was also able to work with Mike Brady when he came to Oxford from MIT. With Mike, I was able to push forward with my research into robotics, particularly looking at autonomous mobile robots. We spent some time investigating different possibilities for mobile robots in the military domain, autonomous tanks and the like, especially closely following research being carried out in the US under their DARPA initiative.

As well as seeing my first book in print – *Control Systems: An Introduction* – I edited a number of texts and continued to produce academic papers. In my first full year at Oxford, one seventh of the total published output of the Engineering Science Department was down to me. As we had around one hundred academics and researchers at the time, my one seventh of the total output seemed quite good. Most of my papers were in the 'quality' academic journals as well – the sort of papers that, if you're lucky, four or five other academics might read.

By 1987, Somerville's student intake for Engineering was looking good with four students entering each year. This may not sound much, but it was the upper target we had been aiming for, and very much the sort of figure expected at Oxford where one tutor has four tutees a year. I had realized what I had hoped to achieve. My position at Oxford was, however, only a temporary one, and although I still had one year to go, I started to look for something not only a little more permanent, but that would also be a step up the professional ladder.

I was very fortunate to see a senior lecturer's post advertised at Warwick University. It was in Electrical Power Systems, which wasn't really my subject, but I applied for it and got the job. It was certainly a step up the ladder, and to a good university as well. It meant that we could stay in Witney, although I would have to endure a hundred-mile round trip by car every day. So, in the summer of 1987, we bought ourselves a second-hand Fiat automatic, and I transferred my things from Oxford to Warwick. I don't usually have regrets, but I was sad to leave Oxford. Whatever I think about it, it is a very special, magical place to be, and the two years I spent there, and the people I knew, left me with wonderful memories.

Just as Oxford is steeped in tradition, sentiment and obedient structure, Warwick is, in many ways, the opposite. The general attitude is, if you want to do it then go and do it! As a potential student eleven years earlier, this was the university I had declined in favour of the place at Aston. But the university had come a long way in those eleven years, and so had I.

Power Systems was not my favourite subject at university, yet here I was lecturing in it. Student numbers were not that high, so I spent a bit of time reading in and around the subject and putting together some course notes, as I wanted to liven up the subject and make it a lot more accessible and enjoyable for the students. I must have succeeded because, by the end of the first term, student numbers were well up. In fact, three students were taking the course who weren't supposed to be there at all, simply because they enjoyed the lectures.

But I hadn't been at Warwick for more than about three months when I was told about a professorship soon to be available at Reading University. I sent off for details and discovered that it was in Cybernetics – robotics, systems, control, communications, computers, and even humans – all the things I was interested in. Coupled with this, for sometime now my dream had been to obtain a professorship (a Chair) at a university in the London peripheral belt. Reading University and Cybernetics fitted the bill perfectly. But I was still fairly young and didn't think I had much chance. However, five years after my PhD, I thought it was a good time to judge how far I'd come, and if I got to the interview stage it would be good experience. I therefore applied and was invited for interview.

The interview was in late November 1988. It was cold and I had raging toothache. When I arrived and checked in at the porter's lodge I saw the list of applicants for interview. It was at this point that I decided my chances were slim – at least one was a professor elsewhere already. So, when it came to my turn, I boldly claimed that in five years I would put the Cybernetics Department on the national map, and in ten years it would be an international player. I was bragging, but I did believe I could do it. To put it in perspective, the department had only five other staff, very few students with falling numbers, and it resided in some Clerk of Works huts left over from the Second World War on the far side of the campus. It was on its knees. I got the job.

I now had to tell the officials at Warwick, where I had only just arrived, that I would soon be leaving. I decided to finish one complete year there though, and start at Reading in August 1988. This gave me a bit of time to get ready for the new challenge, but also to put something back into my job at Warwick.

Along with Keith Godfrey at Warwick, I was successful in obtaining one of the US Strategic Defense Initiative (Star Wars) grants that at the time were extremely controversial. Winning the grant meant that Keith could have one researcher with him at Warwick and I could take one with me to Reading. I recruited Paul Fox, who had been an under-graduate at Oxford when I was there. Along with the professorship at Reading, I was also given a Research Fellow position, and recruited one of my former Newcastle PhD students, Karam. So, in the summer of 1988, with Paul and Karam in tow, off I went to take on the challenge of a knackered university department in Reading.

Chapter 4

In August 1988, I not only became Professor of Cybernetics at the University of Reading, I also took on the role of Head of Department, flag waver and hoped-for Messiah. Several other departments at Reading, particularly Engineering and Computer Science, immediately offered to take over the Cybernetics Department. Statistically, in terms of research income, student numbers etc., they wouldn't have been gaining much. In the three-year period before I arrived, the total published output from the department amounted to twenty-one articles. To put this in perspective, my own output just for the previous year had amounted to twenty-four articles. The Cybernetics Department at Reading was a Sleepy Hollow, and effort, they said, had been put into teaching, not research. However, there were few students to teach.

Looking back, it is difficult to realize that the department which now has the eyes of the world looking at it for its cyborg research was, not so long ago, on its knees. In 1988, with the department in this state, suggesting that we might do the 2002 cyborg experiments was beyond my wildest dreams.

But for me, the department was the most wonderful present

imaginable. What research should I do? The decision was entirely up to me. I had a honeymoon period, possibly lasting a year or two, in which to turn things around. That meant bringing in money to do research, bringing in students and, most of all, boosting the morale of the staff and students present. From what I had learned when Mike Brady arrived at Oxford, we also had to relate what we were doing to what was going on in the world outside.

So, with the help of Paul and Karam, the first few months were spent rallying the troops and desperately looking for money to do research. The answer to the latter was found in Brylcream, made just down the road at Maidenhead by the toiletries production wing of Beechams, later to become SmithKline Beechams. I noticed in a local newspaper's jobs section that they were looking for technical help, so I contacted them and asked if we could be of assistance. After some gentle persuasion they said yes, but we needed finance.

For some time, the UK government had been running the Teaching Company Scheme, whereby it puts up some money to get a university to work on a specific project with a company to make them more profitable. Increased profits mean more jobs, more taxes, and hence more money for the Teaching Company Scheme. I had learned about the scheme while at Warwick, where they had brought in enormous amounts of money in this way. With Beechams we went for a small, two-year, £40,000 project, employing one researcher.

Beechams' problem was that after the Brylcream was splurted into a white pot, a seal was automatically put in place so that the Brylcream didn't escape in transit. Sometimes the seal didn't go on correctly, which meant Beechams had to have a person standing by the production line checking for the occasional faulty seal. As the pots flew past at a speed of six per second, it was difficult for a human to spot the faulty ones. They therefore wanted a computer-based system to replace the human. I told them we could build one that, via a camera image, could learn what a perfect seal looked like, and could deal with fifty per second.

As Christmas 1988 approached, I was hoping to hear that we had got the Beechams grant. In fact, not only did we get that, but we were also successful in capturing one worth about £100,000 from National Grid.

That project involved looking into a computer-based system to deal with alarms on the power transmission network, caused by broken cables or lightning strikes. With names like Beechams and National Grid on the books, and the US SDI grant I had brought with me from Warwick, in a few months we had started to motor. Within my first twelve months at Reading I had raised almost half a million pounds in new research grants.

Sylvia and I moved to a four-bedroom house in Reading, not far from the university, and the children had a good-sized bedroom each. Unfortunately, problems were arising in our marriage yet again. We had simply grown incompatible in many ways, and our marriage had become something for the kids rather than for ourselves.

I began to put more time into my university life, and often went out running. During our time at Witney I had run a few half-marathons, my fastest time being a sedate 1 hour 40 minutes. I had even attempted to enter the London Marathon, but without success. However, my third such entry proved fruitful and I was offered a place on the 1989 London Marathon start line. Running long distances doesn't come naturally to me; in fact I found it really tough. But the challenge of doing a marathon was too great and I was of the opinion that if you're going to do one, then it has to be London. It was a fantastic experience, but definitely a one-off for me. It's the one event on the sporting calendar in which just about anyone can take part, and I made it. But never again. My personal best would remain.

In September of 1989 I had an opportunity to visit Czechoslovakia, still behind the Iron Curtain and still one country. In 1981, while in London, I had met Mirek Karny, who worked at a research institute in Prague and was on a visit to Imperial College. In 1988 I met him again at a conference in Oxford, and by 1989 I felt it was about time I paid him a return visit. The British Council was prepared to fund it so, in September, off I went for two weeks.

The group in Prague was a lot more theoretical in its work than what I was used to. It was very useful for me to strengthen the theory underpinning my work and to look at things from first principles. But the trip was destined to change my life in a completely different way.

Early every morning at the institute in Prague they held an aerobics session. I thought it wouldn't be a bad idea for me to join in while I was there, as it would be good exercise. Little did I know that also attending would be an extremely attractive blonde-haired woman, whom I fell for immediately. Her name was Irena. But I was a married man with children, and so did not make contact, other than to pass a message, via Mirek, to say goodbye when I left. After all, the chances of me going back to Prague were pretty slim.

Back in the department I was keen to push forward projects on two fronts. Firstly robotics, particularly autonomous mobile robots. Following my time at Oxford, this was something I had really got into, and there was now an opportunity to get some things underway with the Reading students. Secondly, I wanted to address the area of designing technical aids for people with disabilities. After all, cybernetics is about humans and technology working together.

As a result of the latter, a range of projects was brought to life whereby specific problems were targeted. The first was the design of a walking frame to help people get up and about again after an accident. As the person's muscles grew stronger, so the frame had less and less of an influence, until the person was able to walk out of the frame altogether, Forrest Gump style. Another project that soon got underway was a telephone system for deaf people to use. This was based on sending a simplified sign language over normal telephone links, using a cheap camera input and a standard television output. A third project which quickly followed was the design of a bath that could be used by someone with epilepsy, whereby if the person had a seizure while in the bath, it would automatically empty. This project was sparked when a woman in Reading died having had a seizure in her bath. Our solution was remarkably simple: the person merely had to wear a pair of clear glasses when having a bath, a small discomfort. As soon as the glasses went underwater this sent a signal to a pump to empty the bath within a matter of seconds.

I was very keen to raise the profile of the department and spread the word about the good stuff we were doing. It turned out that my running provided an answer from an unexpected source.

From time to time Jimmy Saville would run the same half-marathon as me, clocking a similar time. After one such event I trundled up to him and asked him two things: would he like to visit the department and see what we were up to, and would he be interested in a Visiting Fellow's position with the department? I was thinking in particular of his own work with the National Spinal Injuries Unit at Stoke Mandeville Hospital, and was delighted when he said yes.

In a very short space of time Jim visited the department and was made an Honorary Visiting Fellow, being presented with a scroll by Ewan Page, the Vice-Chancellor at the time, to commemorate the event. His visit was broadcast on the Meridian TV news, while the presentation appeared on his radio programme, *Saville's Travels*. Before his visit, Pauline, the departmental secretary, had pointed out that on his BBC TV programme, *Jim'll Fix It*, he used to have a mechanical chair, and suggested that I ask him if we could build a new 'robot chair' for the show. He thought it was a great idea, and, along with John Walsh, a researcher, and Mike Hilton, a technician, we set to work to design and build Jim's Magic Chair, which appeared regularly on his programme.

The chair made its debut on the show in 1990. It housed a powerful computer and a robot arm, which gave *Jim'll Fix It* badges to the children who appeared on the show. It was operated by a touch-sensitive flat TV screen, could make tea and coffee, and had all sorts of other doors and openings. It could even speak (via the computer), saying 'Jim has fixed it for you' – which was a synthesized version of the voice of the producer, Roger Ordish.

When a young boy wrote to Jim asking how the robot worked, I went on the programme and talked about robots, showing how a number of different ones operated. In the rehearsal Jim went through the three or four questions he would ask me at the end of my section. I practised my lines thoroughly, only for Jim to ask me completely different questions when we were on air. I immediately learnt the importance of spontaneity on television, but I learnt a lot more than that from Jim. He is a very clever man, who can look at a complex problem and make it look instantly simple. He knows how to manipulate the media and never seems to stop performing. A complete showman.

A short time later, a couple of our students built an electric platform that could be used by a child in a manual wheelchair. Using a joystick, the platform could be driven around by the child, and was put together for use by children at the Avenue School, a special school in Reading. The students and the platform also appeared on *Jim'll Fix It*. It took a lot of hard work to get it ready in time for the programme, but they made it. I actually tried driving it around myself, and found it very difficult. I kept crashing into things. Then one of the children with profound cerebral palsy had a go and was able to drive round perfectly at hair-raising speeds.

In early 1990 I was approached by the Department of Trade and Industry (DTI): they were keen to foster links with the Central European countries now that the dominance of Russia had been stifled. They were aware of my links with Mirek and asked if I would be willing to organize a meeting in Prague to discuss new technology. It sounded like a good idea, so, in May, Mirek and I put on a week-long workshop, that discussed the use of computer control in industry.

I took up the regular morning aerobic exercise once again, and was pleased to see Irena wearing a new outfit. I thought about saying something to her, but my Czech and her English gave us about a five-word joint vocabulary – hello, goodbye, that sort of thing, so I sent a message, via Mirek, inviting her to join me at the reception being held on Wednesday night by the British Ambassador. She said yes.

So Irena and I got together for the first time in the presence of the British Ambassador. It was a formal affair, but it was good that the DTI had gone to so much trouble. After an hour or so a large group of us left and headed off into the centre of Prague for a meal. It became quickly apparent to me that language was not going to be a barrier between Irena and myself, and towards the end of the evening we were able to split away from the rest and go for a romantic walk along the banks of the Vltava river. On Friday night we went out again. We had a wonderful evening and sadly, the next day, I flew back to England.

I wasn't able to visit Prague again until September, four months later. However, during that period, Irena and I grew very close, writing and phoning regularly. She rapidly learned to speak English very well and I slowly learned to speak Czech very badly. I returned in September and November, and it was on the second trip that we realized it simply wouldn't be possible to keep visiting each other and meeting in this way – after all, we were both still married to other people. So, in December, we told our respective partners and families that we wanted to be together.

But Christmas that year presented something more of a shock. On 27th December, Sylvia, Maddi, James and I went up to Ryton to visit my parents. My father seemed in a strange mood, and he took me to one side and tried to tell me what a terrible father he'd been – he was, in fact, a great dad. He'd been taking some tablets to speed up his heart, some to slow it down, and a bagful of others, some to deal with illnesses that hadn't been discovered yet. He felt he took so many tablets that he rattled when he walked, so that day he decided not to take them any more. About an hour later he was rushing around with the kids. Then he decided to move some furniture about. Then he decided to die.

Although I only saw my dad three or four times a year, I felt very close to him and we got on well. You think your parents will always be there, and when he died it was a shock. I'm sure he'd probably decided to 'hand in his dinner plate', as he would have called it, when I was there, so that Mum would be able to cope more easily. It was quite an experience – not a case of one second my dad was alive and the next he was dead, but rather a gradual process over an hour or so.

In February 1991, I moved out of the family home and into a place in Purley that I rented for six months with Paul. Irena was still in Prague at that time. It was terrible being separated from Maddi and James. I missed them desperately and felt dreadful for 'walking out' on them. Maddi and James never said much about it though, they didn't have to. Any time I had with them, any time at all, became extremely precious. Fortunately, Sylvia was good about them staying over with me, so I managed to see them fairly often.

Irena and I got married in August 1991. Maddi and James remained with Sylvia, but visited me fairly often. Petr, Irena's son, stayed with his father in Prague, and Lenka, her daughter, came to live with us. We extended the rent on the house in Purley for another six months as Paul had decided to move on.

Back in the department things were moving on apace. Student numbers continued to increase and the projects continued to roll in. By the summer of 1991 we had several million pounds worth of research going on in the department. That summer we were rehoused in a new building, purpose-built to our specification. It was an exciting time. In September, at the British Association meeting in Plymouth, I made the statement that robot machines would, at some stage, be more intelligent than humans, and therefore they, and not humans, would be making all the decisions. I don't think that folk were ready to hear it at the time.

The year 1991 was also when the first of the Seven Dwarf robots appeared. One of my research students, Mark McGrath, was working on a project to get a camera system to track a ball flying through the air in real time. The idea behind this was to see if a person could throw the ball towards the robot arm, which would then catch it. It wasn't a simple problem, but it wasn't a particularly impossible one either. Mark came up with a very effective tracking procedure, which worked very well, but he was side-tracked from his main research goal on to the Seven Dwarfs project.

Mark produced some little robots on wheels, with ultrasonic sensors – like those of a bat – by which means they could hurtle around at great speed. Initially, they were programmed simply to move forwards until they detected an object and then to move left or right to avoid an object if it appeared. The first versions were extremely dangerous, with open gearboxes that could chew up fingers faster than their wheels could turn. There was also the problem that the switch to turn a robot off was on top of its head. As a person moved to switch them off the robot would sense the person and move away from them, which meant that you had to chase a robot around from behind in order to try and catch it.

It was quickly apparent that the Seven Dwarfs were something quite special. Some of my research income was immediately diverted to their development, and Brian Wickens, who regularly visited schools for the department, set to work on building a number of the robots for demonstration purposes. Television was very interested in these cute little robots too, and so began a string of appearances, particularly on techno and children's programmes. The Seven Dwarf robots also opened up nicely our own research into autonomous mobile robots, which I had first entered into during my time at Oxford with Mike Brady. Many of these projects are described in my book *In the Mind of the Machine*, where the mode of operation of the Seven Dwarf robots is described in much more detail.

My own research interests include neural networks, which is essentially all about trying to build, from the bottom up, machines that act like brains. Standard computers can also be reconfigured to behave in the same sort of way. It's particularly exciting because when you design a machine brain and cause it to operate a robot, so the robot starts to think in its own way. Humans sense the world in a number of ways, through our eyes and ears and so on. Our brain then makes a decision on what has been sensed and we carry out an action – for example, maybe we put up an umbrella because it is raining. A robot senses the world in different ways – ultrasonic sensing is different for a start, as is infrared sensing – its brain makes a decision on what it has sensed and it carries out an action. If it's a robot with wheels, then the wheels will probably move.

Robots with a neural-network brain therefore provide a fantastic research tool that enables us to ask all sorts of questions. How do they sense the world? How does a robot combine information from different sensors? How does a robot think and learn? How does all of this compare with other creatures? What should be made of a particular robot's behaviour? How do they compare to humans and what can we learn with regard to human behaviour?

By 1992, I had several research students working with me in the area of neural networks and several others in robotics. There was a lot of overlap between what they were doing, and it was because of this sort of overlap that the Seven Dwarfs had appeared in the first place. The students were strongly encouraged to mix their research and pick up ideas from the work of their peers. New ideas, particularly very different ones – off the wall, I suppose – were strongly encouraged. The view was, let's try it out, for real, and we'll see.

Nigel Archer developed some robot legs that thought about how they were walking, particularly how gravity was affecting them. Nigel Ball, meanwhile, designed robot organisms within a computer simulation. These robots had attitude, they had to locate food sources by searching around their environment, using energy up as they went. They were essentially Artificial Life creatures. Subsequently, Ebrahim Al-Gallaf developed CybHand, a four-fingered hand with a neural-network brain, which could be taught to hold objects. One thing all of these projects did was allow me to study both physical and mental differences and similarities between humans and machines.

It became clear that just as machines are usually very different from humans in a physical way, so too they are very different mentally. These differences can be extremely important. Just as machines can carry out many physical actions that humans can't, and vice versa, so machines can carry out many mental actions that humans can't, and vice versa. Mankind's position on earth depends on our physical and mental being, particularly the mental aspects. So it seemed important to me that we should thoroughly investigate the capabilities of machines, particularly in terms of how they think, with as little bias as possible.

Over the next few years, research into neural-network learning and robotics went hand in hand with more technical projects to help people with disabilities. The link with Jimmy Saville continued, not only through *Jim'll Fix It* and our Magic Chair, but also through his work at Stoke Mandeville Hospital, and suggestions from him as to which technical developments would be particularly useful for disabled people. Often this might amount to a simple interface between the person and a computer.

Industrial project work also flourished. We worked with the Bank of England Printing Works to use neural networks in an attempt to ensure that bank-note production would be of higher quality. The aim was to make sure the Queen's picture didn't end up with black marks all over it. We also worked with Brooke Bond at Trafford Park, doing a similar sort of thing to ensure that tea-bag production went smoothly. We were essentially exploiting a problem with human operators – namely the ability to think in only three dimensions, as opposed to the computer's ability of potentially dealing with hundreds of dimensions at the same time. In the industrial-production scenario this means that the computer (neural-network) machine operator can make the equipment run to its best performance by balancing lots of pieces of information, lots of measurements, at the same time.

Under the auspices of the Institution of Electrical Engineers, the professional body of which I'm a fellow and through which I'm a Chartered Engineer, we ran a workshop on neural networks at the university. Out of this came an academic book, each chapter written by one of the various presenters of the workshop, and I was fortunate to be one of the editors. It was called *Neural Networks for Systems and Control*, and has been cited many times in academic papers. One year later a collected text appeared on robotics, published by Oxford University Press. This time I was the sole editor. Because publications such as these had been appearing in addition to my journal and conference articles, I found at that time that I already had around two hundred publications. I therefore sent some collected papers to the University of London for my DSc. You get your PhD for writing and defending a thesis on an original piece of work. Several years later, if you have a substantial body of high-quality research that follows on, you can then apply for a higher doctorate, the DSc (Doctor of Science). Because I had done my PhD at Imperial College, part of London University, I was able to apply for my DSc there. It was successful and, as a result, I had to wear a flowing, bright red and yellow gown and a pancake hat at the degree ceremony at the Barbican, London.

Because of my links with Prague, I submitted a completely separate set of my research papers to the Czech Academy of Sciences there. It took quite a while for them to process the paperwork, but in the end I had to defend my research in front of twelve top Czech academics. It was a nerve-racking experience. At the end they popped the champagne corks and we all had a drink, which made it much more enjoyable than the English version. I therefore was duly awarded my second Doctor of Science, this time a DrSc, from Prague, which I collected at an award ceremony in the Karolinium in the centre of Prague, one of the oldest university buildings in the world.

At the 1995 British Association meeting in Newcastle-upon-Tyne, I presented material indicating the distinct possibilities of machines being more intelligent than humans in the future and in ways that really matter. We also had quite a few of our Seven Dwarf robots up at the meeting for the kids to interact and have fun with. The combined effect of a good 'scary' robot story along with visuals provided by the robots was too good for the media to pass up. All the national newspapers ran something on it, with a nice picture, and a story went out on the main BBC news.

The resulting media attention was enormous. *Time* magazine did the first of their features on our work, and *Newsweek* followed close behind. Several other TV programmes did in-depth reports, including a *Newsnight* special with Peter Snow and Krishnan Guru-Murthy. It seemed from that moment on that no one could do a robot-type report on TV, radio or in a newspaper, without referring to our work at Reading. As well as the Seven Dwarfs, CybHand and robot legs, we now had Walter, a six-legged walking robot that had been put together as a student project. Walter made a one-minute cameo appearance on a quality BBC documentary on insects called *Alien Empire*. He didn't put a foot wrong!

I was approached by Peter Tauber, a London agent, to see if I'd be interested in writing a more general, more popular, less academic book on robotics and the possibilities of robots becoming more intelligent than humans. Until then I had only written academic papers and books, and hadn't tried anything in the more popular line. The result was *March of the Machines*, the paperback edition of which was renamed *In the Mind of the Machine*.

In the department our portfolio of robots continued to grow. As Walter started to develop one or two problems, Darren Wenn, a researcher, set out to work on Elma, a new six-legged robot with intelligence distributed around her body rather like a spider. Each leg therefore had its own artificial nervous system. Elma's central brain would say, 'Let's move forwards', and it was then up to the legs to sort themselves out accordingly. Elma was made to be novel, reliable, and to show how she could learn to walk. She was scheduled for completion in March 1997, at the same time as the publication of *March of the Machines*.

But before then we carried out a couple of distinct experiments. In the first of these we set up a link, via the internet, with the State University of New York at Buffalo. Iain Goodhew took one of our Seven Dwarf-style robots out to New York. It had been built in the same way as one that remained in Reading in that it had two key features: first, a radio link between its microprocessor brain and a personal computer, and via that to the internet; and second, it had been set up to learn a particular behaviour set. Essentially both robots were given the goal of moving forwards but not hitting anything. With ultrasonic sensors on their faces they could detect when something was close by to the left, front, or right. They had to learn what to do with their wheels in order to meet the goal, by a process of trial and error.

Because we were trying to achieve robot learning across the internet for the first time, a Reuters correspondent appeared at the university for the experiment. We switched on the robot in Reading, and it proceeded to learn how to move around in the corral we had set up for it. After about four minutes, the robot decided that it was doing well enough to teach the other robot in New York. So via its radio link to the personal computer, and over the internet to New York, and out to the other robot by a radio link, the robot in New York was programmed, by the robot in Reading, to behave in exactly the same way.

We could have got the robot in New York to learn by experience from the robot in Reading, but, partly for the media who were watching, we wanted things to happen quickly. So the robot in New York was firstly hanging around, like robots do in New York, without a method of behaving, until suddenly it was programmed by the robot in Reading, and started to move about. The robot in New York was not programmed by a human, but rather by another robot, across the Atlantic, based on what that robot itself had learnt. The New York robot then performed in its corral in the US, with the habits and tendencies that the robot in Reading had learnt from its own environment in the UK.

This experiment, which was carried out in November 1996, was not only reported by Reuters, but also appeared in the robotics section of the 1999 *Guiness Book of Records*. What is not reported there though is that when we carried out the experiment there were quite a number of newspaper and radio folk at the New York end. When the link was successfully completed, there was much cheering in Reading and the champagne flowed. But the message came back that at the New York end the media were not overly happy with an English robot programming an American robot. We therefore had to power down and do everything in reverse. Switching the power off cleared the brain in both robots, and allowed us to start the experiment up again, this time with the robot in New York doing the learning and subsequently programming the robot in Reading. Very quickly the message came through that the US media were now very happy with things and felt they had a good story.

In hindsight, this experiment was a major milestone in a number of ways. Just as we passed the brain state of a robot, across the internet and down into another robot, I speculated as to what might be possible with humans in this way. Might it be possible to affect the way a human thinks and feels by sending signals across the internet? Our 2002 experiment was to provide results along these lines that no one could have foreseen.

In March 1997, *March of the Machines* appeared and went straight into the Hardback Top 50. A lot of publicity surrounded the book and I spent quite some time doing bookshop presentations to promote it. Just prior to publication it was also serialized by the *Daily Mail*, becoming the first science book that they had ever serialized, which was fantastic, and opened up our work to a whole new audience.

We attended the Robotix event in Glasgow around that time, and it was there that I was approached by Jonathan Renouf, a producer from the BBC's *Tomorrow's World*. He said he was putting together a programme on robots and intelligent machines, and asked me if I would be willing to take part. The programme turned out to be a special in the *Future Fantastic* series hosted by Gillian Anderson of *X-Files* fame. Unfortunately, I didn't get to meet the woman myself, as she did the links and fill-ins after all the other material had been shot. But when the programme was aired, my street-cred with the students went sky-high. Rather than asking me questions about the robots shown in the programme, they only wanted to know what Gillian Anderson was like.

I said that I couldn't tell them much, other than the fact that she snored! The programme included a lot of talking heads from US universities, with me flying the Union Jack for the UK. In the programme Gillian Anderson called me 'Britain's leading prophet of the robot age'. Not bad praise indeed from someone who snores.

That year a Dalek appeared in the department. It was actually put together as a final-year undergraduate project, to wander autonomously around the building and fight fires. It had ultrasonic sensors around it, just like our Seven Dwarf robots, so that it could detect objects and not bump into them. In the eye on top of its head was an infrared sensor through which it could detect strong heat sources such as fires. Instead of an exterminating gun, it had a fire extinguisher.

While the Dalek in its firefighting mode was fun, it was clear that it could quite easily have been made to operate in a different way. Instead of its infrared sensor, it might have had a camera through which it could recognize faces. It could also have had a neural-network brain with which to learn positive and negative associations, on its own terms, with different faces. Instead of the fire extinguisher it could have had a weapon of some kind. With some very slight modifications the Dalek could have become an autonomous robopoliceman or an autonomous fighting machine, with its own values and decision-making.

Examples such as this brought home to me the potentially enormous dangers of autonomous military fighting machines. It was plain to see that we could quite easily build a very nasty piece of machinery if we really wanted to, as all the technology was in place. What then of political and military powers with much more money than ourselves and a possible desire to do just that? A critical factor in this was the capability of a machine, such as our Dalek, to learn and as a result come up with its own set of decisions and values based on what experiences it had had. How could a human possibly reason or bargain with such a creature?

While the Dalek and the Seven Dwarf internet-learning experiment served to show how a machine can learn and hence exhibit its own behaviours, a second distinct experiment was scheduled for 1997. The philosopher George Berkeley pointed that how humans perceive the world depends on how they sense it. The same is true for all creatures.

This experiment, the building of a robot called Rogerr, has been covered in detail in my previous books, but I will recount it here in brief, as it highlights what it means for a robot to sense the world in a different way from humans.

Two students, Ben Norris and Jim Wyatt, took on the task of building the world's first half-marathon robot. We entered it into the Great Sam half-marathon taking place at Bracknell in October 1997, having obtained special permission from the Amateur Athletics Association, and they sent an inspector periodically to check on things. They wanted to be sure that our robot wouldn't injure other (human) runners.

The robot was called Rogerr (Roger Robot) after Roger Bannister who ran the first mile in under four minutes. I also told the Vice-Chancellor at Reading University, Roger Williams, that we had named it after him. Rogerr was a bright-red robot on wheels. I like to think of it as Ferrari red, but in truth it looked like an upside-down Turkish bath.

The students designed an infrared transmitter to fit on a bum bag around my waist. Rogerr then had a couple of infrared receivers fitted on his front face. The idea was that I would run along in front, emitting an infrared signal behind me as I ran, which would be picked up by Rogerr. Rogerr would then track me, its goal being to stay two metres (about six feet) away from me. If I went faster, Rogerr would go faster, and if I went slower, Rogerr would go slower, always staying two metres away. Rogerr also had ultrasonic and touch sensors in order to detect objects, such as other runners, and was designed to do an emergency stop if necessary. In case it was raining for the half-marathon, Rogerr's electronic circuitry was made watertight, and on the remote chance that it was sunny, Rogerr was given a little peaked cap in order to keep out the sun.

The day of the half-marathon arrived and we were very excited. Quite a few TV and radio crews wanted to see what would happen, including a crew from the main Japanese TV network that had been monitoring our progress for some time. It was a beautiful morning, with a very bright sun lying low in the early morning sky.

The sun is a fantastic transmitter of infrared, which is essentially heat. Certainly it was a much more powerful transmitter than the device on my bum bag. But Rogerr behaved perfectly at first, tracking me nicely, staying two metres away. However, when he caught sight of the sun, he hurtled off towards it as fast as he could go, trying to get two metres away from it. He crashed into the kerb, bent his axle, and that was the end of our half-marathon. So instead of achieving the world's first half-marathon run by a robot, we had in fact achieved the world's first robot athletic injury. It did make the main evening news in Japan though, which was really something.

From the Rogerr episode we could clearly learn that robots sense the world in different ways from humans, and make decisions dependent on what they have sensed. In Rogerr's case, he could sense in the infrared and ultrasonic signals, neither of which are senses that humans have.

While we could witness differences in sensing and learning between robots and humans through the projects being carried out, the question had been lingering as to what could be done about it. What might be possible in terms of mixing robot and human capabilities together? This was a line of research which, for me, had been more of a background task until that time. But, in late 1997 and early 1998, it took off in a way I simply could not have imagined.

CHAPTER 5

5 NOVEMBER 1997: Jim's Magic Chair takes pride of place on the Reading University students' bonfire.

Of course, we removed the robot arm, TV screen, computer and lights before putting the chair on the fire. I'm not sure what happened to the Teasmaid, though. The chair had just been taking up space in the department and nobody seemed to want it since *Jim'll Fix It* had been taken off the air. We had telephoned several museums around the country but no one had showed any interest.

7 November 1997: The Discovery Centre at the Science Museum, Bristol, telephone me to ask how much I want from them to buy Jim's Magic Chair for a permanent display.

That's life!

But I'm jumping ahead a bit and I don't want to do that. In September 1997 the annual British Association meeting was held at Leeds University and the organizers asked me to put together a debate on the possibilities for machines to be more intelligent than humans.

Professor Roger Penrose, the British mathematical physicist, had published a couple of books that took a distinctly opposing view to my own, coming to the conclusion that machines will always be subservient to humans – a view with which I profoundly disagree and have argued against in a number of works. Roger said he would take part in the debate, as did Brian Stableford, a science-fiction writer who lived in Reading, and Rabbi Francis Berry from Newcastle. Angela Lamont, a presenter on BBC TV's *It'll Never Work*, whom I first met when she came to the department to film an item for the show, agreed to chair the debate.

In the early afternoon of 11 September, Brian and I drove to Oxford to pick up Roger Penrose. From there we went to Coventry to collect Angela Lamont, and finally on to Leeds, where we met the Rabbi at the railway station. It's not far from the station to the university, so the five of us walked there together, stopping off at Burger King on the way.

Just before the debate we were asked if we'd like coffee or tea. To most people this question would be pretty straightforward, but Roger Penrose answered, 'That's a very interesting question.' He then took quite some time to weigh up the pros and cons of each option before coming to his selection. It was the first time I had seen Godel's theorem and sustained philosophical argument employed to decide on a beverage. It's lucky that they didn't offer him a biscuit as well, otherwise we would have had to call off the debate.

But the evening was absolutely electric. The debate was a stormy one, and we had a thumping good philosophical argument that covered robots, cows, quantum physics and religion. In many ways it turned out to be a microcosm of much of the discussion in my book. We all seemed to agree on a number of points: first, that the exact actions and resultant awareness of a human brain cannot (yet) be exactly simulated by a computer; second, that the actions of a human brain and a computer are somewhat different; third, that human brains are stuck (roughly speaking) with the number of cells and performance that they have now, whereas computer brains, even if they don't have a power advantage yet, will have one before long. But that's just about where our agreement ended, apart from all of us believing intelligence to be a vitally important feature.

Roger and I nearly came to blows on a couple of points. First, he contended that because a computer cannot exactly simulate a human brain it could therefore be expected that computers will always remain subservient to us, no matter how far they advance with respect to speed, capacity and logical design. I felt that was utter balderdash, with no basis in either logic or science, and said that I regarded it as pure Hollywood – simply what we wanted the ending to be. There is no reason whatsoever why computers will remain subservient to humans. Second, he contended that genuine intelligence requires genuine understanding, and as computers cannot genuinely understand, so they cannot be genuinely intelligent. My own argument suggested that when a cow moos to another, a human listener does not genuinely understand what is happening, therefore, by Penrose's own argument, humans are not as genuinely intelligent as cows. Such an argument, I proposed, did not hold water, and was seriously flawed. Clearly I felt that different creatures are intelligent in different ways, which Roger agreed with!

The philosophical discussion continued in earnest in the car back down the M1. By defining my car as our sole form of reference, questions were raised as to my continued existence when I got out of it to fill it up with petrol at Leicester Forest East Services. Despite the minor problem of not existing, I succeeded in not only filling the petrol tank but also paying by credit card. When I got back into the car I was relieved to find that the discussion had moved on, Roger having unearthed a serious flaw in the thinking process that had caused him to plump for tea several hours earlier.

We dropped Angela off and then, at about midnight, said goodnight to Roger. Forty minutes later I said goodbye to Brian and managed to be in bed by one o'clock. It had been one of those evenings.

Soon afterwards I gave a talk on the subject of *March of the Machines* at the Royal Society for Arts (RSA) in London. The chairman for the night was Igor Aleksander, Professor of Neural Systems Engineering at Imperial College, and a hugely important individual in his field. We had started a debate earlier in the year at Robotix 1997 in Glasgow, along with Mark Tilden from California, and I was very pleased that we were able to continue it at the RSA. My own stance is that robot machines, with computers for brains, can be, and indeed are, conscious in their own way – just as a bat or a slug is conscious in its own way – although such consciousness is most likely to be different from that of humans. Igor appears to agree with me in terms of, as he puts it, 'artificial consciousness', although he shies away from claiming that his own computer, MAGNUS, is conscious in any way. He also describes himself as an incurable optimist, in concluding that conscious machines, more intelligent than humans, will always treat humans kindly – something I simply cannot agree with.

Philosophy aside, 1997 was an important time for yet more robots. The Science Museum in London held a special, three-month, exhibition called 'Thinking Machines'. Sponsored by the Engineering and Physical Sciences Research Council (EPSRC), its aim was to show off some of the research that the Council was sponsoring in different universities. One of our own robots was centre stage in the exhibition – in fact, as far as I was concerned, apart from our robot and Igor's colourful neural-network exhibit, nothing else seemed very exciting. A signature-recognition system was found to be broken by the end of day one, and a video on autonomous vehicles had broken by the end of the first week. But Igor's brain kept working, as did our robot.

The robot was the first museum exhibit that we had put together for permanent display. When a member of the public pressed the start button, the little Seven Dwarf-style robot would swan around using its ultrasonic sensors, taking about three minutes to learn how to move forwards without hitting anything. It was doing the same thing as the robots in the *Guinness Book of Records* experiment, described in the previous chapter. After it had learned enough it stopped in its tracks, waiting until someone else pressed the start button, at which point it would spring into life again.

A particular problem that is faced when running a robot continually for a museum exhibit is its power supply. Normal battery packs run out after a few hours and replacing them regularly is not a working option. A novel power supply was therefore designed using the flooring of the robot pen. Here, positive and negative pick-up tracking rails alternate with the flooring. Special ball-bearing contacts on the underside of the robot then ensure that it can receive power at all times.

Before the year was out, we finished helping OXIM, a company in

Oxford, put together a fish-handling robot for Iceland. Handling large cod on the quayside in freezing-cold weather is not the most popular of jobs for humans, but even getting a robot to do it was not easy. The robot had to pick up the cod from a conveyor belt, decide which way up each one was, then place it in a de-heading and de-tailing machine.

I also went to Bogota, Columbia, for a week, with Chandra Kambhampati, a lecturer in the department, Elma the walking robot, and several of the Seven Dwarfs. It was a very busy week. As well as making at least one major presentation every day, we were interviewed for a large article in *La Tiempo*, and for several South American TV channels. Robots certainly help make you media friendly wherever you go.

The end of January 1998 saw me at the World Economic Forum in Davos, Switzerland, an annual meeting attended by a lot of influential and powerful people from around the world. Each year they invite a group of academics to make some presentations on issues felt to be of international importance, and I was there to present my views as explained in *March of the Machines*. The first night there we had dinner with Jeff Bezas and his wife. Jeff had sprung to fame and fortune when he started amazon.com, the online book retailer. It was amazing how many people in Davos wanted to share in his experience.

Irena and I also met up with the Berkeley philosopher John Searle and his wife Dagmar. I instantly warmed to John as a person and, both being of Czech origin, Irena and Dagmar got on very well. On the whole though, my view on philosophers is not that complimentary. I feel that we are all philosophers, and that those who describe themselves as 'a philosopher' simply do not have a day job to go to. However, in John's case I am almost prepared to relax my definition slightly and, as a result, we met each other quite a lot during the week.

In the middle of the week, along with Hugo de Garis (then at the STAR Labs in Belgium, now Professor at Utah State University), John Searle and I took part in a debate about whether or not machines could be conscious. John put forward the view, which I liked very much, that a shoe is not conscious, therefore a machine is not conscious. My own argument was, and is, that consciousness comes with complexity and organization. As far as I was concerned, the analogy John used was similar to saying if a cabbage is not conscious, how can a human be conscious?

But my most cherished memory of John is when he wore his philosopher's hat squarely on his head. Bill Gates was making a presentation towards the end of the week, something that John indicated on several occasions to be the talk he was really looking forward to. Unfortunately when the time came I couldn't go because I had to do a robot presentation about half an hour into Gates's talk.

After we had lunch, John went in to Bill Gates's discourse while I remained next to a table outside, preparing my own presentation. Not more than ten minutes had gone by before John came storming back out of the room. 'What's the matter?' I asked. 'I thought you really wanted to hear Bill Gates talk.' John informed me that rather than give a presentation, Bill Gates had opened up a question and answer session, inviting questions from the audience. Very early on someone had asked Gates what was the secret of his success. Gates had answered that he had always followed one motto, which was 'don't waste time'. John took Gates at his word and left the room immediately.

Another abiding memory I have of Davos is when Irena squarely bumped into Archbishop Desmond Tutu. She was going upstairs as he was going down. Neither of them wanted to give way. In the end it was the Archbishop who lost the battle. Even God has to step aside for a Czech woman!

Two days after returning to England I was at Imperial College, running a discussion involving George Dyson, who had just released a book entitled *Darwin Among the Machines,* and his elder sister, Esther Dyson, whose own book *Release 2.0* had not long been out. George and Esther are the offspring of Freeman Dyson, the mathematical physicist. But while Esther followed a more traditional route, becoming what might be described as a computer guru, George headed off into the Canadian wilderness and became a kayak builder. He then proceeded to observe the world from afar – from the inside of a kayak, presumably.

While my own book indicated the emergence of intelligent machines as an evolutionary step from humans, George's book pointed to symbiosis, a collective. He said, 'In the game of life and evolution, there are three players at the table: human beings, nature, and machines. I am firmly on the side of nature. But nature, I suspect, is on the side of the machines.' Like me, he sees the emergence of an intelligence greater than our (human) own. As he puts it, 'Technology, hailed as the means of bringing nature under the control of our own intelligence, is enabling nature to exercise intelligence over us.'

Surprisingly, the discussion proved to be an important milestone in my own thinking. I had looked to the future with some trepidation; machines more intelligent than humans will appear, and far from those in power – politicians and commercial managers – stopping such an event, it is they who are actually bringing it about in their desire to get one step ahead. We cannot look to politicians for some global treaty against intelligent machines, so what hope is there?

Perhaps George was right – we could go the symbiosis route. Humans and technology could evolve together. If you can't beat them, join them – isn't that the expression?

In fact, to a cybernetician, none of this was particularly new. Andre-Marie Ampere used the word 'cybernetique' in 1843 to describe the operation of an overall human-machine system. As 'Cybernetics', the term was reinvented with a much more technological orientation by Norbert Wiener in 1947. A spluttering of science-fiction books and films, particularly in the 1980s and 1990s, had taken a look at the whole concept of humans and technology merging. *The Terminator*, *Blade Runner* and *Robocop* were very good examples of these films, while William Gibson's book *Neuromancer* presented the idea of a silicon-chip implant enhancing the workings of the human brain (although linking technology to the human brain had in fact been discussed before, in Michael Crichton's *The Terminal Man*). But recently, and most importantly, a number of scientists had been pointing to this as a likely way forward – principally Hans Moravec, Ray Kurzweil and Peter Cochrane.

Apart from using technology to assist those with some sort of medical problem – heart pacemakers, cochlea implants, artificial hips, etc. – nothing seemed to be happening with regard to upgrading humans. Yet with the research we were doing in the department I was bang in the middle of the field – firstly, robot technology, particularly intelligence, and secondly, technical aids for humans. After all, that was what my job was all about. I quickly realized that I was in an excellent position to do something about it myself. Little did I know at that stage just where it would take me.

I suppose what we were really looking at was the actual creation of cyborgs, Cybernetic Organisms. A popular culture had recently grown up in both literature and films looking at the whole issue. Some, such as Steve Mann, and Thad Starner, seemed to feel they were cyborgs merely by wearing special glasses linked to computers, and some definitions clearly allow for this: for example, Chris Butlin defines a cyborg as 'a person whose physical capabilities are extended beyond normal limits by a machine'. In the film *The Terminator*, meanwhile, a cyborg is defined as part-human, part-machine (with reference to Arnold Schwarznegger at the time).

My own definition is that a cyborg is something that is part-animal, part-machine, and whose capabilities are extended beyond normal limits. This is much more general than other definitions and includes creatures other than humans. It allows for mental upgrades as well as physical upgrades and allows the extension to go beyond the normal limits of either the animal or the machine. I can't really see that it includes wearing a wristwatch, a pair of glasses, or riding a bicycle – to me that's a cybernetic system.

In particular I could look with jealousy, as a mere human, on the capabilities of machine intelligence, both in its form in the fairly low-powered microprocessor brains of some of our robots and in its potential future. The key advantages include:

1. Machine intelligence is easily networked.
   The human brain is stand-alone.
2. Computers can process information in hundreds of dimensions.
   Humans can only conceive of space as consisting of three dimensions at most (four if you count time).

3. Computers can sense the world in an enormous variety of ways.
   Human senses are relatively poor – there is a lot that goes on that we never know about.
4. Computers are fast.
   The human brain is slow.
5. Computers have good, long-term memory storage capabilities.
   I can't remember how good human memory is.

And perhaps the two biggest differences of all;

6. Machines can communicate in parallel, over long distances, with little or no error.
   Humans communicate in serial fashion, over short distances, with enormous errors in message passing.
7. Machine brains of the future appear to be unlimited in the number of cells and complexity of connections.
   Human brains will very slowly evolve. In the short term, the number of cells will remain roughly constant.

There are probably many more of these. However, those listed are conclusions drawn from our own research, and gave me a tremendous drive to do something about upgrading myself.

As a starter, in the Cybernetics labs at Reading we had in our possession a relatively small radio-frequency identification device (RFID) in a small glass capsule which, under certain circumstances, might be used as an implant. I contacted the company who made them and they said they were happy to supply as much detail as we needed about the device, along with the technology itself and any technical support we wanted in order to carry out an important trial. However, publicity-wise, their head office in the US did not want to be seen to be associated with anything we did. We therefore had a good start – a possible implantable device about 2.5cm long – not too big.

At the same time a group of researchers in the department, including Grant Foster, Neil Glover and Darren Wenn (Darren originally built

Elma, the walking robot), were working on an intelligent-building project. The same sort of intelligence used in Elma was being employed in the Cybernetics building. Where Elma had six legs, each one of which could look after itself, so the building had various nodes (doors, lights, voice generators), each one of which could look after itself.

In spring 1998, the building was being wired up so that at different points the central computer could detect the presence, at a certain time, of devices such as the radio-frequency identification device (RFID). At various doorways, fairly large coils of wire were neatly tucked away on either side of the doorframe. These induced electrical power into the RFID, an effect discovered by Michael Faraday of the Royal Institution in the early nineteenth century. Electricity in the coils realizes a magnetic field, and when another coil is placed in the field, the process is reversed and an electric current appears in the second coil. In our case, the second coil was in the RFID and provided power for the RFID, so it didn't need its own battery. The RFID then transmitted, by radio, a unique signal which was picked up by the coils of wire in the doorframe and thence on to the computer. The RFID would therefore send a unique identifying coded radio signal to the computer every time it passed through any doorways with the large coils of wire in place. Re-programming the RFID from the computer could change the actual code, but largely the unique signal transmitted would stay the same.

The next step was to see if we could get it implanted. I therefore went to see my local GP, George Boulos. In the six or seven years George had been my doctor, we had always got on well. I didn't visit him very often but when I did, he was always interested in the robots we were building and the research that was going on. I suggested to him that I wanted to consider implanting the RFID in its glass tube, and asked if this would be possible and, if so, what problems might we have to overcome. I put myself forward as the patient although at that time, nothing had been finalized. I think he was, to say the least, shocked by the suggestion, but at the same time seemed very excited by the whole idea. He went away to find out more.

It was only just spring, the intelligent-building work was still several months from completion and that would need to be up and running before we could go ahead with the implant trial. After all, when the implant was put in place, it would have to *do* something. So back in the department we started to discuss the project more seriously. One thing George Boulos had made clear was that there were quite a few dangers associated with the operation itself. Although he felt local anaesthetic would be sufficient, it was possible that infection could set in. Also, the body might not like a glass object fixed inside it and might react in a whole host of ways. I considered the possibility of one of the researchers being the recipient, and in the department we joked about who it might be, as we would know where they were in the building at all times. But I realized very quickly that if something went wrong in the experiment and the researcher concerned became seriously ill, there was no way I would have been able to live with it. On top of that I wanted to experience the implant myself. If we were going to go further in our cyborg studies, then I wanted to witness the experiment at first hand.

In the meantime, I had achieved some success on another front. Following the death of Peter Tauber, I had been without an agent. It had been suggested that I try Robert Kirby, who was part of Peters Fraser and Dunlop, the literary agency, in London. Robert and I met up and instantly got on. I had a new agent.

It was decided that the paperback version of *March of the Machines* should be called *In the Mind of the Machine* to try and appeal to a wider audience. I wrote a new opening chapter and generally updated the book. It was scheduled to appear in August 1998, about a year and a half after the hardback.

Since *March of the Machines* appeared I had been working on new book called *QI: The Quest for Intelligence*, which was aimed at answering one of the main issues that had arisen in the first book: if machines came into existence that were more intelligent than humans, then we would have a problem on our hands. It would be machines that inherit the earth. That logic all hung on the one question: what does one mean by intelligence?

I had continued to work on a number of projects with local companies, particularly small ones. One good link was with OXIM, at Oxford, for the fish-handling robot. Then there was Plint at

Wokingham, making control test-rigs for oil companies, and Sondex, who make measuring equipment to go down bore holes for deep drilling. Many of these projects were funded with help from the government's Teaching Company Scheme, which had provided us with the original Brylcream grant. But now we had so many projects at Reading that we set up as a centre for the whole university, with myself as its director. Very quickly the centre was bringing in over half a million pounds per year to the university. It wasn't long before this rose further, to over a million pounds – about 7 per cent of Reading University's total research income.

By this time, one increasing part of my daily life was dealing with the media. A lot of interest had been generated by my claims in *March of the Machines* that robots were going to take over the world. This, coupled with the fact that we had quite a few nifty robots, meant that I was regularly asked to contribute to radio programmes and newspaper articles. Each week saw a different one, many from the other side of the world. Every year the undergraduate students would come up with a new robot that the media would like: 1998 saw a hopping robot and a robot playing with a yo-yo. The former appeared on Meridian TV news, and the latter in a Channel 4 schools programme on robots.

Peter Tauber had once informed me that the film producer Stanley Kubrick had read *March of the Machines* with a view to making a film based on the ideas. Unfortunately he opted for *Eyes Wide Shut* with Nicole Kidman and Tom Cruise instead. But now Satel Doc made a documentary called 'March of the Machines' for Channel 4 – not quite up to Kubrick's level, but never mind. As a result of this documentary, Jonathan Margolis wrote a national newspaper feature on me, then James Geary interviewed me and wrote a long piece for *Time* magazine.

In 1997 Ian Kelly had obtained his PhD in the department with a project that involved getting the Seven Dwarf robots to communicate with each other using infrared. For one robot this enabled it to locate a charging station, such that when its power was getting low, it could hunt for food. But we also had several robots communicating with each other, and Ian had researched flocking and leadership capabilities. As a result of this work, the Ars Electronica Museum in Linz, Austria, approached us with regard to producing a permanent exhibit. The powered-flooring trials with the 'Thinking Machines' exhibit for London's Science Museum proved useful again, and Ian was put in charge of getting an exhibit up and running in Linz. What materialized was a five-robot permanent exhibit that showed flocking behaviour. The exhibit is still in operation today.

Because of the success of our robots and the increased high-profile media coverage, requests for lecture presentations came in thick and fast. I had to say no to many, and merely squeeze some in when I could. I always felt school visits were important and therefore I tried to put those on top of my list and find the time whenever possible. An evening presentation sometimes meant that I would spend my day in the university, travel two or more hours for the presentation, and then travel back again, getting home in the early hours of the morning. It was exhausting, but worth it. I made many presentations, among them visiting some of the traditional English public schools.

In the first half of 1998 I went to Stowe School and then on to Shrewsbury, where Charles Darwin spent his school years. At Uppingham School in Rutland, when I demonstrated the Seven Dwarf learning robots, the children crowded round and stopped it moving. The robot was trying to learn what to do with its wheels in order to move forwards but not bump into anything, as that was its goal. But, with the children stopping it when it moved this way or that, it was always wrong, whatever it tried to do, and in the end it just stopped moving altogether. I checked it out, only to find that it was still fully functioning. But it had simply received so many negatives and had therefore, on that occasion, decided that everything it did was wrong, and that it wasn't going to do anything anymore. Effectively, it had committed robot suicide, overriding its life goal. When the robot was switched off and on and started again, it worked fine. Interestingly, this was the only occasion on which we have ever been able to achieve the suicide solution, despite many subsequent trials.

Whenever possible I enjoy a good philosophical debate. I had particularly enjoyed the meetings with Roger Penrose and John Searle. But in May 1998, I had another opportunity for some fun. Alan Bundy from Edinburgh University had been having a bit of a go at me – one or two letters to papers, that sort of thing – with regard to my views on machine intelligence. The students on the Edinburgh University Artificial Intelligence course therefore arranged a debate between myself, Alan, and Chris Malcolm, a lecturer at Edinburgh with different views from both of us. Irena and I travelled up to Edinburgh for the Friday night debate, and when we arrived, the room was packed. The debate was a hot one, and a lot of the students joined in. For me, that sort of evening symbolizes what universities stand for – good intellectual discourse.

Alan's views appear to be that it is not possible to get very far with artificial intelligence, and hence we cannot see robots as being very intelligent until we have a much deeper understanding of human intelligence. My own views are, along with many others, that humans behave intelligently in the world without having a theory of it, so why should robots have to have one? I'm sure that such debates will continue, and so they should.

That spring of 1998 also saw a fleeting love affair with the BBC's *Tomorrow's World* programme. Although one or two of our robots had previously appeared, I had not been on the programme. But the BBC initiated a five-minute slot called *Visionaries*, and I was one of the first people to be invited on. Phillipa Forrester and the crew therefore came out to the department for a day and filmed me, along with some of the robots, talking about how robots could be intelligent – generally, the stuff of *March of the Machines*.

A few weeks later they were back again for another day's filming for what I think was a *Tomorrow's World* Christmas special for cable or digital. This time all the presenters came out to Reading, Phillipa amongst them, with a make-up team and the works. This time they filmed every conceivable thing in the department that could be called a robot in the broadest sense. For me though, the highlight was that Roger Penrose popped down from Oxford, and we had a mini-debate, with Phillipa acting as chairperson. I had learned my lesson from Leeds – I just offered Roger coffee! But whereas I felt I had sneaked a vague win in the debate that was held in Leeds, on my home patch in Reading I felt that Roger probably got a slight philosophical upper hand and put his argument over in a better way.

The *Tomorrow's World* filming didn't stop there. We had been working on a new form of genetic algorithm – a method of getting a computer to operate based on the ideas of genetics. In addition to this, one of my research students, Justin Gan, along with Iain Goodhew and myself, had developed a computer system we called Gershwyn. Gershwyn's role was to create new musical arrangements that would be meaningful to humans. As a result of *March of the Machines*, numerous people had asked me how robots could be creative. They needed to see an example, and Gershwyn was just such an example.

In the normal process of producing a finished song from a music recording, eighteen tracks or more are initially recorded – including different vocals, drums, guitars, etc., on each track – which, in the usual run of things, are mixed together by a human producer by balancing volumes, fading, lifting and enhancing. Gershwyn's role was to replace the human producer. So Gershwyn started with two different mixed versions of the same set of 18+ tracks. These two versions acted as first-generation parents. They were combined in a number of ways and listened to by a group of people who indicated which they felt were good choices and which not. Gershwyn then took characteristics from the best of these and produced another generation ready for human feedback, and so on.

From time to time, mutations were introduced, in terms of a random element, to change some aspect of the mix completely. If the mutation had a negative effect then the new version affected would most likely not be accepted by the people choosing. Meanwhile, if it turned out to be well received, then Gershwyn could quite easily have achieved a completely different final sound to that which a human producer would have realized. Gershwyn would have created a new piece of music.

So Gershwyn takes music that is initially recorded by humans and mixes it in a way that humans can appreciate, adapting towards likely good selections. The finished article is certainly something that humans can listen to.

We decided to give *Tomorrow's World* an exclusive on Gershwyn, such that the programme was the first to show, in any form, what

Gershwyn could do. We worked with a rock band called Manus, who consisted of the four younger brothers of Declan McManus, who is perhaps better known as Elvis Costello. They were a very good band, extremely accomplished, but they had not yet really made it big on the music scene and hadn't got signed up with a record company. I think they hoped that a TV appearance on *Tomorrow's World* might make a difference.

We worked with them down at a recording studio in Kent for a couple of days. Elvis had pulled a few strings and we were teamed up with some of the best music-production facilities and people available. The toilet walls were lined with platinum discs from Wet, Wet, Wet and the Pet Shop Boys, who also recorded there.

For the *Tomorrow's World* item the band went into the BBC studios at White City and played 'Star', the song they had recorded, followed by a brief interview. Phillipa and the gang then came out to the department to record a sequence about Gershwyn, giving an indication of what Gershwyn was all about. The BBC played two versions of the song, one as recorded by the human 'expert' producer, Pete Moore, and the other as recorded by Gershwyn. Pete Lewis, who had produced Elton John's tribute to Princess Diana, was then recorded in the department giving his views on just how good he felt Gershwyn really was. He said that he felt that the human version was still better but that Gershwyn could take a lot of the drudgery out of the producer's lot.

Over the space of a few months, there had been three separate appearances on *Tomorrow's World* and it felt as though Phillipa and the crew were almost part of the department. With Gershwyn I thought we had a nice system and a nice story – a robot machine being creative in a way people could understand. So I was surprised when there was very little feedback from the item. A follow-up article did appear in the *Daily Express* about two weeks later, but that was all. No magazines came looking for a story, no companies for research. Even with some previous small stories in the local newspaper we had had more interest. So what was the problem? Perhaps people were just not ready to hear, or simply not interested in hearing, that robots could be creative. Alternatively it might have been that giving Gershwyn to *Tomorrow's World* as an exclusive story was not such a good idea. They had pushed the human-produced version as being better, yet Gershwyn had had very little time to carry out only ten generations of mixes, when often such systems take thousands of generations. Disappointed with the lack of public interest in Gershwyn I decided not to go the *Tomorrow's World*-exclusive route with our next project, which would be the implant experiment later in the year.

In early June, I was in Vienna for a robotics meeting, right in the heart of the Old Town. It was a joint art–science event and they had several exciting names on the presenters list. One of the leading lights was Stelarc, an artist who wires himself up to a computer by means of electrodes on the outside of his body. The computer then programmes his movements by stimulating different muscles in a sequence. I not only enjoyed his performance but also chatted with him during breakfast on a couple of occasions. I realized that, as far as muscles go, there's no real need to stimulate them directly inside the body, as you can achieve most of what you might want externally. This made me think that in the future, with implants, direct muscle stimulation might be a waste of time.

I also shared a discussion meeting with Hans Moravec. I had liked the ideas about uploading the human brain into silicon he had expressed in his book *Mind Children*. Our ideas seemed to be similar in terms of machines becoming, before long, more intelligent than humans, but Hans suggested that as humans we could fight back by becoming machines ourselves. This got me thinking again more about the potential not so much of humans becoming robots, but rather linking ourselves more closely with technology. This was particularly relevant with the upcoming implant experiment.

A couple of weeks later Irena and I went across to Philadelphia for the annual American Control Conference. It was generally quite a theoretical conference, and I had attended every two or three years since the 1983 conference in San Francisco. But I could now see that my interests had moved on: my mind was clearly on intelligent robots and implants, not on theoretical control. From Philadelphia we moved on to Pittsburgh. Although part of the reason for travelling there was to see the town again, it was also so I could meet up with Hans Moravec. Hans is housed at Carnegie Mellon University, along with the team that has developed a lot of the autonomous vehicle robots that travel on motorways. I was a little disappointed to find that none of the autonomous vehicles were there. Not only that, but no one seemed to know Hans Moravec. Even in his own department we had a devil of a job to find him, but eventually we did, tucked away in a little back office.

We discussed the philosophy of a human brain being 'programmed' into a robot machine brain, and the resultant robot (human type) walking away as a metal person – essentially his ideas in *Mind Children*. But he also talked about the soul and after-death feelings, which I didn't particularly relate to. He seemed to be doing little or no technical or design and development work with robots anymore, which I felt was a great shame. I unashamedly used the opportunity to throw around some of my own ideas that had been developing since the Vienna meeting, ideas more along the lines of humans merging with technology rather than humans becoming technology. The question of what it would feel like if you were a robot or a cyborg was strongly on the agenda.

On my arrival back in Reading, a barbeque was held with the new graduate students to celebrate the 'successful' end of their studies. This was a momentous occasion in that it signalled the end of the half-marathon robot, Rogerr. Rogerr was used as the barbeque, and was piled high with coals, and I have to say that he was much more successful as a barbeque than he was at half-marathons!

Meanwhile, the implant experiment was progressing and it looked as if we might be able to go for it by the end of the summer. At the end of June, I had another talk with George Boulos. He explained that the main danger was of infection setting in. The implant might get broken or the body might reject it. I dropped the news to Irena that I was going to have an implant. I don't know that we had talked about it seriously before, so at first I don't think she had much of an idea of what on earth I was talking about. We discussed the whole project, what it would entail, the pros and cons, and after a while she was fully in the picture and knew exactly what was likely to happen.

Neil, Darren and the rest of the team working on the intelligent-building side of things were doing a fantastic job and it looked as if we would have a number of demonstration points in the department by late July. This would involve several doorways at which the implant would be recognized. The door to one of my research labs had been mechanized and could be opened by computer control, potentially when the computer recognized me, via the implant, walking towards the door. In the entrance foyer a light was being rigged up in the same sort of way, along with a voice box, so that when I came through the front door the computer could talk to me. A number of other things were, at this time, mere possibilities – it would just depend on how smoothly things went over the next few weeks.

By mid-July George Boulos and I had met several times and had settled on the implant being positioned in my upper left arm. This suited me because we really weren't sure how well it would work and I didn't want to do my right arm any permanent damage. In order to be recognized the implant needed to be implanted at a fairly specific angle to the coils of wire in the doorways. The feeling in the lab was that if the computer was not picking up the implant then I could waggle my arm all over the place until things lined up and we achieved success. George felt that the upper arm was also useful because of the protective fatty tissue present. He was therefore firming up on the procedure involved, the nurses who would help out, and any other issues.

One important point was sterilizing the glass implant to make it as inert as possible. George had suggested that we brought the transponder implant in so that he could get it done, possibly using alcohol. But first we decided to have a go in the labs ourselves. So, rather like schoolboys, we tried dropping the transponder in boiling water. It exploded, shattering everywhere. We even had bits of chip and wire splattered on the ceiling. I made the decision: we were ready to go for the experiment.

CHAPTER 6

Just a small piece of silicon under the skin is all it would take for us to enjoy the freedom of no cards, passports, or keys. Put your hand out to the car door, computer terminal, the food you wish to purchase, and you would be dealt with efficiently. Think about it: total freedom; no more plastic.

From *Tips for Time Travellers*, Peter Cochrane, then Head of British Telecom Research Laboratories, 1997.

IN JULY 1998 I did a lot of run-of-the-mill academic work. I acted as external examiner for PhD vivas in Sheffield and York universities, I continued on a number of projects with different companies, and pressed on when I could with writing *QI*. But on my mind all the time was the implant experiment – planning, organizing, and bringing it all together. It became completely engrossing.

One thing I realized was that when we were ready to go ahead with the implant the media might well be extremely interested in it. The university had shown itself to be worse than useless at putting out a media story. Normally I was media reactive, in that newspapers, TV and radio came to me and I fielded their requests, but in this case I felt that we needed to be proactive instead.

At the beginning of August I therefore contacted Debbie Pogue who worked at INS, an international news agency. In the past she had contacted me for a story, but in this case I asked for her advice. She suggested a two-pronged approach: first, give a TV company and a news agency (INS perhaps) an exclusive on the operation itself, and then make a general announcement to any press who might be interested. That way I would make sure the story went out to as large an audience as possible. I took her advice and immediately gave INS the exclusive in terms of still photographs of the operation. They would also get a little more time to put the story together before I passed it on to any other media. It was an arrangement that suited me quite well. Brian, one of the INS photographers, had done one or two things with me before, and we got on very well. He was a very good photographer.

It was agreed that Maddi would help out with the publicity, as there was no one in the department who would be able to do the job. At the time she was sixteen, on school holidays, and seemed quite amenable to a bit of work experience as long as I paid her something for it. So we agreed on a figure, I signed her on, and she started immediately. I knew I could rely on her completely, that she would pick things up pretty quickly, and she'd do a good job.

Everything seemed to be coming together nicely. Darren and the team hadn't quite finished wiring up the 'intelligent' building, but they promised it would be ready in the next couple of weeks. All that was left now was to settle on a date and make sure everything happened when it was supposed to. Because my diary was incredibly full over the next few months, we opted for the last week of August, which was only ten days away. A critical factor was booking George Boulos and the surgery. Would he be ready by then? Would the surgery be available? A visit to the surgery indicated that they could release a little time late on the afternoon of Monday 24 August, but that was about the only possibility. George was absolutely fantastic about it all, even though it really put the pressure on him to get things ready, finalize the method to be used, the sterilization procedure (following our own failure in the lab), and get his team ready.

One thing that hadn't really been considered until that time was how long the implant would stay in place. But the problem was quickly solved. George said that the stitches to hold it in place would last about ten days. If the implant was left in any longer than this it would probably work itself loose quite quickly and migrate elsewhere in my body. To find it might mean that several incisions were necessary in order to track it down. I didn't much like the sound of this, so we decided that nine days after its insertion, George would take the implant out again.

The dates were roughly set, but were certainly not ideal. On Friday 28 August I was scheduled to fly up to the Edinburgh Book Festival for the pre-release of *In the Mind of the Machine*. As I would have the implant in place at that time it would mean that I would have to go through airport security in both London and Edinburgh. This provided me with a distinct worry as I had witnessed one implant explode in dramatic style when we heated it up for sterilization, yet here I was, giving the implant a tester as far as the pressures in flying were concerned. Having the implant explode in my arm was obviously not something that appealed to me.

With this experiment I really didn't want the story getting out, in any way, ahead of time, so I had to be careful whom I talked to. Sue Nelson was a TV reporter for BBC News 24 and had already done one or two stories with me, including the coverage of Rogerr, the half-marathon robot. I therefore telephoned her in confidence, filling her in on what the experiment was all about. She went for the story like a shot, particularly because the BBC could have an exclusive on the operation.

The operation was due to take place at Tilehurst on 24 August at 4p.m. As long as things went well, we would then do the 25-minute journey back to the university with the BBC and INS and test how well the computer could track me around the building and see what else might happen. Then, mid-morning on 25 August we would give a press release in the university and show invited press who turned up just what the implant could do. For Sue it would mean that the BBC could put the story out on the news ahead of the field on the afternoon or evening of 25 August if they saw fit.

In the meantime, Maddi had a job to do. Put a press pack together, fax and email an invitation to various press folk, then phone round to check on numbers and see who was likely to come to the press release on the morning of 25 August. She started off with an invitation list that included all the major national newspapers, local newspapers and radio, and some useful specialist papers such as the *Times Higher Educational Supplement*. She also invited a few more television teams, such as Meridian, the local independent station.

We really had no idea how many media people would be interested, particularly as we weren't telling anybody what it was all about, just that it was a good story. Although it's not too far from London to Reading, actually getting top reporters to make the trip when they are not sure about a story is not easy. However, we figured that if we got one or two TV crews and reporters to commit, then others would follow. As a result, Maddi worked on more of a bottom up strategy, firstly landing Meridian and the local newspapers, then moving on to the nationals. In fact, the big newspapers came on board very quickly, and committed straightaway. Things were looking very good on the publicity front.

For the press pack we wanted to be sure about whether or not anyone had done a similar experiment in the past. We were certainly not aware of anything in the scientific community. It seemed a little strange that several scientists were pointing to such a thing happening, but nothing seemed to have been done at all. An extensive search revealed that, apart from hip replacements, cochlea implants, heart pacemakers, and the like, the only thing remotely relevant to what we were doing was the work of the artist Eduardo Kac. About one year before, he had apparently barcoded his ankle and read himself into the internet to symbolize the human race being captive to technology. At the minimum, our own experiment would thus be a significant contribution, but even now we were looking at enhancing human capabilities and interacting with an intelligent building, neither of which had ever been done before. The press packs Maddi put together were upbeat.

But we still had a lot of technical work to do in the few days that remained. One big worry was getting the building all wired up. Things had slipped a little and, although the team was working hard to get it all operative, some niggling problems were creeping in. Two main areas needed to be focused on: the corridor to the laboratory, with an automatically opening door and so on, and the main entrance door and foyer, with a welcoming 'hello', a light coming on and the computer switching to my web page. When we got the entrance working, the corridor didn't, and then when the corridor worked, the 'hello' welcome died. The gremlins or bugs certainly seemed to be at work. Then, on the Thursday, everything except for the computer web switch was working until mid-afternoon when the whole lot went down. With four days to go, an implant was due to be put in place; TV and newspapers were coming to see it happen, but when in place the implant didn't look as if it would actually do anything.

Despite the fact that it was all going horribly wrong, I still took the implant across to George Boulos that afternoon because he needed to ensure that it got properly sterilized. We had checked it out, in terms of its operation, earlier in the day when the building system was working, and it was just fine. But I knew that the next time we could check the implant out again would be when it came back to the department in my arm. Only then, as long as the building system was doing something, would we see if it was still operative.

George put the implant into an oven and heated it up to around 80°C, on the grounds that most things would be killed off at that temperature. It was then kept in sterile conditions ready for Monday's operation. He had tried to sterilize an implant in this way a week earlier and when we checked it out in the department afterwards it still seemed to be working. We hoped that the implant for the actual operation would also turn out fine. However, if the sterilization procedure itself ruined the implant, then not only would the whole experiment have failed, but I wouldn't actually know it until I returned to the department.

The weekend of the 22 and 23 August was a busy one, with a group of us trying frantically to get the building's computer system up and running ready for Monday afternoon. Slowly it began to come together.

First the door to the corridor started opening again, then the light started coming on, until gradually everything except the computer web page was working perfectly.

In a coffee break, Darren told me what had brought the system down. The implant I was to receive on Monday emitted its own identifying code signal. Originally it was programmed to emit the code 666 which, in line with Darren's humour, is the 'mark of the beast' from the Book of Revelation in the Bible. For some reason, though, when 666 was tried nothing worked. The code for the implant was therefore changed to 161, and with this everything worked perfectly. Earlier in the week Darren had been trying to figure out why 666 caused so much trouble, and then he tried it again; it brought the whole system to a standstill, causing the problems we were having to cure over the weekend. I am not a religious or superstitious person, but there was certainly not a simple solution to the 666 problem. We never tried that particular code again and certainly never will.

By Sunday night things were looking good in the department. When I went home I knew that the next couple of days would be busy ones and that I needed to get a good night's sleep, particularly before the following day's operation. Physically I was tired, but mentally I was already in Monday, playing through what was going to happen, first this way then that. So when Monday morning arrived I was absolutely exhausted and in desperate need of sleep.

That morning Maddi spent her time phoning round to check who from the press was coming on Tuesday. As the day wore on it became clear that everything was going to go ahead. It was quite a nice day weatherwise, and so at lunchtime, to try and relax, I took a stroll around the lake on the university campus. I felt rather sick, but didn't know if it was from my sleepless night or nerves before the operation. With the run up to the experiment being so hectic, I had hardly had a moment to myself to reflect on what was going on. Yet here I was, a few hours before I was to receive a surgical implant and suddenly I had time to think. What on earth was I doing it for? What if I simply walked away from it all now, what would happen?

The first of these two questions wasn't difficult to answer at all. I was a scientist. To me this was a wonderful opportunity to do some experimenting, to do some science, maybe to affect the way people think. Certainly, I felt, I would cause folk to stop and reflect on what I was doing and what it meant to them. Above all it was the first tentative step on the cyborg route. If I was going to do anything more serious in the future, it was a necessary step. I needed to experience what it was like to have an implant, to actually feel it for myself.

As for walking away from it – well, this was merely last-minute panic. It wasn't something I had ever done in my life before, would not do now, and would never do in the future. As far as I am concerned, life contains some testing, but rich, moments. If you walk away from them when they occur, for whatever reason, you devalue your life tremendously. Indeed, you may well not get another chance.

We had agreed that everyone involved would meet at George Boulos's surgery just before the operation. I had to get there a little earlier because George wanted to go over with me exactly what was going to happen before the others arrived at 4p.m.

It takes about twenty-five minutes to drive from the university to the surgery, so I set out in good time, just after 3p.m. I knew I was about to do something a little bit special, perhaps even historic and, as I drove along Reading's busy Oxford Road, I looked at people on the street as they went about their daily business. None of them knew that I was about to do something special – it was a strange feeling.

When I arrived, George sat me down and we had a quiet chat. He was particularly keen to keep an eye on things as they progressed, once the implant was in place. If I had any trouble with it, any subsequent signs of infection or bleeding, I was to return immediately so that George could take care of it. It all sounded very reasonable to me.

By about 3.45p.m. everyone was there except for Brian, the INS photographer. The BBC therefore took some shots of me walking into the surgery and then me walking out of the surgery, getting into my car, and driving away. Then I drove round the corner and came straight back again. By 4 we were all set to go with the operation, except for the fact that Brian still hadn't turned up. We had to wait. He arrived just before 4.30, having got caught in traffic, and the operation took place only half an hour later than scheduled.

The operation itself was not particularly complicated and took about twenty minutes in total. George took things relatively slowly, explaining his actions as he went, hamming it up to the BBC camera. He used a local anaesthetic at the point of incision on my inner, upper left arm, and first of all made sure that I couldn't feel anything in that region. He then made his incision, at which point Sue Newton turned white and had to face the sink. She subsequently asked George and me questions while facing away from us.

George burrowed a hole, just as he told me he would do, through the fascia, the outer layer of the skin, down to the muscle. He then proceeded to try and push the implant into place. Unfortunately he hadn't burrowed far enough, so the implant wouldn't go in fully. He therefore took it out again, burrowed some more, and tried again. This time it went into its new home, lying on the muscle in my left arm without any complaints. George then stitched it into place, so it wouldn't migrate – for nine days anyway – and stitched up the wound. I was ready for action.

A plaster was put over the wound to provide some protection and I relaxed for a few minutes before heading off back to the university. The local anaesthetic was still operating, so I didn't feel any pain at that stage, although George had warned me that it might be very different when the anaesthetic wore off. There was a little bleeding, but that soon stopped.

I gingerly drove back to the university. Changing gear meant moving my left arm, which I did very carefully. As a result I drove most of the way in either second or third gear rather than change gear regularly. But, to be honest, I didn't feel too bad. As I was driving I reflected on things. I'm not overly fond of medical operations, yet I had gone through something purely for a scientific experiment. Now, here I was, with a strange implant in my arm, which we couldn't be sure would actually do anything at all. If it didn't work, how would I deal with it? I had no idea.

Because it was after 5p.m., there was more traffic than before, and it took quite a while to get back to the department. As soon as I got there, I linked up with Darren and we were able to check out just how well the implant operated. It seemed to be functioning well, which was a huge relief.

We had worried that the implant would need to be aligned in the doorframes in order to indicate a strong signal between the coils in the doorways and the coil in the implant. We had tried to deal with this by positioning the implant in my arm so I could move it to the appropriate angle. In fact, we quickly discovered that it performed much better than expected, even to the extent that no matter what contortion I put my arm through, the implant still operated. It also created a good signalling path when I moved very quickly through a doorway. It was interesting to note that the implant operated with 100 per cent reliability up to one metre from one doorframe, but more than two metres away it didn't operate at all. We had certainly expected this take off, but hadn't expected the operation up to the one-metre mark to be anywhere near so reliable. The only immediate conclusion we could come to was that the body fluids were in some way assisting the functioning of the implant.

Sue Nelson and INS soon joined us with the BBC cameraman, who filmed me wandering through doorways and recorded the lights coming on and so on. For some reason the computer was not showing up on my web page in response to me appearing, so that had to be left out. They also took some shots of Sue walking around the department, making a few comments on the experiment. By about 7.30p.m. they had the footage they needed and off they went.

I headed home alone and, as I drove, I realized that the local anaesthetic had worn off, yet the wound didn't hurt much, it merely stung a little. The implant did feel somewhat uncomfortable, but it was nothing I couldn't live with. The whole experiment seemed to be going well.

When I arrived home Irena was extremely interested in how things had gone. Although she wanted to see what my arm looked like, she wasn't overly keen on touching it, which I could understand. It might have been good to relax with a glass of wine, but I couldn't have any alcohol as I had been put on a course of antibiotics. Irena did have a little something though, some Becherovka, a strong Czech alcoholic drink from Karlovy Vary. She said it was for medicinal purposes!

Later, we had yet another troublesome night as we attempted to sleep.

Firstly there was the excitement of the day gone and the one still to come, then there was the implant. Irena didn't want to roll over on top of my arm, and I didn't want to hit my arm in any way – after all, the implant was in a glass capsule which could easily smash. I therefore spent most of the night with my arm out of the bed at a strange angle. It's not easy to sleep that way. I found it strange that I had this implant in place, and that hardly anyone knew about it. The BBC and INS were not putting the story out until the 25th, and it was as if we were holding on to a secret that we weren't sure who would be interested in.

The morning of August 25 duly arrived, and by 10.30a.m. all the big names in UK newspaper science reporting had appeared at the department. Once they had all arrived, they were ushered through into the lecture room and we got started. The room was lit with a spooky blue light, with a spotlight on me when I started my presentation. I opened by talking about Big Brother and the idea of being tracked and monitored wherever a person went. I talked about the sort of things Peter Cochrane had been saying about implants, as quoted at the beginning of this chapter. However, I don't think any of them were quite ready for my announcement that I had been surgically implanted with a silicon chip transponder the previous afternoon. As they heard this news, a communal gasp was clearly audible.

The reporters were given Maddi's press pack, which included technical details about the implant and further background material on the team involved. We then walked round to the department and demonstrated the implant in operation, turning lights on, opening doors, and so on. One computer was set up to display clearly what time I entered various rooms and what time I left, and it was obvious that the Big Brother issue was of much interest. Most of the journalists wanted some specific quotes from me and the rest of the team. Michael Hanlon of the *Daily Express* even interviewed Maddi. One thing I was particularly delighted with was that everything worked. Even the computer in the foyer pointed directly to my web page when I entered the building. The team had worked extremely hard, we'd made it, and I will be eternally grateful to them for that.

Meridian and Sky TV made reports to be shown later in the day. But

BBC1 got the scoop, based on Sue Nelson's report. They pushed out the story, for the first time, on their lunchtime news at 1 o'clock. The item went, 'A silicon chip has been successfully implanted into the arm of a British scientist so that his movements can be remotely tracked by a computer.' That set alarm bells ringing everywhere. By 2p.m. we had a list of requests from TV, radio and newspapers all around the world. *News at Ten*, ITN's flagship news programme at the time, came out to the department straightaway, and I did various interviews over the phone. I had already done one for Richard Hollingsworth who was then at BBC World Service, but they got me to go down to Shepherd's Bush that night to do a live piece for BBC World. Maddi and I rushed up to London by train, getting back at midnight.

The following day all the national newspapers went with the story. Of all the headlines, though, I think my favourite was that of the *Sun* newspaper. It read, 'Hello, Mr. Chip' – absolutely brilliant. In the *Daily Express*, Michael Hanlon had quoted Maddi as saying that she thought I was crazy. *The Times*, the *Guardian* and the *Telegraph* all ran excellent articles, as did the *Daily Mail*. As a result, the rest of the day was spent fielding more media enquiries. ABC TV from the US did a piece, as did CNN, and NBC followed a day later. German and French TV companies were also very quick to send someone out, along with countries that you might not expect, such as Korea and Chile.

I also received around one hundred emails a day. One nice message came in from Eduardo Kac, the artist who had done the barcode hook up. He sent his congratulations and we exchanged emails discussing each other's work. I also appreciated emails from scientists around the world, particularly the younger sector.

On Friday 28th I had to fly from Heathrow to Edinburgh for the launch of *In the Mind of the Machine* at the Book Festival. I had worried not only about the possibility of the implant exploding, but also that I might set off alarms when walking through the scanner. I need not have worried. No alarms were set off and no explosions took place. In fact, as a result I felt a little less confident about the whole scanning procedure. If my implant got through airport scanners, then what other things might be sneaked on to a plane?

The Book Festival proved something of a relief, although one cynical journalist from Edinburgh suggested that I had carried out the implant experiment merely to provide publicity for the book. It came as something of a shock to me that anyone could think that way, although as things turned out it was probably just the tip of an iceberg. From my own perspective, I always seem to be doing a lot of things, and it is difficult to cram them into the time available. In this case, we had gone for the implant experiment at that time even though for me it meant I would have to take time out to do the paperback launch. I had actually seen the Edinburgh Festival as getting in the way of the implant experiment.

If we had done the experiment a few weeks before, it would have clashed with or complemented Gershwyn and the *Tomorrow's World* item. If we had left it for a couple of weeks it would have clashed with the annual British Association meeting. Which ever way we went, it would have to be at roughly the same time as something else, unless I stopped doing so much.

Back in the department we were able to do some more tests on how well the implant operated. We looked closely at the power it was taking, the range of signalling, and the frequency of operation. All of this experimentation would prove to be extremely useful in the months ahead. We were all amazed at how accurately I could be monitored. Very quickly a picture of my habits emerged and the computer acquired a pretty good idea about my routine visits in the department, which all pointed back to the Big Brother issues we had tried to raise.

I wasn't in the slightest worried or even upset about the computer monitoring my movements. After all, it was opening doors for me, switching on lights, and even greeting me. These were all nice and positive things. Perhaps if the computer had been doing negative things to me, such as switching off lights or locking doors to deny me access, I might have felt differently. But I was gaining rather than losing something. The computer was only giving me extras and this was something I was happy with. Maybe it's a bit like having a credit card: you gain the ability to buy things quickly and easily and perhaps even gain some credibility because you hold such a card, but at the same time, for every transaction, various computer systems gather more information about you, your buying patterns, and just exactly who you are.

If this is correct, in general it would mean that George Orwell's negative view of a human dictatorial Big Brother is not really the sort of thing we are likely to see in the future. Rather, we are looking at a computer network to which humans are linked because it gives us benefit. Essentially, we are happy to allow such a system to spy on us and monitor us because of the positives it brings. Big Brother therefore becomes a positive that we choose and that we want, rather than a negative and something we want to get rid of. Orwell's Big Brother was also a political entity, whereas in reality we are heading towards a commercial, Big Company Big Brother.

I was learning much more than I could ever have imagined or bargained for with the implant in place. Certainly, it felt physically uncomfortable at first, but after only a few days, this feeling died away and I really didn't notice it was there – apart from all the things that were being done for me. Physically my body seemed simply to accept the implant, with no intention of rejection.

The biggest surprise, though, was how I felt mentally. Very quickly I regarded the implant as being a part of me, part of my body, just as much as my arms, toenails or skin. A wristwatch or jewellery you can be fond of and like, but they are separate from you, they are not part of you. With the implant it was clearly *me*. When talking to people as I gave presentations later on, I discovered that this is a feeling shared with those who have heart pacemakers and artificial hips or transplanted organs. In fact, if people with transplants do not regard their new organs in this way, it can lead to the body's rejection of the organ. Mental suggestion and thought are very powerful tools.

The implant's direct radio link with the computer in the department meant that the computer was connected to the inside of me and was therefore also part of me, but at the same time was not part of me. It was such a strange feeling it is difficult to describe. I certainly felt that it gave me an affinity with the computer, so much so that by the weekend of 29 and 30 August, Irena started to worry about what was going on. She began to feel that there were now three of us in the marriage: Irena, me and a computer.

A few days later, on the afternoon of Wednesday 2 September, the implant was removed. It was a very strange feeling. On one hand I felt relieved that nothing had gone wrong medically – no infection, no explosion, no breaking loose of stitches. But on the other hand, my link with the computer was suddenly taken away. Perhaps the feeling between the computer and me had been a bit like Siamese twins. I felt as though a friend had died – very down and very sad. However, it was probably a good time to have the implant removed. We had carried out all the experimentation, and collected all the data we wanted. Indeed, the experiment had been tremendously successful.

Despite feeling rather low now that the implant had been removed, I had to drive to Swansea that night, a two-and-a-half-hour trip straight down the M4 motorway from Reading to attend a conference organized by the Institution of Electrical Engineers (IEE), entitled Control 98. It was poles apart from the implant experiment that I had just been involved in, and even further from my popular-science book presentation at the Edinburgh Festival. It was all about theoretical control, which involves quite a bit of mathematics. My own PhD had been very much in that sort of area, back in 1982. Now, nineteen years on, I still had roots in the field. A couple of research students were working further in this area and, at the time, I was editor of one of the top journals in this field, the *IEE Proceedings*. I therefore had to present a paper, and was scheduled to do so the next day.

Due to the rigours of yet another operation, plus the fact that I had been working, one way or another, non-stop for about four weeks with no days off, I was exhausted. After about half an hour of driving down the M4, I stopped for petrol and bought myself a Lucozade and some sweets. I felt I needed to input energy directly. It appeared to have the desired effect and, as I drove to Swansea, listening to my Spice Girls cassette, I generally felt a lot better.

That evening I met up with some academics and administrators with the IEE. It was quite a warm evening, and as we sat down to order a meal I started to sweat. Sarah Hunt, who was my direct link with the IEE for all *Proceedings* work, asked for a glass of iced water, but the sweating worsened and I quickly got through all the paper tissues of everyone present. Sweat was pouring out of me by the bucketload. Nothing like this had ever happened to me before and I tried to make light of it, saying I would be okay soon. But it got worse and a waitress brought me a towel. Iced water didn't help, and apparently I went as white as a sheet. Sarah then telephoned for an ambulance, which arrived very quickly.

Once at the hospital, Sarah announced that I was the man with the implant who they had probably seen on the news. This created a minor panic. Rather than the run-of-the-mill evening casualties, they suddenly had some weird medical case on their hands. I think we managed to calm them down by telling them the implant was no longer in place, however their initial line of enquiry seemed to concentrate on the fact that the situation was caused by the implant doing something strange in my body.

After a while, the sweating calmed down slightly. The doctors did a number of tests, including the checking of my blood pressure and pulse, and pronounced that I was perfectly all right. Perhaps it was the exhaustion, perhaps it was the sugar, or maybe it was some reaction to the operations I'd had. Whatever it was, it looked as though it had passed.

That night I had a light snack back at the university in Swansea, and went to bed early. The next morning I was up and raring to go, giving a conference presentation of the more traditional academic type, with plenty of equations. At lunchtime I climbed into a taxi and was driven to the BBC radio studios in the heart of Swansea to do a live link-up with London for, of all things, a Radio 4 business discussion.

That evening saw the conference dinner at which I was able to relax a bit as I didn't have a meeting to go to, and didn't have to rush off to do a radio interview. I felt that, after my sweating experience the night before, perhaps I needed to calm down a bit, relax more and do fewer things. But by the next morning I had snapped out of it and was back to normal. I drove to Reading and got home at lunchtime. Irena and I packed our bags and set off to catch an evening flight to Prague. I was scheduled to appear at another conference there with my old friend Mirek, for which we had managed to put together a new, good quality, academic textbook that we had jointly edited. Meanwhile, Irena would be able to visit relatives and spend some time with Lenka and Petr, her daughter and son from her first marriage, who were both living in Prague.

During that week in Prague, I reflected on what the implant experiment was all about and what it had achieved. I had built up a good rapport with some Czech journalists, especially one called Martin Uhlirsh, who reported for the quality newspaper *Lidovy Noviny* (*Popular News*). He liked to follow my exploits and so wanted a good story and update on the implant experiment we had just carried out. He also hit me with one or two criticisms that had appeared in the two weeks since the reports on the implant had first appeared in the media.

One criticism was that I had only done it for publicity – not for my book, a criticism I had already faced in Edinburgh – but for myself. While I realized that this is a criticism almost anyone can make about someone who appears in the news, such a criticism was not too far wrong in my case. I had a research goal of creating cyborgs, with myself as a guinea pig, and this implant was a step on the way. I needed funding to continue and I wanted people to be aware of what was going on. As a result, I was certainly not shy to publicize what I was doing, but it was not at all true to say that I *only* did it for publicity.

Another comment was that the demonstration of the intelligent building, with lights coming on, door opening, and so on, could have been achieved with a smart card rather than by having an implant. This one I had to put down to being a bit of a silly comment. As it stood, we could certainly demonstrate such capabilities with a smart card, in fact that was how the building normally operated, and still does. But that is not new; why would anyone want to report on that? The implant was something different, and this was the whole point of the news story – we were looking 'outside the box' of present-day thinking. To me it was the same criticism as if someone had said to Alexander Graham Bell, following the first telephone demonstration, 'Why didn't you walk next door and talk to your technician? It would have been much more efficient than talking down those wires.'

But 99 per cent of the comments that appeared had been tremendously supportive. No one seemed to be shouting for us to stop the research, in fact, most of the world seemed extremely interested in what was going on. And this I had to put down as being one achievement of the implant experiment. Many people around the world were now aware that such a thing could be done, in particular to some regular person like me. No longer was the implant technology something from the realms of speculation of futurologists, such as Peter Cochrane, and no longer was it merely a science-fiction story. In fact, I had received an email from Scott Grusky in California who said that he had just published a science-fiction story entitled *Silicon Sunset*, about someone doing exactly what I had done. But now it was science fact.

I felt that we had also raised popular awareness to implant possibilities as far as tracking and monitoring were concerned. As a result of the experiment, I received several communications from companies, government bodies, military and police forces about my experience and what it might mean in the future. Would we as a society want implants like this to be generally available? Who would control the situation? The technology was now available, so such questions had to be raised, rather than just discussed as a mere futuristic concept that might never happen. Clearly the social, moral and ethical questions behind what we were doing were considerable.

But the main reasons for doing the experiment in 1998 were not so much for public awareness, for publicity, or even demonstrating what you could do with an intelligent building. As far as I was concerned, they were a few steps on the route towards the creation of cyborgs – upgraded humans. From here we would need to take the technology forward and design the next implant to be used. The 1998 experiment provided us with invaluable data on performance and characteristics, but above all it had given me the experience of what it was like to have an implant, what it felt like physically and mentally. My own views of what would be possible in the future had taken a distinct leap forward because of the experiment. The big question now was, where do we go from here?

CHAPTER 7

ON MY RETURN to Reading from Prague I had a lot of work to do: first, I had to catch up on an enormous backlog of university work; second, I had to deal with a mountain of requests from TV companies and magazines for follow-up stories on the chip; and third, I had to promote *In the Mind of the Machine.*

To promote the book, over the next few weeks I did bookshop presentations and television and radio interviews around the country. I was also interviewed by the *New York Times,* a Swiss newspaper, *VSD* (a French magazine), South African radio and RDF German television.

Back in the department, I had meetings with my research students, discussed research projects with companies such as National Grid and Computer Associates, and generally tried to hold the fort with my university paperwork. Lectures started up again at the beginning of October, just to add a little extra to my workload.

But although I had more than enough to do, I decided to take on something else: the Millennium Bug. For some time I had been amazed by the confidence trick that was legally employed by many computer consultants and so-called specialists under the name of the 'Millennium Bug'. The general claim was that a large proportion of computers were going to fail when the new millennium came into being on 1 January 2000. At great expense, the UK government had set up a task force to warn people of the terrible dangers ahead. Many companies were not taking any chances, and at considerable cost replaced all their computers and software (often creating months of havoc), just to be on the safe side.

I couldn't believe what was going on. We were being told our TVs and VCRs would fail, our toasters would stop working, hospitals would have to close and people on life-support machines would die. And the government was spending money on all this. It got to the stage where no one could question it – the Millennium Bug was set to happen.

Meanwhile I was aware that most electronic systems, such as toasters, didn't have anything to do with computers. Most things that did operate on computers used pretty modern systems and wouldn't be affected at all – planes and emergency back-up systems, for example. Of course, there might be some old personal computers that might have a clock problem when 2000 arrived, but if you didn't have anything depending on the clock, other than maybe some financial package, you needn't worry as you could always sort the problem out when it occurred. The only possible realistic problem would be if you had a safety critical system based on a very old personal computer. In that case, and only in that case, would it be sensible to check it out. However, this amounted to about one computer in every ten million at most!

A number of articles really incensed me. For example, Alasdair Kemp wrote an article in *IEE Review* which indicated that some cars would not start on 1 January 2000. A 75-year-old man subsequently wrote a letter in response, showing obvious panic at the lack of mobility and problems he would face. Kemp wrote, 'Hopefully Mr Taylor will not be going anywhere essential on 1st January 2000'. This, to me, was utterly ridiculous and bore no relation whatsoever to the actual problem.

I therefore wrote a number of articles on the subject, saying how stupid it all was and how people were being forced into parting with a lot of good money unnecessarily. Changing one line of software or replacing some hardware can often cause more problems than it remedies. I said that people should check first, in a sensible way, to see if they really needed to do anything. I felt that a number of managers were spending vast sums of money on new systems merely because they felt it was the 'safe' thing to do and they were looking after their own backs.

I appeared on Radio 4's *Today* programme in response to a government directive which said that video recorders could become extremely dangerous on 1 January 2000. Essentially I said it was an absolutely stupid statement and that people should ignore it completely and get on with their lives. I felt it was a great shame the government was wasting so much of our money on all this.

In response, I received telephone and email threats from a number of so-called 'computer consultants', who told me to shut up and not to be so irresponsible. The university's Vice-Chancellor even received a letter asking him to shut me up, which of course he didn't do. I could easily understand it – a lot of consultants were making vast sums of money, simply because most people didn't know enough in the way of technical details and thought it best to play safe. I really couldn't see how such blackmail and extortion could not only be legal, but actually be backed up and supported by government.

Over the months ahead, I made a number of radio contributions along the same lines, and input to several newspaper articles. I was approached with a view to making a contribution to a BBC programme on the dire threat of the Millennium Bug. But I got the impression that, when the researcher realized that I felt it was one big confidence trick, my part in the programme was not pursued. It seemed to me that they weren't looking to question the Bug's existence, but instead wanted to discuss the appropriate level of panic we should be feeling.

Fortunately, it turned out to be hysteria in the US and the UK. In the rest of Europe, they believed much less in the Bug and as a result I did quite a number of radio interviews to such countries as Austria, Germany and France, indicating some of the inane things that were happening in the UK. In Russia, they (quite sensibly) didn't seem to bother about it at all, despite considerable pressure being applied on them to do so from the US.

At the same time I was aware that, for myself, the whole Millennium Bug issue was sidetracking me. It was not a crusade on which I wanted to march out in front, banner unfurled; I had enough things to do. So although I continued to get requests to contribute to various articles and radio programmes on the subject, I tried not to get too embroiled. After all, on 1 January 2000 we would all see. If the extorting consultants were correct, then there was no way that *all* problems would be rectified by that time, and we would certainly have a number of major catastrophes on our hands, particularly in Russia where they had done little or nothing about it. I guessed what would probably happen was that there would be no serious problems and that the consultants would then say that if it hadn't been for them, then there certainly would have been. I trusted that no one would be stupid enough to believe such a comment, whether or not they had been foolish enough to believe the same consultants in the first place.

Over the next few months I travelled a lot. My trips took me all over the world, and included attending the French Science festival in Paris, a trip to Denmark to talk to Lego, who had begun to support some of our work in robotics, the Vanguard Conference in LA, and Delhi, for a Global Communications conference.

As a result of the implant research we were involved in, and what it might mean for the future, not only was I invited to places like Los Angeles, Paris and Delhi, but I was also (and still am) regularly asked to contribute a chapter to a book. The books can have more of a technical or sometimes arts bias to them, and at that time I wrote one chapter on our implant research entitled 'The Man with X-ray Arms and Other Skin Ripping Yarns', and another, 'The Chip and I'. Years before I had read a book by Betty MacDonald entitled *The Egg and I*, hence I felt that the title of my second chapter was quite witty. Unfortunately, no one else seemed to think so. When I explain to someone my reason for calling it 'The Chip and I', they merely nod patronizingly, and change the subject. Obviously my sense of humour is not mainstream.

We also worked with the publisher Dorling Kindersley on a set of books for children on the subjects of Robots, The Future and Media. We also worked with Heinemann, who were updating their A-level physics textbook at the time, and wanted to include material on our implant work. All of this pleased me enormously, as it meant that what we were doing could be put over in a way that was readily digestible for children and teenagers. In fact, the Dorling Kindersley book on Media included on its cover the picture of me from the cover of *The Week*.

Being asked questions by journalists about where the implant research was going actually made me ask myself the same question. While I could toss ideas around with journalists, I was aware that, if we were really going to push things along, we had to do something ourselves. In reality, this meant that *I* would have to kick things into life. The first implant experiment in 1998 had been very successful, particularly in raising public awareness and expectation. Quite surprisingly, we had formed our own niche at Reading. Through one experiment we had planted ourselves firmly on the international stage. But now we were duty-bound to do something more.

At the beginning of 1999, I started off a two-pronged attack. I knew we needed to raise money. In the past we had been very well supported by the UK's research councils, so I decided to concentrate my efforts more on raising funds from companies. Computer Associates had contacted me earlier and, as a result, we quickly tied a number of things together. They decided to support three researchers, one of whom would be able to deal with the software aspects of our implant work. But what I really needed was funding to support a researcher on the hardware side, to help get the new implant built. This was not going to be such an easy job as it would be expensive. However, I had an account in the university in which I had been able to salt away some income from previous projects, and it now seemed to be the time to use some of its money. I therefore employed Mark Gasson as a researcher, to start work on the implant. Mark was particularly keen on hardware work, and had graduated from the department several months earlier. He was excited about getting involved and rapidly set to work to find out where exactly we stood technically in relation to research in the rest of the world.

In the meantime I was receiving a tremendous number of invitations from around the world to give presentations on our work. In April 1999, for example, I went to the Salishan conference with Andrew Burns, a student in the department, which was held in a log cabin resort in the pine forests of Oregon. Like the Vanguard conference in 1998, a lot of top people were present from the US, this time from places such as the Lawrence Livermore and Los Alamos US National research labs.

My overriding memory from the Oregon conference is of Gary Kasparov, the former world chess champion, who gave the after-dinner speech. Later on, four of us, including Gary, met up in his room and attempted to get through as much wine as was possible. Gary espoused a strange theory that Jesus Christ was actually born in the year 1052, which, with the wine, sounded quite a reasonable theory, although in hindsight I have my doubts. It was particularly interesting to talk with him about how he plays chess, and his view was that he can plan twenty moves ahead, whereas his opponents usually only manage nineteen. It all seemed a lot more programmed than people imagine. He was still sore at losing to Deep Blue – IBM's chess-playing computer – a couple of years earlier, and throughout the night continually complained that the computer had been cheating.

In February 1996 Gary had beaten Deep Blue by three games to one. However, in the rematch in May 1997, Deep Blue, which can perform more operations in the blink of an eye that most humans complete in a week, won by two games to one. Gary, who was paid one million dollars for the rematch, stormed off the stage after his defeat, claiming that Deep Blue had been set up specifically to beat his game plan.

After it was victorious, IBM dismantled Deep Blue. During our evening of wine-soaked story-telling, Gary said that this incensed him even more, and that he had demanded, but been refused, a further rematch. I said that I could see why IBM had dismantled the computer, in that once Gary had been beaten, what was the point of another set of games? In any case, I continued, it would be Deep Blue's turn to get the one million dollars – what would it do with the money?

My flippancy was not at all well received and I thought he was going to hit me. I could see the headline immediately: 'Kasparov checks out British Prof. in drunken brawl'. I felt I was on a roller so I sacrificed another pawn and said that I didn't see anything wrong with Deep Blue upsetting the Kasparov game plan, as it seemed to me to be a perfectly honorable strategy. My opinion was not welcome. Nevertheless, later on I seemed to get back in his good books when I gave him a signed copy of *In the Mind of the Machine*. A few months later he wrote to me with a few questions about the book's content, along with a request for money so that he could set up a chess institute in California.

Around this time we were approached by Newcastle's Discovery Museum about the possibility of putting together some exhibits for a new learning centre they were preparing. At roughly the same time it became apparent that the Science Museum in London would most likely want a robot pit exhibit as part of its new Wellcome wing due to open midway through 2000.

Iain Goodhew, Ben Hutt and I had several meetings with the team at Newcastle, all of whom impressed us with their commitment to the museum. As a result, it was decided that we would put on two exhibits. One would be a robot arm which you could remote control to move bricks around or to trace along a wire without touching it. The second exhibit would be a couple of autonomous robots, rather akin to our Seven Dwarf robots, which would communicate with each other using infrared signalling. The idea was that a person visiting the exhibit would be able to control remotely, with a joystick, one of the robots, and the other would respond in some way. So either one robot could be controlled to chase after the other one, like a predator, or that robot could be the prey and the other robot would chase after them. The space dedicated to the two autonomous robots turned out to be absolutely enormous and surrounded by a big glass case; this would definitely challenge our abilities in making a special powered floor for the robots. We had until September to get everything done, the official opening being on 7 October 1999.

In the spring of that year I once again gave invited lectures at both Oxford and Cambridge universities. Such lectures had become almost annual events. Usually the talk is to that university's Scientific Society, but sometimes it is to the artificial-intelligence group, or possibly a particular department. Apart from Oxford and Cambridge, Edinburgh and Reading also offer me annual invitations. Every time I go to Oxford or Cambridge I feel that perhaps this time there won't be so many students in the audience, that by now they must have heard it all before. But every time I am proved wrong, and the spring of 1999 was no exception. The audience was bigger than ever before, which I was delighted by. I really feel that if the students at these universities are interested in what I'm doing and are happy to give up their evening to hear me talk, then this is perhaps the best honour that you can achieve. The occasion was particularly special in that I gave the Robert Boyle lecture, named after one of the greatest scientists of all time.

I had learned from my own experiences at Oxford, and from those of others, such as Dave Clarke, who later went on to be an FRS and Professor of Control at Oxford, that if there is someone elsewhere whose work you do not think much of, then you simply ignore them and don't recognize their existence. Therefore, being commented on or questioned by an Oxford academic, whether it be in a positive or negative regard, means that they actually look on your work as being of some value at least, to the extent that it is worth them spending some of their time on it or you. If your research is not up to much, they simply won't say anything. Yet here I was, being regularly invited to give presentations – it meant a great deal to me.

On the TV front I was invited to take part in a BBC *Watchdog* programme, at the time when Vanessa Feltz was the main presenter. The item was about how domestic appliances, such as washing machines, are designed to last a certain time, and after that many different things can go wrong. The insurance that gets tied into such appliances is directly linked to when the appliance is most likely to fall apart. The insurance companies make money on this, obviously – they wouldn't do it otherwise – which means that it is clear common sense *not* to take out the insurance offered on domestic appliances, as on average it is simply going to lose you a lot of money. Some companies had claimed that domestic appliances were not designed to fall apart after a period and that the insurance link didn't exist. I went on TV to 'tell it how it was'. In my normal working life I *never* wear a white coat; this can be a caricature of a scientist. On this occasion the BBC got me to wear a white coat. It was something that I had never done in the past, and it is something I am very unlikely ever to do in the future.

In 1999 I took part in filming a programme called *Robocritters* for the BBC, which looked at how robots could be designed based on ideas from animals and insects. It was to be shown early in 2000. Our six-legged robot Elma clearly fitted the bill, as did the Seven Dwarfs with their bat-like ultrasonic sensors. I also took part in a programme called *Ripley's Believe It or Not* for US television, discussing the implant project. They even got me to make a trailer for them. I said directly to camera something like 'I am about to become the world's first cyborg. Find out how on this week's *Ripley's Believe It or Not.*'

In July I was asked to give a presentation to children at the Royal Institution of Great Britain. For over two hundred years it has been at the centre of scientific research and the popularisation of science in England. Some of the major scientific discoveries of the last two centuries have been made there, and one of the most famous scientists to have a connection with it was Michael Faraday, who is, undoubtedly, my scientific hero. From his experiments came devices that led directly to the modern electric motor, generator and transformer. He was an excellent communicator, and founded the annual Royal Institution Christmas Lectures for young people in 1826. He was a true pioneer of scientific discovery. The Royal Institution houses a wonderful lecture room that appeared, with Faraday, on the old £20 note. It is also the lecture room used for the annual Royal Institution Christmas Lectures. So, in July 1999, I was able to stand where Michael Faraday once stood, and talk about robots and cyborgs to a lecture room packed full of children. It was absolutely fantastic.

Back in the department, research was going well. Not only were we progressing on the new implant front, although we quickly realized there was an awful lot to do, but in other projects some good results were also being obtained. Some of my research students were working on more theoretical, mathematical projects – for example, Justin Gan was investigating niches in genetic algorithms of the type that we used for Gershwyn. Meanwhile, Ben Hutt and Iain Goodhew were looking at different aspects of autonomous robots.

In September I went over to MIT in Boston, where I had been invited to make a presentation at the annual 'Future of Health Technology' meeting. It was not only good to be invited to present at such a prestigious event, but I seemed to be the only UK representative. The other distinct bonus was that I presented next in line to Marvin Minsky, the MIT professor who became famous as the father of artificial intelligence. It was quite a nerve-racking experience, but Marvin is a very nice guy, and afterwards I had dinner with him and his wife, Gloria.

While still in Boston, I was contacted by Katrina Heron of *Wired* magazine, asking if I would be interested in writing an article for them on the implant experiment. *Wired* is a top-notch, very trendy magazine that sells around half-a-million copies in the US alone. I agreed, setting to work immediately on the first draft, and discussing what was needed with Michael Behar who was assigned to be editor of the piece. They were strict with the deadline, giving me the carrot that it was potentially the cover story for February or March 2000. I therefore spent my time in Boston either attending the meeting in MIT, or putting the *Wired* article together. I wasn't sure if they would actually want to go for a cover with some little-known scientist from the old country, but I kept my fingers crossed anyway.

On my return to England, I finished off the *Wired* article. Just after that, Mark Alesky, who had been assigned as the photographer by *Wired*, spent the day with me. The day finished with Irena and me in bed, semi-clothed, with Mark and an assistant, and a lot of lights and cameras. It was a very strange experience being photographed in bed with Irena, in particular because, although it was now October and our bedroom is not enormous, with four of us in there, along with several lights, the room became unbearably hot.

October 1999 was a busy month in many ways. On the 7th, several of us took a trip up to Newcastle for the grand opening of the Discovery Centre, where our robots were – and still are – fully operating on a regular basis. I was also called upon to say a few words, before setting it all under way, and I was surprised to see that quite a few school groups had turned up to watch the opening.

In October, along with Claire Whitehead, who was helping me put together my book *QI*, I had a difficult day organizing IQ tests and activities for two hundred students. We were looking at the question: if you have an hour or so to go before a vital examination, what do you do to maximize your performance? We had recruited one hundred male and one hundred female volunteers. We gave them all an IQ test then sent them off in groups to do a different activity and to partake of a different beverage. Then they all returned and we gave them another IQ test.

We were not interested in how well anyone did, but rather in how their test scores increased or decreased depending on what they were doing. Also, we were not trying to look at any particular cross-section of the community, merely a couple of hundred students. The results of the experiment were published in their entirety in *QI*. Some of them were quite understandable: for example, drinking coffee increased IQ scores in all concerned, and on average by three points, which is quite good. Meanwhile, the activities turned up quite a shock in that watching a chat show on TV was the winner, ahead of such things as reading a book or listening to classical music. All in all though it provided us with an interesting study, as well as being the final chapter to *QI*.

At the end of the month, Iain Goodhew and I were scheduled to visit Russia, having been asked by the British Council to give a number of lectures in Moscow and St Petersburg, at various universities. They wanted us to take several of our robots with us, including one called Hissing Sid, a large robot cat that two students had put together as a final-year project. It walked in a most ungainly way, wagging its tail from side to side for balance. As it operated on compressed air, each time a leg moved a loud hissing sound could be heard, hence its name. But, maybe because it was a little different, and quite large, it had already appeared on a number of TV programmes including *Blue Peter*. Hence the Russians wanted us to bring Sid in particular.

But Sid was a fairly delicate robot and took quite a bit of looking after to make sure it remained operative. A couple of times previously it had fallen over and had ended up with a pronounced limp for a week or so until it could be fixed. As a result, we didn't want Sid to go into the hold of the plane on the flight from London to Moscow, in case it was damaged in transit. However, our travel agent couldn't actually get a ticket for Sid as it didn't seem to fit an appropriate category. On our suggestion, therefore, the British Council wrote to British Airways asking if they could give our robot Sid a seat on the plane. BA's reply was to say sorry, no, but they didn't allow animals in the cabin.

Naturally, within a couple of days the story, along with a photo of Sid and me, appeared in the UK national, and several international, newspapers. It even made page three of *The Times*. BA changed their minds, perhaps not surprisingly, and actually gave Sid three seats for the flight out to, and back from, Moscow. When Sid arrived in Moscow, he was already a celebrity. His fame was further enhanced as he appeared on every major TV channel, at least once, during our week-long stay. All of this turned out to be very useful publicity for my book *March of the Machines*, the Russian translation of which the publishers decided, quite sensibly, to put out at the time of my visit.

Apart from Sid and my book launch I have two main memories of the Russian trip. Firstly, on our arrival at Moscow State University (amid a backdrop of Stalinesque buildings), we were met by a collective of frosty Russian academic professors, who were extremely formal – with no smiles – in presenting us with their business cards. We were then shepherded into a large austere auditorium in which I had to give a lecture as well as demonstrate the robots. The Russian professors settled down on the front row – still not smiling – then they let the students in. It was clear that we were very popular with the students. The room quickly filled, many were crammed into window arches, on stairs, anywhere to get a view, while others were simply locked out. There were probably six hundred or more in a room designed for four hundred maximum. We had a wonderful time, and when we demonstrated the robots, the students cheered and hollered. The frostiness went from the professors, and we ended up, after the lecture, having far too much to drink with them. Everyone had to have a photo.

My second memory is that I had to give a presentation at the St Petersburg Academy of Sciences, housed in a really enormous, grand building in the heart of old St Petersburg. At this lecture I was made an Honorary Member of the Academy of Sciences, which was completely unexpected, and an absolutely incredible honour. Apparently the only record they had of ever bestowing the same honour on an Englishman was well over a century before to a chap called Michael Faraday. Sometimes life throws up little gems like this.

From the academic rigour of the Academy of Sciences in St Petersburg I returned to attend, with Irena, Maddi and James, the London première of the Hollywood film *Inspector Gadget*. The invitation said, 'Come and meet the stars'. When we got to the Odeon in Leicester Square, crash barriers were in place to keep the crowds back, but apart from one guy taking a breather while walking his dog, no one else seemed to want to form a crowd.

We watched the film and then went to a nightclub on the other side of Leicester Square, where we thought the stars must be hiding out. Nibbles and drinks were available, as were a lot of noisy kids who had also been invited. I was asked if I'd mind presenting prizes to some children who had designed special gadgets as part of the film launch, and of course I agreed. I was joined by Angela Lamont, Johnny Ball and Rex Garrod (from Robot Wars) in presenting the prizes, and it turned out that the four of us were the stars they had been claiming would be there. What a disappointment for everyone!

But in November 1999, I received a pleasant surprise when I appeared as one of 'Thirty Great Minds on the Future' in a book entitled *Predictions*, edited by Sian Griffiths. It wasn't so much that I was included in the book, discussing as I did *In the Mind of the Machine*, but that the other contributors included such heavies as J.K. Galbraith, Arthur C. Clarke, James Watson (of DNA fame), and some guy called Paul Davies, with whom I'd done an Australian satellite link up a few months earlier. Also included in the book of thirty was Susan Greenfield, Director of the Royal Institution, who I met up with on a couple of occasions as 1999 and the old millennium drew to a close. The first was when we took part in a debate at the RI as part of a two-day event, which also included Stelarc and Igor Aleksander. The second time was in December, when I was invited along to a buffet reception to kick off the 1999 Royal Institution Christmas lectures, which were entitled 'Arrows of Time', and were presented by Neil Johnson. I had, in the past, watched the lectures when I could and had been completely fascinated by the series given by Carl Sagan, the physicist. Some years, though, I had felt I could do better myself. Now here I was getting a little closer to it.

To me, the Christmas Lectures represent a signal honour for the scientist selected, much more than any medal or fellowship. Started by Michael Faraday in 1826, the aim was, and still is, to provide an exciting opportunity for children to learn directly from scientists who are recognized as among the best in their field. Presenters have included James Dewar, the inventor of the vacuum flask, Frank Whittle, the father of the jet engine, David Attenborough and Susan Greenfield. So, when Susan asked me to give an evening presentation, I put everything into it.

We took along all of the robots that we could, we used videos and planned the lecture to perfection. Partly the thought was, that if we put on a good show, there might be an outside chance that in the years ahead I might receive an invitation to do the Christmas Lectures. However, in reality, I thought this was unlikely. But the evening lecture went brilliantly, the lecture room was packed out, and at the end of it I felt that I had given it my best shot. Even the Dalek and Hissing Sid performed out of their metal bodies.

While I was having fun, the implant design was coming along well. Every week or so the group of us involved would have a head to head to see where things stood. Getting money to support the project was vital. Following several meetings with Nortel Networks, it looked as though we might get some sponsorship from them. They had a base at Maidenhead, no more than ten miles away, and had asked me how much I wanted. When I replied, half a million pounds over three years, they had responded quite favourably, but had not yet committed to anything.

All I really needed was some money to pay for Mark Gasson, who was doing the technical work on the implant – actually putting it together. Once the signals were in the computer, then support from Computer Associates paid for researchers to do something with them, such as display them in colour. Until now I was still funding Mark out of the money I had built up in an account in the university, but that wouldn't last much longer.

But at this time we received an astonishing, major positive into the project from an unexpected source. Brian Andrews was a professor at the

University of Alberta, Canada, his specialist area being implant design. He was looking to return to the UK and we seized on this opportunity. Stoke Mandeville Hospital in Aylesbury had a number of charities associated with it that were looking to set up a university position in the biotechnology area. Stoke Mandeville also housed, for part of the week, a certain Jimmy Saville. It seemed too good to be true, but very quickly paperwork was being circulated to create a position, as professor, for Brian in the Cybernetics Department at Reading, which would bring him over from Canada permanently. On the back of William Harwin having recently joined the department from a top medical centre in Delaware, we were creating our own reverse brain drain.

Things moved quickly, and Brian's position soon materialized. He immediately started to input vital ideas into Mark's implant design, making sure the right signals were being selected and that noise was reduced. But Brian also brought to the project a key individual, the man who would carry out the operation – Ali Jamous, one of the world's top neurosurgeons, situated at Stoke Mandeville.

As 1999 left by the back door, I welcomed 2000 in through the front door with a major decision. I didn't want to drop my robotics work completely, but there was only one thing driving me forward now with a vengeance, and that was the next implant project, the next stage of becoming a cyborg. And, what is more, it was looking very likely to happen. So, at the end of 1999, I decided that the implant experiment would be my number one priority. I knew then that, more than anything else in the world, I wanted to become a cyborg.

CHAPTER 8

SCIENTISTS AROUND THE world swap information at conferences and presentations, pick up lines of attack from others, even borrow some good ideas from time to time in order to push forward their own work or steer it in a more fruitful direction, so keeping an eye on what other people are doing is a necessary part of the action. Although it is important to spend some time developing your own research direction, it is also good to devote a little time to peer over the shoulders of others.

In the realm of cyborg research the variety and extent of ongoing work is astounding. Some of it – such as that in the military domain or work tied up with commercial confidentiality – is almost impossible to find out about. Other work, particularly in the US, needs to be translated in order to discover what is going on or what has actually been achieved, and I am often left amazed at what others have done.

In a new area of science, as indeed the study of cyborgs is, very little concrete evidence exists, there are few equations and the rules are yet to be drawn up. Subject boundaries are ill-defined: what is a cyborg and what is not? Most of what exists is a wide variety of experimental results from scientists around the world. Largely though things are yet to be mapped out, and facts need to be sorted from mere speculation or old-wives tales. Each experiment steps out into the unknown. To me, it is the most exciting science of all.

In this chapter my aim is to give an idea of the related research projects that have given us ideas for our own cyborg research or have opened up our minds as to what we might be able to achieve. Some are directly related to what we are doing, whereas some have acted merely as inspiration. Others point a finger into the future, in the direction in which we are heading. Finally there are a number of projects detailed here that serve to indicate that what we wish to do is not only possible, but is very likely to result in our success.

One of the problems we faced, in the Department of Cybernetics, with the 1998 implant was its potential to migrate from its starting position. Indeed, this was perhaps the main reason why the experiment was of a relatively short duration. So I was delighted to discover that this might not be a problem. A porous polymer sheath, named Bio-Bond, had been developed for the same type of radio frequency devices I had implanted. Using this sheath, 148 beagles were implanted with a radio-frequency identifier. After a two-year period thirty-seven of the beagles who remained had their implants evaluated and all implants were found both to be fully functional and in exactly the same position where they were originally placed. Although the company concerned with the research stated that the beagles were 'normal residents of the research facility', 111 of them were nevertheless killed in order to 'rotate their genetic program'. In each case the tissue surrounding the implant was investigated. I surmised that Bio-Bond might well be useful in my own case, although if I had a 111 in 148 chance (75 per cent) of being slaughtered during a two-year period, I would most likely opt for the stitches that I had.

Quite a large amount of research exists where technology is positioned *on*, rather than *in*, the body, and yet, in one way or another, it can be seen to enhance the way in which the body operates. This gives us some idea as to what sort of technological upgrades might be possible and what we might be able to achieve by taking things further with an implant.

In fact many problems can be avoided if we don't consider implants in the first place, but instead look at linking up technology with the outside of the human body. Stelarc, the Australian digital artist, who causes programmed movements to occur in his own body through external electrodes which stimulate his muscles, said: 'We try to design our instruments so that our body can use them . . . now we have come to the point where we have to think about redesigning the human body to match the capabilities of machines.'

Stelarc uses a technique called functional electrical simulation (FES) by means of surface electrodes. The same method is used to improve the quality of life of spinal-cord injured subjects, so that they can live a more independent, everyday life. By this method an electrode-connected neural prosthesis operates by the generation of a series of short, electrical pulses in order to cause a muscle contraction. By activating a group of muscles in a specified order, a subject can control the motion of a limb which could not otherwise be moved.

Meanwhile high-tech 'wearables' are being developed to augment everyday items such as glasses and shoes with mini computers. In this way it is felt that we will be able to extend our senses, improve memory and add to the wearer's social life. Some recent developments are directed towards medical wearables to assist the elderly, particularly to monitor high-risk medical problems and give an early warning.

A lot of this research is taking place at MIT. However, of the work being done there, the most exciting and the most relevant, I feel, to our own research, is that being carried out by Roz Picard, who is looking into active wearables. She is investigating a system to track constantly indications of alertness and stress – such as those caused by anger, shock or excitement – by witnessing changes and effects going on inside the body and even on the human nervous system. These signals could be loosely described as those attributable to physical emotions, and the hope is that it may be possible to help the individual stay calm and collected.

Perhaps the best-known work in this field is that of Steve Mann, who appears to have been immersed in wearables for several years. His goal is to develop computing that is worn like clothing and therefore always ready for use. For example, he has a miniaturized computer screen fitted into an otherwise normal pair of glasses. Similarly a small camera, also fitted on to the glasses, allows for remote vision. With the computer systems networked it means that with multi-users, one person can witness what another person is looking at, and can therefore share in decisions, or the computer can be used to provide information to the viewer. For example, if a human face is being viewed, the computer could send a message to the wearer informing them of the name of the person – very useful if you're not very good at putting a name to a face. Mann considers that, as humans get used to such wearable computers as everyday items, interaction will become natural.

For the most part this wearables research is extremely practical. In many cases actual trial systems exist and experiments are underway. Some speculation does take place as to how such systems might be used socially in the future, but these are generally well-founded ideas of what might happen if society was to run with the technology – something that I don't think any scientist can ever really know.

In some ways, I feel that my 1998 implant went much further. Wearables research is very interesting to us in terms of what humans want or what they will accept, though perhaps of much more interest are technological connections directly affected by what is going on in the body or that themselves affect the internal workings of the body. The combination is then working much more as a cybernetic system.

When we consider technology placed inside the body, namely implants, research tends to follow two main lines. First, where experimentation involves human subjects: in this case the implants, thus far, have almost exclusively been designed to deal with a patient's particular medical problem (although my own implant in 1998 was an exception to this). The second line involves experimentation on animals.

I do not experiment on or with animals. However, many others do, and it is well worth keeping an eye on what is going on in order to relate it to our own research. Although some animal research is directly linked to the potential for dealing with medical problems in humans, most of it appears to be much more scientific and aimed at pushing back the frontiers.

What follows is a brief look at some of the recent experiments that have changed the way I look at our line of investigation. In each case it is worth speculating what the likely result might be and what the potential is, when the same technology is applied to a human.

In 1997 a team at the University of Tokyo connected a microprocessor directly into the brain of a cockroach in a widely publicized project. In effect the microprocessor was piggy-backed on to the motor neurons of the cockroach and was worn as a backpack. Artificial signals sent to the neurons through electrodes were then used to propel the cockroach despite what it might have itself chosen to do. At the Max Planck Institute in Germany a similar experiment has resulted in the controlled movement of a leech by means of a computer, and in the spring of 1999 there were reports that a rat's movements were directed by remote control in the same way. Although the rat walked under its own control, its direction of travel was decided by the researchers.

Meanwhile, in an amazing experiment at Northwestern University's Rehabilitation Institute in Chicago, Sandro Mussa-Ivaldi used the extracted brain of a tiny eel-like lamprey to control the movement of a small-wheeled robot, to which it was connected with electrodes. A lamprey has an innate response to light, which it usually uses to keep itself the right way up in water. However, the team at Northwestern surrounded the lamprey-brained robot with a circle of lights such that when a light was switched on, the brain directed the robot to move towards the light. As different lights were flashed on and off the robot dashed back and forth.

In an experiment reported in 1999 by John Chapin at the MCP Hahnemann School of Medicine in Philadelphia, an initial arrangement was set up so that when a rat pulled a lever, it received a tot of water as a reward. Electrodes were then implanted into specific positions in the rat's brain such that strong signals were emitted when the rat thought about pulling the lever before it made a physical movement. The signals were then used to deliver the treat to the rat, before it had a chance to pull the lever. It appeared to be the case that the rat quickly caught on that it did not need to pull the lever in order to get its water treat, but simply think about the act.

Perhaps an even more astounding experiment was that carried out by

Miguel Nicolelis at Duke University Medical Centre in North Carolina. His team connected ninety-six electrodes to the motor neurons of two owl monkeys. As each monkey reached for a piece of fruit in front of them the signals transmitted from the electrodes were used to control the movement of a robot arm that mirrored the monkeys' movements. With identical success the team also transmitted the signals from each monkey's brain 600 miles across the internet to another robot. Perhaps this research more than any other made me think, couldn't we do this sort of thing with a human?

Well before this though, a furor was caused by an experiment carried out by Olds and Milner in the 1950s, who implanted electrodes directly into the lateral hypothalamus area of the brain in several rats. Each electrode was connected to a stimulator that was activated by the touch of a button. The electrical stimulation caused feelings of pleasure. The rats were taught how to press the button themselves, giving them the feeling of pleasure. They were then given the choice between the pleasure button and a button that would result in them receiving food. The rats continually chose the pleasure button even when they were hungry and even as they starved to death. Very similar results have since been achieved replacing rats with monkeys.

While it is clear that we should not immediately extrapolate these results directly to humans, it would be stupid in the extreme not to believe that not only would the human brain be capable of such feats but, because of its complexity and power, would also be capable of much more. It would be foolish to feel that in the future humans will not be able to control technology merely by means of thought. After all, if monkeys, rats and even lampreys can do it, then surely humans can too?

Most research of this ilk, centred on humans, involves patients with a medical problem, often of considerable seriousness, for which they are only too happy to try new approaches to its correction. By contrast my own research involves self-experimentation. While this is certainly not the norm, it is by no means without precedence. The following cases have inspired me in different ways.

Over the years, numerous scientists have carried out experiments involving themselves in order to prove a point. One famous example is

US Colonel John Stapp who, in the early 1950s, repeatedly strapped his body to rocket sleds and propelled himself to more than 600 mph before hitting the brakes and stopping in less than two seconds. Stapp, a military physician, wanted to improve safety in aeroplanes, spacecraft and even cars. Although Stapp survived these perilous experiments into the human body's tolerance of crash forces, he suffered numerous broken bones, a permanently impaired sense of balance, eye damage, a hernia and concussion.

In 1984 Barry Marshall, a resident at Royal Perth Hospital in Australia, wanted to show that stomach ulcers are not caused by stress but by bacteria. He proved it by swallowing large quantities of the organism and shortly afterwards was able proudly to announce his theory to be true. However, he then had an ulcer problem to deal with. In 1929 Werner Forssmann, a German physician, was attempting to learn about the intricacies of the human heart and its accompanying blood-flow system. He therefore inserted a catheter into an artery in his arm and snaked it all the way to his right auricle heart chamber.

With all these experiments, the individuals put themselves in considerable danger in order to prove their theories correct, and they have been successful. In other cases the danger was too great and the individual did not survive, although in such cases it can be difficult for others to decipher what exactly the experimenter was setting out to prove. Naturally, the experimenters can sometimes start with an incorrect hypothesis and their experiments are thereby bound for failure.

One example of this is Max Von Pettenkofer, another German doctor who, in 1892, drank a culture of bacterium that causes cholera. His aim was to show that certain environmental factors must also be present before the germ produces the disease. His hypothesis was entirely wrong and, as a result, he was seriously ill for about a week. Fortunately he lived to tell the tale. Then there is the story of one of the most famous scientists of all time, Isaac Newton, who, for a number of years, stuck needles into his eyes. This seemingly strange activity is further embellished in that a number of stories abound as to exactly why he was doing it. In my own view none of the versions is particularly plausible, so it may well always remain a mystery.

Animal experiments, wearable-computing research and human self-experimenters all, in their own way, influence our own project, even if it is only in terms of driving us forward, telling us not to give up. But by far the largest body of research concerned with our own interests involves experiments on human individuals (often patients) by physicians. In this research we are given a clear direction of what we are likely to expect. This in turn influences the technology in terms of signalling between the human body and a computer, in terms of implant positioning, materials used, expected lifetime of the implant, and so on.

The best-known researcher from an historical viewpoint is José Delgado. Delgado started his investigations under the fascist regime in Spain during World War Two but continued them well into the 1970s while holding the position of Director of Neuropsychiatry at Yale University Medical School. He designed what he called a 'transdermal stimulator' which was, essentially, a computer-controlled remote neural transceiver (i.e. it could send signals in and out of the brain) and stimulator. He showed that it was possible to transmit and receive electrical messages to and from the human brain. In his work a small number of terminal wires were implanted within the brain, with further wires leading to the radio receiver/transmitter positioned outside the scalp. One of the worries of his research was always infection, something that we have also been faced with.

Although well cited, Delgado's practical results on humans were extremely limited, and most of his research was either merely stated without a results base, or has been reported on second hand. Partly this is due to the fact that he received substantial financial support from the US military, and the validity of the output must therefore be questioned. Reports have been made on his work on the 'Pandora Project', which involved modulating electromagnetic fields to a soldier's head so that the soldier would lose self-control on the battle field. Reports also include how work was carried out to induce schizophrenia artificially through electrical stimulation of the septal zone in a human brain. It was stated that, as well as hallucinations, various emotions such as anger, love, solitude, euphoria, fear and depression were all produced through electrical stimulation. It is very difficult to judge whether these goals were ever realized, were only conjecture on the part of Delgado, or were mere speculation on the part of others.

Delgado said: 'It is possible to induce a large variety of responses, from motor effects to emotional reactions and intellectual manifestations, by direct electrical stimulation of the brain. Also, several investigators have learned to identify patterns of electricity localized in specific areas of the brain and related to determined phenomena such as perception of smells or visual perception of edges and movements. We are advancing rapidly in the pattern recognition of electrical correlates of behaviour and in the methodology for two-way radio communication between brain and computers.' Clearly Delgado seems to have been ahead of his time in many ways, seeing a distinct and exciting path ahead that research could follow. Perhaps it is only in recent years though that the technology has become sufficiently advanced to allow us to follow this path, and it is interesting to conjecture what he might have been able to achieve with the micro and even nano circuits of today. But his inspirational foresight should propel us along the path to achieve the two-way communication he suggested.

Perhaps the largest body of research in the field that exists however is in the replacement, rewiring or reinvigoration of body parts that have ceased to function. So rather than the two-way connection foreseen by Delgado, emphasis has been placed more on a uni-directional channel from computer to brain. One good, and relatively straightforward, example of this was the work of Eugene de Juan and Mark Humayun of Duke University in 1992. They introduced an electrode into the eye of a completely blind patient, Harold Churchey, and then caused a spark at the end of the electrode by introducing an electric pulse. Churchey said, 'I could see it. Just a little light. That's all it was.'

This spark was sufficient to ignite a considerable amount of research directed towards the realization of an artificial retina. The clear aim was to move from hand-held electrodes, as used by Juan and Humayun, to actual implants with their own, built-in, power supply. By 1996 the two researchers, having by that time moved to Johns Hopkins University in Baltimore, conducted another experiment with Churchey, who was seventy-five years old by then. They placed a 25-electrode array, lined up in a 5 by 5 square, in Churchey's eye, and attempted to display an image of the letter 'U' by lighting up an appropriate pattern of electrodes. Unfortunately it was difficult to replicate the curved edges of the letter and what Churchey actually reported seeing was the letter 'H'. Nevertheless the experiment was a considerable success, as, for the first time, a blind person had been able to take in a simple image.

Since then a number of different research groups have been working on artificial retina projects. Joseph Rizzo and John Wyatt have been working on a system that involves a small digital camera mounted on a pair of glasses. The image captured is turned into an array of pixels which are then sent to the implant inside the eye. Human trials with this system have produced mixed results and it is extremely difficult to ascertain from reports what has actually been tested and what hasn't.

But a similar approach, taken by William Dobelle, has achieved considerable success, a big difference being that signals are passed not to the eye but instead directly stimulate brain cells via an array of small electrodes on the brain surface, just behind the right ear. The trial patient, named only as 'Jerry', wears a pair of sunglasses with a tiny pinhole camera mounted on one lens. This communicates with a computer carried on Jerry's hip, which highlights the edges between light and dark regions in the image. The computer in this technique is used to send image-edge information to Jerry's brain, the aim being to give him a caricature-type line-drawing image. The device provides a type of tunnel vision, allowing Jerry, who is otherwise completely blind, to pick out, for example, a black cap on a white wall. At any one time it covers an area of vision around 1.5 metres ahead, and about 20cm high by 5cm wide. Jerry, who is a walking laboratory, only uses the device two or three days a week, and the 64-electrode array is now being worked on in an attempt to provide some depth perception.

One problem at the present time is that it has taken Dobelle's team several years to put together and modify the software in order to produce satisfactory results for Jerry. It is certainly not the case that the electrode array was simply plugged in and operated fully from the first day.

The situation with cochlea implants is very different, in that it is far more developed. Over the last twenty years tens of thousands of people have successfully received such implants. Initially some scientists believed that at least one thousand electrodes would be necessary in order to create coherent sounds. However, it turned out that as few as six electrodes were quite sufficient in many cases. As has been found with other studies, the human brain has enormous plasticity and can take in a fairly crude input generated by a computer and then make sense out of it. Indeed, when presented with a new opportunity the human brain adapts well and modifies its mode of working to make the most of it.

Cochlea implants provided the first reliable and successful interface between the human brain and an external, technological device. However, a lot remains to be learned about the implants and the cochlea they are assisting, but at the present time a success rate of well over 50 per cent is being achieved. Unfortunately not every deaf person can use a present-day cochlea implant, as they operate as a replacement for a disfunctioning cochlea in a person who is deaf; this means that the individual must have completely intact and functioning auditory nerves.

For those whose auditory nerves are not operational, newer implants are now being researched, which involve the placement of an array directly on to the cochlea nucleus in the brain stem or alternatively into the auditory cortex. A number of human trials have taken place and results are encouraging. However, the technology is lagging ten to fifteen years behind the well-established cochlea implant approach which is itself commercially viable.

Something more off-the-wall is the work of Theodore Berger at the University of Southern California, who is trying to achieve accurate silicon models of the hippocampus, the cortical area of the human brain directly involved in memory. His ultimate aim is to implant artificial hippocampi into people with memory problems, i.e. to implant memory chips. This work immediately begs the question that if it does become possible to implant such chips, will it therefore also be possible to give people extra memory capabilities – in other words, to enhance someone's memory?

Berger is presently investigating thin slices of the hippocampus and trying to 'copy' an individual slice on to a silicon chip. At present he claims to be able to get at least one hundred neurons on to one chip and can readily see how that number will soon increase eightfold. There is still a long way to go, however, to replicate the whole of one slice in which potentially millions of neurons (certainly thousands) are involved. Then comes the problem of connecting together different chips representing several slices. This will require wires and contacts and will take up a lot of space. Berger's hope is to use photonics, to direct lasers to transmit information precisely between the slices by means of light signals.

But the biggest problem still to be faced by Berger is how to connect an artificial hippocampus into the rest of the brain so that it can actually be used. His view is to culture human neurons on top of a specially designed chip, which then functions as a set of electrodes. In itself this is not as speculative as it sounds, as other brain implants are now applying such a technique with some success. He expects to be conducting animal experimental studies in the next few years.

It is work like this that really causes you to think. Yes, the interfacing is a problem to be overcome. But why is he trying to model the functioning of the hippocampus in silicon? Would it not be possible to try to connect standard memory devices on silicon with the human brain? Such trials could go ahead much sooner and it may even be found that the human brain quickly adapts to the alternative memory source it is coupled with, perhaps even sharing functions with a much simpler input/output signalling procedure between the hippocampus and a computer. This would link in more closely with Delgado's ideas and could provide a great deal more flexibility in memory accessing and storage. Indeed, the external computer could also come into play as a complementary external memory device.

Nevertheless, the research of Berger is both interesting and highly relevant to our own project, particularly if we move forward to brain implants in the future, which is highly likely. Mapping the nervous system – and in particular the human brain – could give us vital indications as to where it is best to connect in technology. There are two big unknowns that are important questions for the future. The first is, how individualized will Berger's maps be? Will the map of one person be very different from that of another? The second question is how much and in what way will a map change when technology is connected?

Another Dobelle success is the use of implants for bladder control. This is an important requirement for paraplegics, who may have no immediate bladder-control capability. The overall neural prosthesis consists of a radio-frequency stimulator which is positioned outside the body, and an implanted radio-frequency receiver connected to platinum bipolar stimulating electrodes. The electrodes are placed on the conus medullaris nerve, which is responsible for contracting the bowel.

A patient who has such a prosthesis carries with them an external transmitter, about the size of a small Walkman. It has a looped antenna which is held over the receiver site when stimulation occurs. At a press of a button, impulses are transmitted through the skin to the implant receiver which forwards appropriate signals to the electrodes that bring about the stimulation of bladder contractions. In a matter of 45 seconds a bladder can empty about 100cc. So rather akin to opening a garage door with a remote-control button, an individual can empty their bladder.

As well as the FES systems mentioned earlier, which externally activate muscles, implanted versions exist. One approach is to implant electrodes into the wrist and forearm muscles of one arm of a quadriplegic in order to restore hand grasp. A joystick controller is also implanted in the opposite shoulder. The quadriplegic then learns how to move their shoulder, and hence the joystick, in order to move the appropriate muscles to grip and hold a cup and pick up objects between thumb and forefinger. The muscles need to be exercised for a period before such functions are possible, as they are often out of condition at the time of implant. It is interesting that muscles may well get out of condition through lack of use, but they don't actually waste away, as some people think.

It was found that the external stimulation method using electrodes on the skin surface, as in Stelarc's case, didn't provide the necessary precision for stimulating the individual muscles to grip and hold objects. Implants are therefore required for the accuracy necessary to achieve the coordinated movements for grasp and lift.

One of the most incredible things I have ever witnessed was seeing the effect that electronic stimulation can have on a person who suffers from Parkinson's disease. With Parkinson's, diminished levels of the neuro-transmitter dopamine cause over-activation in the ventral posterior nucleus and the subthalamic nucleus, which are tiny parts of the brain. This over-activation causes slowness, stiffness, gait difficulties and the hand tremors commonly associated with the disease. The younger you are when you get the disease, the worse it gets, as it gradually takes hold. To some extent the condition can be treated chemically, but after a few years the effect of chemical treatment does wear off.

In 1995, pioneering studies by Dr A.L. Benebid, a French doctor at the University of Grenoble, demonstrated that high-frequency stimulation of the ventral intermediate nucleus of the thalamus disrupts the tremor. By implanting the electrodes into the subthalamic nucleus and stimulating the regions in question, the over-activity is inhibited, and the symptoms are reversed. Implanted units at the top of the patient's chest contain the main circuitry and power and these are connected to the implanted electrodes in the brain. When switched off the symptoms return and the disease takes full effect, but when switched on (which can be done externally by induction), the results are, to understate the case, dramatic. With the implants operative it is as though the disease simply doesn't exist in the patient. The patient is completely free and can move around, drive a car, dress themselves and so on, in the normal way.

The complete neural prosthetic is manufactured by Medtronic Inc. of Minneapolis, and I have been fortunate in that the company have allowed me to use video footage of an implanted patient in my lecture presentations. The video indicates in the clearest possible terms how the workings of the human body can be distinctly changed by the introduction of electronic signals. First the video shows a man with an acute case of Parkinson's disease and how he cannot walk and has great difficulty moving around. The implants are then switched on and his transformation into a disease-free individual is immediate. Every time I have shown this video it has had a profound effect on the audience.

But results such as these have not stopped just with Parkinson's disease. It has also been found that by implanting an electrode into the ventral lateral thalamus – another part of the brain – a similar approach can be used to suppress the tremors caused by cerebral palsy and multiple sclerosis.

In the last few years various techniques have also appeared in an attempt to deal with epilepsy. One device, called the Neuro Cybernetic Prosthesis System, provides intermittent stimulation of the vagus nerve by means of an electrode implanted in the neck. It is claimed that activation of this nerve considerably reduces the likelihood of seizure occurring. However, it is still not clear how successful the method is and a wide variety of different claims have been made to its efficacy.

An alternative approach based on EEG (electro encephalographic) data seems also to produce good results. In this case the EEG signals can be used to successfully predict the onset of an epileptic fit. It is simply an algorithm which takes EEG data and warns of an incipient seizure. Many believe that the main cause of disability in epilepsy is the unpredictability of when a seizure will occur, so once you can reduce or even remove this unpredictability, the patient is helped enormously – particularly if they can take some protective action to avoid embarrassment and minimize injury. Further, it is felt that such a system can also be used to indicate when electronic stimulation of the brain should be used in order to counteract the effects directly. Nowadays research is going on to find the best method and location for such stimulation to take place.

Perhaps the most stunning research that relates to my own interests is that carried out by Philip Kennedy and his team at Neural Signals Inc. and Emory University in Atlanta. They have used brain implants to enable people to operate a computer merely by the power of thought. The aim of the research programme is to allow people who are totally paralysed not only to operate artificial limbs but also write letters, send emails and generally control their environment via a computer. By the end of 1999, two incapacitated people had received implants that gave them the ability to control a cursor on the computer screen by thinking about moving parts of their body. By pointing the cursor at different icons the patients could get the computer to voice phrases such as 'I am too cold' or 'Turn off the light'.

Electrodes consisting of two gold wires attached to hollow glass cones, each one about the size of the tip of a ballpoint pen, were implanted into the motor cortex which contains cells controlling various muscles. Ordinary movement is initiated when neurons in the motor cortex fire. The patients, one of whom was Johnny Ray, a paralysed war veteran, were asked to think about moving. A magnetic resonance imaging (MRI) scanner was then used to detect where the brain activity was at this time. The electrodes were therefore positioned where the activity was most noticeable.

Once the electrodes were in place the patients were again asked to think about moving. This time the responses from the electrodes were amplified and transmitted to the computer by radio. Here they were translated into signals used to command the computer cursor.

The cones were laced with neurotropic chemicals, originally extracted from the patients' knees, to encourage nerve growth in the brain. Over a period of several months, the implant became a natural part of each patients' brain as their neurons grew into, and attached themselves to the electrodes. Depending on exactly which nerves grew into the cones, each patient had to think about moving a different part of their body in order to bring about cursor movement. The patients learned to use the device by thinking about movement, and receiving feedback not only through seeing the cursor move but also through a buzzer which became faster and louder when they were thinking along the right lines. In Ray's case it was his thoughts about hand movement that operated the cursor.

Interestingly the implants used by the Emory team shared two similarities with my 1998 implant: both used radio-frequency signalling and the same means of powering the device. Rather than the large coils of wire in doorways that I used in my experiment, the Emory team use a coil worn outside the skull in a cap which needs power sent to it in the usual way by means of wires. The coil then induces a current in the transmitter–receiver, which is positioned just inside the skull, and it connects to the electrodes themselves. Neural activity signals are sent from the electrodes to the transmitter–receiver, from there to an amplifier positioned in the cap, and thence by radio to the computer.

By looking closely at research such as this, it can helps us firm up on ideas for the research we are doing ourselves. In the case of the Emory project, it was clear that as they were using the same signalling procedure as ourselves, this was not a bad route to be taking. It was also clear that less than 5 per cent of the technology used for their experiments was actually implanted. The powering device, the coil of wire and the vast bulk of the electronics were situated not inside the body, but outside in a cap. In our case, trying to get all our technology into an implant was creating difficulties. To implant everything you need it to be very small. But this adds all sorts of pressure as today's technology doesn't allow for a great deal of miniaturization. This is especially true as far as the power supply is concerned. The fact that in Emory's case most of their interface was not implanted was to have a major impact on our own research. After all, the most important topic for Emory was getting signals from the nervous system to the computer. Whether or not this was by a piece of technology that was completely implanted was irrelevant. In our case we were also looking at sending signals from the computer to the nervous system, thereby requiring more technology and making the problem worse.

Another interesting feature of the Emory research was that each patient's neurons grew not only into the electrodes and joined with them, but when experimentation started they strengthened around their new opportunity, making themselves more capable of taking advantage of what was on offer. This brain plasticity, on which I have commented before, was also a vital observation for our own work, particularly if we wanted to consider sending signals on to the nervous system that the brain had not witnessed before. It would need to adapt in some way.

With this ongoing backdrop of related research, we were given ideas as to what might and what might not be possible with our own project. Most of the work with insects or humans involved direct connections to the brain. However, our next experiment was to be along a different line and would, like the 1998 investigation, involve me as the subject. There appeared to be more than enough dangers in going for another experiment, even if we stuck with a second arm implant, so going for a brain hook up seemed unnecessarily risky at this stage. Indeed, very little appeared to be known about connections between the human body and the computer, so there was much still to be learned from an arm implant.

But what method should we use, and what sort of connection should we make? An FES system, externally connected, such as that used by Stelarc would not get us very far as it would only allow for muscle stimulation. It seemed that even connecting up to muscles inside the body would only allow for a very limited range of experiments. Yet this approach had a number of advantages. Firstly it would be a lot safer than a connection on to the nervous system. Second, the signals required to stimulate muscles are of the order of millivolts. With this signal strength we were unlikely to have problems with noise. Conversely, nervous-system connections would require microvolt signals – much smaller in amplitude and therefore much more prone to be affected by noise. However, nervous-system signals would allow us to look at not only movement signals, which would be the case with muscle connections, but also to sensory signals and even possibly body state/emotional signals. But if we did go the nervous-system route, what sort of connection could be made with the nervous system?

One fairly well tried-and-tested method makes use of a cuff electrode. Such a technique has been used on numerous people who have been paralysed due to illness, a stroke, or because of an accident, in an attempt to activate paralysed muscles. The particular application target areas are for hand grasping and to overcome a drop-foot, where control of the foot has been lost.

In simple terms the cuff electrode fits as a collar around the nervous fibres. Signals travelling along the nerve fibres can be picked up and transmitted to the computer. For a fully-implanted device we would need a power supply and an associated radio transmitter and receiver, as well as the cuff. The cuff picks up whatever is happening in the nerves it has surrounded. This means that for the median nerve, the main nerve that goes down the centre of the human arm, the cuff actually picks up a roughly average signal from the 10,000 nerve fibres that exist. True, we can stimulate particular movements and senses, but even if the signals that appear on the nervous system associated with these stimulations are strong, it still gives an amalgamated signal.

Several forms of the cuff electrode can be obtained. Perhaps the most useful version is one in which two or three electrode pick-up points exist along the 20mm length of the cuff. With this device it is possible to pick up the same signal at several points, thereby gaining an indication of how a nerve signal travels down the nerve fibres.

For our purposes, one problem with the cuff was the danger it would cause to the nerve fibres. To make a good connection the cuff is fitted tightly around the fibres. Firstly, this means cutting off the links with the blood vessels around the nerves, and second, actually crushing numerous nerve fibres to make a good connection. Someone once said to me that fitting a cuff electrode was rather like fitting a size 10 foot in a size 6 shoe – it is a real squeeze. For a person whose nerves in question are not functioning normally as a result of a break in the nervous system nearer to the brain this is, of course, not a problem. However, for me it would most likely mean losing quite a few nerve fibres. One plus was that the technology was readily available and quite simple to use, but a negative side was that the information we would be able to obtain from it would be fairly limited.

The only alternative technology available appeared to be a miniature array of microelectrodes, about 4mm by 4mm in size, invented by Richard Normann and his team at the Moran Laboratories in the Department of Bioengineering at the University of Utah. The array contains one hundred electrode silicon spikes, each 1.5mm long and connected to a very fine wire, thereby providing an electrical connection. The array has been described as having the appearance of a hair brush and is fitted into the nervous system with a special gun so the electrode spikes penetrate easily. At the end of 1999 it was also apparent that the Utah group were about to launch a new form of the array: a slant array. In this case, rather than all the spikes being of the same length, they were stepped, so that the first row of ten were only 0.5mm long, the second row a bit longer, and so on, until the final row is at the 1.5mm depth.

The array seemed a much better idea. Firstly, it offered the possibility of picking up one hundred signals from the nerve fibres. Out of the ten thousand fibres in the arm this didn't seem to be too low a proportion.

Second, all the tests seemed to show that the resultant nerve damage was relatively slight in comparison with that of the cuff. But the key thing with this array was that we should be able to obtain patterns of nerve-fibre activity associated with some movements and sensory information.

It therefore seemed to be a better idea to go for the array, keeping the cuff as a potential back up if we met with any problems. If, however, the team at Utah came through with their new slant array we would probably use that. In either case we still had to design the remainder of the implant, namely the electronic circuitry to take the signals from the electrode wires and transmit them to the computer by radio, and also to pick up signals from the computer and play them down on to the electrode array. Along with incorporating a suitable power supply, this was essentially the reason Mark Gasson was on the team.

One slight problem with both the slant and original arrays was that they had not yet been used on humans. Experiments had only taken place with animals, particularly cats. In addition to this, the usual procedure appeared to involve firing the array into the nervous system of a cat and carrying out experiments over a three-month period. The cat would then be killed and the researchers would investigate nervous-system tissue to examine the after effects. As a result, even the work with cats meant that it was not really known what would happen if the array was simply removed at the end of the experiment. Would the cat return to life as normal?

Making ourselves aware of other ongoing research not only opened up the range of possibilities, but also pointed to a range of gaps. We quickly discovered that only a very basic understanding of the human nervous system had been obtained during the twentieth century. This understanding had come from experiments using single micro-electrodes, usually inserted through the skin. Recordings were then taken either when nervous-system activity was enforced, or in response to various stimuli applied through the electrodes. I had previously thought that it was just the human brain about which relatively little was known, but we quickly discovered that the same lack of knowledge applied to the human nervous system as a whole. As for the nerve fibres we would be connecting to – most likely the median nerve in my arm –

there really was very little to go on. It appeared that three separate theories existed as to how the nerve fibres were structured and operated. Each theory seemed to be contradictory and in direct opposition to the others.

While we didn't have much of a starting point, we knew that firing in the array should allow us to collect a lot of data through our experiments, that may enable us to come up with our own theory about the nervous system. Certainly it was expected that we would acquire unique data to prove or disprove any of the existing theories.

One worrying aspect of the first implant had been the possibility that my body would reject the glass capsule. This hadn't actually happened, and in fact the opposite had occurred. However, for this experiment, with the new implant, the Utah array seemed perfect. It was made of silicon, which is extremely biocompatible, and it had been shown in tests to be able to cope with the corrosive environments it was likely to encounter. In addition to all this, mechanically it was very strong. So, in terms of reliability in the body, the Utah array definitely seemed the way to go.

Keeping our eyes on what research had gone on before and what was ongoing was therefore both a good and necessary thing for us to do. Essentially we had to collect all the knowledge we could from other experiments, particularly those carried out on animals that we hadn't done ourselves, and bring together the technology we needed in order to carry out the experiment we wanted to do. Once we got signals from the body we knew we had the technological know-how in the lab both to work with them and send the signals of our choice back into the body. However, for the actual hook up to the nervous system we would have to lean very heavily on the technology with which Utah would supply us.

This, however, presented us with something of a problem. If we told them we were going to fire an array into my arm, would they supply us with the technology? After all, to that point the array had only been tried out on animals. We therefore had to purchase an array from Utah, perhaps without them knowing exactly what we were going to use it for.

Another problem was that Ali Jamous, the neurosurgeon, would be undertaking a procedure that had never been done on a human. Would he be happy about this? Would he get it right? Would the array actually make good contact with the nerves? Would human nerve fibres respond differently to the array than animal nerve fibres? Most importantly though, would I be in excruciating pain once the array was connected into my nervous system? Although reports from Utah had indicated that the experimental cats did not seem to be suffering a great deal of pain, how obvious would an understanding of their pain be, and what about the experiments that went wrong that Utah might not have reported?

We had to look back at the pioneering work of Delgado and listen to his words again with comfort. By sending signals to and from my nervous system via my arm, we were merely taking a step on the path he had suggested. How far might we go down that path?

With the work of Philip Kennedy and others, the plasticity and the adaptability of the human brain had been highlighted. On the one hand that was excellent news. We wanted to send different signals on to the nervous system and hence up to the brain and it would be fascinating if my brain changed, albeit slightly, in order to deal with those signals more effectively. But at the same time this would mean that my brain would change from its present state. Would it change in a beneficial direction? Would it be able to cope nonchalantly with the new data it received?

As far as I was concerned, the pain and danger aspects of the implant were merely a hazard of the experiment. This was something I very much wanted to do, in order to find out what it was like, what was possible and what was not. Irena was more worried about the potential mental effects. While the chance of these being particularly disruptive were only slight, she was worried about waking up one morning next to a husband who was different mentally. I remembered my father and how his mental state had changed in all sorts of ways as a result of his agoraphobia operation. Would the same thing happen to me?

All the practical research on humans that was there for us to lean on was directed towards using technology to help people to overcome a problem. Meanwhile, several animal experiments were pushing back the limits and extending capabilities. This was not what I really wanted to do in terms of the next implant experiment. I wanted to see what might be possible over and above what humans are capable of at the moment, and I wanted to be involved and take a practical step, despite what the dangers might be.

But we still had a lot to do. Not only was it necessary to get hold of certain pieces of technology and design our own to go with them, but we also had to decide what experimentation we were going to do. Ali had to make momentous decisions about exactly where the implant would be positioned and how he was going to carry out the operation. I had to bring in some money to pay for Mark Gasson and other researchers working on the project. While we didn't need enormous sums, the amount was significant. We also needed money to pay for the technology it would all be connected to.

As the new millennium was born, so television, radio, computers and jet engines became something from the previous millennium – old technology. We were about to undertake pioneering research into the new world of cyborgs that was likely to change the world as we knew it. In typical UK fashion we were doing it all on a shoestring, but where was I going to get the money to buy the shoestring?

CHAPTER 9

ON THE FIRST day of the new millennium, our toaster didn't mutate and chase us upstairs, our TV kept working and so did our car. There appeared to be no possible stories for the media. It seemed to be the one moment in the history of the world when nothing of any significance went wrong, and the consultants congratulated themselves that if it hadn't been for them, the world would have been in chaos. All in all I felt sad that so much tax payers' money – openly reported as well over £17 million – had been wasted on the whole affair.

In my own life the Bug was soon replaced by a Bot. On 5 January Maggie Calmels from Eaglemoss paid me a visit. Eaglemoss produce part-works magazines, whereby a magazine is published every two weeks and, at the end of its run, which is often around sixty weeks, you have a fully detailed account of dinosaurs, having a baby, or whatever is the subject of the magazine. Eaglemoss were thinking about publishing a magazine on robots, so Maggie had come to us as leaders in the field.

One idea that came from our meeting was to redesign one of our Seven Dwarf robots into a new robot, a Cybot, that could be given away, in parts, with the magazine. After several weeks, purchasers would therefore have a complete robot, plus the magazine's instructions for putting it together. Although it was far from our implant work, it sounded very exciting. Eaglemoss were funding the project, and I immediately employed Jim Wyatt – who had been involved with Rogerr, the half-marathon robot – as the researcher. Very soon the name of the magazine was settled: it was to be called *Ultimate Real Robots*.

January 2000 also saw more magazine, radio, TV and newspaper interviews. I went over to Lego's headquarters in Billund, Denmark, in an attempt to extract some more funding from them to pay for Iain Goodhew, to cover the organisation and running of some schools' robot competitions. I felt that it was an extremely positive trip and I was very hopeful of some funding later in the year, which duly came.

January also saw the start of regular meetings with Mark Gasson and Brian Andrews, the idea of which was to discuss exactly what we were going to do with the implant experiment, compare notes as far as progress was concerned and pinpoint any hold-ups or problems. In January we had three of these meetings. At first Brian was pushing for a project that would be much more simple. He proposed that we avoid the implant altogether, and simply insert electrodes through the skin, forcing them down until they made contact with the nerve fibres in my arm. This would have been rather like sticking very thin knitting needles into my arm.

There were many advantages attached to this option: it didn't require proper surgery; it had been tried and tested many times before; it was fairly cheap; we would be able to get some useful information out of the experiment. However, the main disadvantage was that hardly anyone would be interested as it had all been done before. In contrast to Brian, Mark and I were united in our resolve to go for an implant. Whether it be by a cuff or array, a connection directly on to the nerve fibres from inside my body seemed to be quite possible technically. Over the next few months Brian gradually came round and agreed that the full connection would not only give us much more data to work with, but as far as an exciting project was concerned it was a clear winner.

Before January was over, the February 2000 issue of *Wired* magazine hit the streets, with a picture of me on the front cover. I first knew it had appeared when my daily number of incoming emails went from being merely unmanageable to completely off-the-planet. By the end of the month I was receiving over 250 emails everyday, the vast bulk coming from the US. Most were saying well done, but asking if I could give them more information on this, or what did I think about that? Often it was college students trying to find out what I was like as a person. I made a rough calculation and found out that, given the average time it took me to answer one email, if I didn't sleep, eat or breathe, it would take me about two weeks to answer one day's emails. I concluded that, unless I quickly discovered a means of warping time – something that the world's physicists had uniformly failed to do – my best bet was to only answer the few emails that I felt needed to be answered. Another knock-on effect of the *Wired* piece was that even more reporters and TV programs wanted to do an item on what we were up to.

In February Irena and I appeared as guests on *Esther*, Esther Rantzen's afternoon programme on BBC2. I also did some filming with BBC Arts, talking about robots and androids during the interval of a screening of the ballet *Coppelia*. Coppelia is about a doll that comes to life, and the BBC recorded footage of some of our robots dancing around in unison and set it to Delibes' music. It was beautiful, and seemed as though Delibes had our robots in mind when he wrote the music. In the same month I worked on an *Equinox* program on self-experimenters and did an evening presentation at Harrow School.

The next implant meeting mainly centred on what I had said in the *Wired* article. I had written the article back in September 1999, and we had learned a lot in the five months since then. In the article I had said that the next implant would be encased in a glass tube as it had been in 1998. However, by February 2000 we had discovered that glass was far too brittle, and I had been extremely lucky that the first implant had not broken into small pieces when it was in my arm.

Until February 2000 a lot of our practical work on the project had been experimental, attempting to sort out the basics. The original implant was a glass capsule, which is inert but very easy to break, especially when not in the form of a fully enclosed tube. Also, we needed to have wires running in and out, which raised a number of problems with regard to the implant's overall strength and reliability. We therefore firmly ruled out the possibility of a glass implant.

In the *Wired* article I said that the implant would be connected to my body through a band that wraps around the nerve fibres in my arm and looks like a little vicar's collar, but by February our strong preference – and the implant we were including in our designs – was the array. I also claimed that we would again power the device by means of a copper induction coil rather than a battery, yet Mark Gasson had just come up with some figures which showed that to obtain the sort of power we needed, the induction coil would have to be about the size of an orange – we would therefore have to use a battery. But apart from these slight anomalies, the article was quite a good summary of the experiment we were planning to do, and what we were hoping to investigate. What follows is what we were hoping for at the time.

The main difference between the 1998 implant and the new experiment was the connection that would be made with the nervous system, most likely using the Utah array. The main body of the implant would be a radio transmitter/receiver to send the signals from my nervous system by radio to the computer and to receive signals sent, again by radio, from the computer and play them on to my nervous system via my arm. In one way it would be like listening in to a telephone conversation, although we wanted to send our own signals in to the connection as well.

A straightforward example of this is that if I was to move one of my fingers, electronic signals travel from my brain down the nervous fibres in my arm to activate the muscles and tendons that operate my hand. The plan was that the implant would pick up the signals en route, even though the signals would still reach the respective finger. Because of the number of connections we were going to be able to make with the array, it was unlikely that we would pick up all the signals for a whole finger movement, only those concerned with a small proportion of the muscles involved.

These signals on the nervous fibres would be continuous, analog signals that would be converted to digital on an interface, and trans-mitted out. Similarly in the reverse direction digital signals would be sent to the implant where they would have to be converted to analog so they could be played down on to the nervous fibres. Mark was working on this interface. The idea was to store in the computer the signals associated with a finger movement and then, at a later time, play the sequence of signals back again from whence they came. There was also the possibility that we would try and manipulate the signals before posting them back. One question arising from this was would we be able to re-create any of the original movement in my fingers by repeating the same set of signals? In the *Wired* article I said I would consider the test a fantastic success if we could record a movement, then reproduce it when we sent the signal back to the arm. Another question though was what would my brain make of the returned signals and what was happening in my arm in response to them? With muscles being remote controlled by a computer, would my brain merely accept the occurrence, would it try to counteract the movement or would it not be able to cope? Little did we know at the time that we would get some answers to these questions in the most dramatic of ways. We hoped that the results would contribute to research into the retrieval of movement for those with a break in their nervous system due to an accident or illness such as multiple sclerosis.

We also wanted to investigate the addition of a whole range of senses for humans. With the human collection of senses so limited, our brains do not ordinarily process signals such as X-rays, ultraviolet, infrared or ultrasound. Might it be possible for us to feed extra-sensory input on to the sensory nerves in my arm, and therefore up to my brain? We knew we would be able to use ultrasonic (high frequency) sound sensors, with which we were very familiar, having employed them on a wide range of robots from the Seven Dwarfs, to Rogerr and the Cybot. Like our robots, would I be able to learn, purely from ultrasonics, how far objects were from me? Would I ever learn how to perceive the signals? Would I 'feel' the ultrasound? Would my brain cope with it?

One hope was that if we could get some success with the ultrasound signal (essentially similar to the sense a bat uses to fly in the dark), it had the potential to provide a really useful alternative sense for a blind person. For this possibility alone – not to repair a person's blindness, but to give them an extra sense – the whole experiment, with all its risks, seemed well worth doing. We simply had to find out.

Pain was another element we wanted to investigate, as it creates a clear electronic signal on the nervous system when it moves from its point of origin to the brain. We wanted to see what would happen if the pain signal was stored in the computer and then played back again on to the same nerves. Would I feel the same sensation? Would it feel like the phantom pains felt in the missing limbs of amputees? As our brains associate an ache or pain with a particular region or part of the body, we were interested to see what happened if we sent the same signal down via a different sensory nerve. Would I feel the same pain somewhere else?

Rather than actually creating pain, the big question was, would we be able to send in an electronic signal that would be able to negate or equalize an original pain signal? While this was doubtful, we thought it might be possible to use electronic signals from the computer to reduce a pain signal, albeit only slightly.

At this point, most research on the human nervous system had involved stimulation via one signal electrode at a time. By using the array we would be able to try out a variety of patterns, using the array to send signals on to the nerves via different electrodes at the same time, or by sequencing signals to the electrodes. The results of this, even at the minimum, would provide us with some unique results.

A new area we wanted to examine was the range of signals loosely associated with physical emotions, particularly anger, shock and excitement. An overall aim was to record signals from my nervous system when I was happy; then, if my mood changed a day or so later, play the happy signal back down on my nervous system to see what might happen. Would my brain be fooled in any way? This area would be difficult to conduct experiments in, but it was an extremely exciting one that could open up a whole field of study and research, opening a window on the possibility of sending electronic signals on to the nervous system to change the state of a person's mind: e-medicine. Using electronics for medicine rather than chemicals would revolutionize the traditional approach of western medicine.

While this could be seen as an extremely positive contribution, I did point to a potentially enormous negative in the *Wired* article. Before I wrote the article a number of people asked me if it would be possible to get high from drugs, store the signals from the nervous system and then return the same signals to the nervous system at a later time to re-create the original sensation. While I didn't fancy the idea of taking drugs, I certainly felt that I could have a glass or two of wine, and record my body's reaction. The following day I could play back the recorded signal.

Things then started to get slightly speculative as we had no idea what the results might be. As a 'drunk' signal appeared in my arm, what would my brain do with it? As my brain tried to make sense of the signal, it was possible that it would search for the past experience, trying to put the sensation in the context of what it already knew, and might therefore believe that I was indeed, to an extent at least, intoxicated. By varying the theme it might then be possible to transmit different electronic patterns on to the nervous system to bring about a sensation equivalent to that of drinking bourbon, rum or even coffee!

If we achieved even a small but positive result in this area, it had the potential to send antidepressants stimulation, vaccines, or even contraception in a similar manner. Clearly this would completely alter the face of medicine and therefore to my mind was worth a try. If we could provide an alternative to the concept of feeding people chemical treatments with all their side-effects, by using clean, electronic signals, this would be wonderful and a huge breakthrough. It might be that in the future such cyberdrugs or cybernarcotics could be used to cure cancer, relieve clinical depression, or merely be programmed as a pick-me-up on a bad day.

The human brain is quite good at adapting to unfamiliar information coming in through the nerve branches, and the brain of a young child is particularly pliable. An interesting possibility for the future is that if a young child received an implant, they might have the ability to take in new information in their own right. In response to additional input, it is probable that the nerve fibres linked to the implant would grow thicker and more powerful, thus developing the ability to carry more, and different kinds of information. At this stage, however, it is simply conjecture, but interesting nonetheless.

On 9 February 2000 I had my forty-sixth birthday. When we carried out the experiment it would be interesting how much my 'older' brain would be able to adapt. It was clear, particularly with the amount of noise that might be present, that the experiment could be dangerous. One concern was the possibility of damage to the nervous fibres in my arm, which could result in the loss of some movement and feeling. But most likely this would only be slight. Infection was another possibility, and it was difficult to know what effects that might have. But perhaps the biggest risk of all appeared to be a mental one. Feeding signals that went directly to my brain could have disastrous affects: I might go crazy, I could even end up as some sort of vegetable.

When the *Wired* article appeared, several people sent me emails asking why I would want to put my life at risk. As a result I thought about it deeply.

But I am a scientist, and having an opportunity to do pioneering research, to step forward into places nobody has been before, where we don't know what to expect, was the most exciting thing in the world for me. I felt it was my duty to do some new science, and I couldn't even begin to think about passing up such an opportunity. There were dangers, but I didn't need to think about them for more than a few seconds to know that even if there were greater risks, I would still go for it. When I had worked for the GPO many years before, the story of the telegraph and then Bell's invention of the telephone was quite inspirational for me as far as scientific research was concerned. Yet it now appeared that we might be on the threshold of a whole new means of communicating, not only between humans but between human and machine.

Humans have many diverse and complex ideas in their brains. These actually amount to numerous electro-chemical signals that link the brain's neurons together in a particular way at a particular time. To communicate with another human these complex signals are converted by our mouths into simple, mechanical pressure waves. They are then slowly transported by sound to the ear of another individual where they are converted back to electro-chemical signals and an attempt is made to understand them. In the process many errors can occur, especially as the method is one that takes a relatively long time. For a start things get in the way and the signal may not travel the short distance clearly. If it is in a difficult coding system, a foreign language, then the recipient may not understand anything at all. But most of all humans can only transmit and receive one (maybe two at most) signals at a time, only communicating with others in a serial fashion. Speech is therefore a relatively poor way to communicate.

Human interaction with technology is no better, however. Using a keyboard or a computer mouse is also very slow because the complex issues in our brain have to be converted into slow mechanical movement signals. Yet we know technology can communicate, in parallel, with very little error over enormous distances. Wouldn't it be good if humans could do that too? We humans have clearly evolved, over thousands or more years, to communicate as we do, but technology offers us more if we can link more closely with it. As a human I was becoming embarrassed to continue communicating in such an old-fashioned way.

The possibility to send signals, by radio, directly from brain to brain or from human brain to technology and vice versa certainly seems to be within our grasp. After all, we are simply considering transmitting electronic signals from place to place by radio. Surely it would not be too difficult for one person to learn to recognize another person's motor-neuron signals – the electronic signals associated with movement? Indeed it would not appear to be pushing things too far for one person to learn how to send particular movement-related signals – rather like Johnny Ray as discussed in chapter eight – and for another person to learn to recognize those signals. Humans are good at learning.

While it appears clear that with radio-transmitter electrode technology we should be able to learn a basic form of brain-to-brain communication, a lot of research will still need to be done to decide the best positioning for, and number of, such electrodes. Nevertheless, controlling technology, just by thinking about it, would appear to be a relatively simple step along the way. Much more difficult is the concept of sending abstract ideas from person to person. Might it be possible for one person to think about an ice cream and for that thought to be transmitted to, and understood in, the brain of another? Could we even communicate abstract ideas, in parallel, in this way?

Perhaps our experiment could change things. I was going to have an implant, so all we needed was someone else to have a connection on to their nervous system to enable us to look at sending signals not just back down on to the nervous system from whence they came, but rather from one person's nervous system to another, possibly via the internet (just as we had connected up some robots a few years before) and possibly from continent to continent.

I often discussed the experiment with Irena. She had been shocked when I first mentioned the original implant, but since had become progressively more excited about the whole project, especially as she saw the enormous potential that might be opened up. One night Brian, who had been the photographer for the original implant experiment, was round at our house taking some more photos for a magazine article. When I talked about the communication possibilities, Brian asked why Irena didn't get involved. To my great surprise she announced her enthusiasm for getting involved. The experiment instantly took on a whole new meaning.

With Irena joining me in a his-and-hers implant experiment, we had to quickly modify our plans. Most of the original ones involving myself wouldn't change, however we needed to bring in some new aspects involving communication. Whether Irena had the full implant like mine remained to be seen. One thing though was clear: because of the significant dangers involved I would have my implant first and then, if everything looked all right, Irena would have hers.

Initially I toyed with the idea of doing the experiment twice: I would carry out an implant experiment on my own first, and then do the double-implant experiment with Irena. I telephoned Ali Jamous to discuss the options with him. He was completely clear: there was no way he was going to put one implant in me, remove it, and then a few months later put in another implant – the dangers would be immense. One implantation and extraction, that had never been done before, was risky enough. My body, my nervous system in particular, would adjust to the implant and then have to adjust back again. A further implant would leave my nervous system battered, not knowing what was going on. The decision was therefore made: I would have my implant, then a few days or weeks later Irena would have hers. Some weeks later still they would both be removed. I had decided that the experiment should last for a few weeks, maybe two months at the extreme limit.

With Irena on board we would be able to do a lot more investigating, and could start by sending movement signals from person to person. Immediately I realized that if I could move my finger and Irena felt something on her nervous system, then I moved my wrist and she felt something else, we could have the basis of a new means of communication, a form of telegraph morse code between our nervous systems. But would I be able to move her muscles simply by moving my muscles, and vice versa? If so, this could open up possibilities for remote-controlling patients with a nervous-system problem. The electronic signals on my nervous system that were moving my muscles would be picked up, as they happened, by my implant and transmitted simultaneously, by radio, to the computer. The computer could then be employed to relay them on immediately, or at a later time, by radio, to Irena's implant and thence down on to her nervous system. This in turn would cause her muscles to operate, in response to the signals from my nervous system. Exactly the same thing could of course happen in the reverse direction. Also, by transmitting the signals from one computer to another, by means of the internet for example, Irena and I could be quite some distance apart for this experiment.

Despite the fact that this seemed to be technically possible and well within our grasp, it also posed new problems: would the movement signals from my nervous system have a similar sort of effect when they appeared on Irena's nervous system? Would there be any extra dangers involved in transmitting signals that had not previously been witnessed by the other person's nervous system? When a signal was transmitted from Irena's nervous system to my own, would my brain be able to deal with it? In particular it would be very unlikely that we would be fortunate enough to link up the exact, equivalent nerves on both our nervous systems, if such nerves even existed in the first place.

But what about emotional signals associated with being happy, depressed, shocked or even sexually aroused? Irena said that if anyone was going to jack into my limbic system, she definitely wanted it to be her.

Looking at the communication issues raised a whole new range of questions. If we sent a pain signal from Irena's nervous system to mine, would I feel the same thing or would we find that there was some truth in the rumour that women are tougher than men? It is known that different people have varying emotional responses to the same stimulus, so if a particular emotional signal was sent from my nervous system to hers, would her brain recognize it in anything like the same way? It was possible that we would start to gain some idea from my own reaction to having emotionally related signals replayed in my own nervous system, but it was clear that with the his-and-hers hook up we would be entering completely uncharted territory. My own feeling was that if Irena's brain could make out, even roughly, my incoming signals, then her own stored knowledge would be used by her brain to create a way of deciphering the information as it appeared. What sort of solutions it would come to, we would only find out once the experiment was under way.

In order to demonstrate the sending of signals between us across the internet, I decided it would be a much better demonstration if we were able to transmit the signals across the Atlantic Ocean rather than the laboratory. While the implant was in place I was hoping to travel to New York. If Irena remained in Reading, we could send real-time movement and emotional signals from person to person, continent to continent. I am scared stiff of high buildings, so what better than to arrange for a connection at the Empire State Building? I would attempt to go to the top of the building in the lift, and my nervous-system signals would be transmitted to Irena. What would she feel when signals associated with my vertigo appeared on her nervous system? With the roles reversed, Irena has a complete dread of spiders, so what would I feel if signals from her nervous system were transmitted to mine when a spider was somewhere near her?

Irena expressed an instant worry that if it did turn out to be anything like we expected, then it might be very difficult to have the implants removed at the end of the experiment, and return to a normal life.

Irena's thought made me understand things in a more general way. Once you have a technology that enables you to do a lot more, that empowers you, it is very difficult to do without it at a later time. This was a general point where cyborgs were concerned: once you've been upgraded you would not want to return to being a mere human again. With the 1998 experiment it had been quite traumatic having the implant removed, so it was intriguing to me to see whether Irena and I would be able to return to normal after this one.

One result of the *Wired* article was an email I received from an investor called Geoff in the US. He told me he ran a venture capital enterprise scheme and asked how much money we wanted in order to do the experiment. He was speaking in terms of millions of dollars, or even more. I talked to Brian Andrews and William Harwin about it and we all agreed that we should follow up with an email conversation. After all we shouldn't, as the proverb goes, look a gift horse in the mouth.

On 17 March 2000 our gift horse flew over to the UK and came to stay in Reading. Brian, William, Geoff and myself met up and went to the local tandoori for a meal. Geoff filled us in as to how the deal would work – that his company would invest the money we wanted and his backers would reap their rewards when it was a great success and the new technology could be marketed.

It was refreshing to discuss the possibility of having so much money that we didn't know what to do with it, particularly as at that moment I was still paying for Mark Gasson from an ever-dwindling pot that would not, I knew, last for more than a few months. However, although extra money would be very useful, we really didn't need the amount Geoff was talking about. Another problem was that we weren't actually developing a new technology that could be marketed, in fact we were buying in or borrowing the technology. It was simply that we were doing something with it that was completely different and pioneering. Nevertheless the meeting and the meal seemed to go well and Brian, William and I spent the rest of the night trying to think of what we could do with so much money. New cars for each of us sprang to mind instantly as definite necessities!

The next day I was scheduled to meet up with Geoff again at his hotel before he headed back to the US. Unfortunately, when I arrived at the hotel I received a message to say Geoff was sick. He tentatively came down to the lobby about twenty minutes later looking incredibly white.

Apparently the tandoori had not agreed with him, he had had to call a doctor in and had been up all night. So we only had a quick meeting, going over non-tandoori details from the night before. Geoff then left for Heathrow and the US. We never heard from him again. I concluded that the next time someone offered me millions of dollars they would have to settle for fish and chips.

The upshot of that incident was that it still looked as if we would soon run out of money. It was difficult to say exactly how much money we required to carry out the experiment. We needed around £50,000 for equipment for the lab, a further £50,000 for the technology and electronics for the implant, and a further £50,000 for incidentals such as travel, telephone, design work, outsourcing and so on. By far the biggest cost I estimated was the £400,000 needed for researcher salaries over a four-year period. A total of just over half a million pounds would be about right. However, with the university putting around 40 per cent of overheads on everything, this actually meant a figure of around £750,000, which we were certainly some way away from. The work we were doing was far too blue sky for any government research council support which meant we had to look to companies. However, they generally want something in return. The easiest way to deal with this was by providing publicity for the company on the back of what we were doing. Computer Associates were exceptional: as a result of being based in Slough, they were interested in supporting the local university, and Reading was less than ten miles away.

Even though the money situation did not look good, I continued to make presentations in which I outlined what we planned to do. Generally the presentations were very well attended and seemed to be equally well received by the audience. The implant plans frequently concluded with the sex scenario, which usually brought the house down. At the end of March I visited Colombia for the second time, on this occasion making four presentations at a congress in a city called Bucaramanga, about a one-hour flight over guerrilla country from the capital, Bogota. This congress was particularly memorable because I had to give a presentation in a very large auditorium with a seating capacity of 1500. When the presentation began, every seat was full and the theatre was overflowing. The atmosphere was electric, and the adrenalin flowed freely.

In April I gave presentations for the British Council in Zurich, an academic conference in Dublin, New Orleans and then one Friday night at a Jewish Synagogue in North London. I arrived at to the synagogue with Irena and some robots and then we discovered that we could not, because of the Jewish religion, switch the robots on. I didn't fully understand the reason, but apparently at certain times technology cannot be switched on or off. However, despite a few grumbles, the rabbi in the driving seat gave us a special dispensation and the robots were demonstrated. My presentation was followed by a Jewish meal, and lots of singing and chanting. It was a fantastic evening, and a night that was culturally very different from anything that either of us had experienced before.

On the morning of 25 April I received two telephone calls that would have a dramatic effect on my life. The first call came from Susan Greenfield, the Director of the Royal Institution, and the second from Alan Winter, the Administrative Manager of the Royal Institution. Both calls were, in essence, about the same thing: to invite me to give the year 2000 Royal Institution Christmas Lectures. It was a dream come true, something that, as a child, I could only imagine others doing, and then as a scientist I felt I was not Oxbridge enough to be invited to do. But that clearly wasn't the case. I didn't need to think about it, and accepted the invitation instantly. Up until then, BBC2 had televised the five lectures at Christmas time. This year Channel 4 had taken over the reigns and they would be broadcasting the lectures each day between 26 December to 30 December. I was on cloud nine.

Although I had given a number of presentations at the Royal Institution in 1999, I had held out some hope that I might get a chance at the lectures, but I hadn't been that confident. I had been assured that the 2000 lectures had already been decided, so if I was fortunate enough to be selected I thought it would be for 2001. Yet here I was, the lecturer for 2000. I knew that I would be creating a first, because I would be the first person from Reading University ever to give the lectures. It was a fantastic feeling.

In the next few weeks I gave invited presentations at Oxford, Cambridge, Warwick, Keele and Nottingham universities. I also talked to the Sociology Department back at Reading. I never ceased to be amazed at just who was interested in what we were doing. In May I also met up with Moi, a research student from Thailand, who was sharing her time between the Royal College of Art in London, and our department in Reading. She was looking at making techno-jewellery that changed shape and colour depending on the body state – such as the mood or emotion – of the person wearing it. Moi instantly struck me as a very conscientious worker, artistically gifted and willing to put in hours over a new design. We discussed how her designs could be powered and the type of signal, such as pulse or temperature, that could be monitored to change the jewellery's appearance. She quickly put together some intricate flower designs containing light-emitting diodes. It was a fascinating project. Moi also received help from Mark who, as well as pushing forward with the implant, helped her from a technical viewpoint when she visited the department. Moi's area of wearable computing was very much in vogue in the US, at MIT in Boston in particular, and I felt it provided a nice contrast to our work to be involved in the field as well.

Meanwhile Mark had unearthed a major problem with the implant design, largely due to the level of noise that was being picked up. In terms of design, it was fine for picking up signals from the nervous system, but when playing down the signals, if the noise affecting the implant was of a certain magnitude it simply saturated the receiver. This meant that if I was in a slightly noisy (electronic noise that is) environment, a full-scale voltage would be played down on to my nervous system which would, in practice, probably cause me excruciating pain. Using radio-signalling pick up of electromagnetic noise was always likely to be a problem, but if a small amount caused the circuitry to apply the maximum voltage, then a small amount of noise could cause a maximum pain signal, probably equivalent to someone constantly drilling a nerve. It therefore seemed to be quite a good idea for Mark to spend some time trying to sort out the problem.

At the beginning of June, while Mark was working hard in the department, I went to a four-day conference in Sardinia, taking some of our robots with me to demonstrate. In my presentation, apart from talking about the implant experiment, I described the operation of our robots based on ultrasonic signals. I described how the robot uses ultrasonics to judge when something is nearby and how far away it is. In explaining the ultrasonics I described how a high-frequency sound signal is transmitted, 'Ping', and if no object is nearby the signal merely travels and travels. However, if an object is nearby, the signal is bounced back, 'Ping-Pong'. I had used this description before, to little reaction. But on this occasion everyone in the theatre erupted with laughter. I immediately had the feeling you get when everyone is laughing and you're the only one who doesn't know the joke. One of the organizers spoke to me after the presentation and told me, quietly, that Pong-Ping is the common description in Italy for, if I remember correctly, oral sex.

Thankfully, in the first week of July 2000, Mark Gasson told me that he and Ben had solved the noise problem with the implant. This cheered me considerably, as it meant the experiment could go ahead without the danger of my suffering constant pain. No sooner had I heard this news when Stewart Bruyn from Nortel Networks contacted me to say that they would be very happy to fund our implant work for a three-year period, at £25,000 per year, to take effect immediately. It also came in the nick of time as my own money pot had by that time just about dried up. While it wasn't the sort of much larger sums that Nortel had entertained me to ask for earlier, it was enough to be going on with, and I was extremely grateful. At least I would now be able to pay Mark.

August saw the release of my book *QI*, with a big publicity drive that began with a launch at the Edinburgh Book Festival. As well as promoting my own book, I had to take part in a panel session with Andrea Dworkin. She is a very large, Jewish, feminist. Not much in common with me you might think, but we were just two of the '30 Great Minds' included in the Oxford University book *Predictions*, so the panel was aimed partly at promoting that book as well as our own books. It actually turned out to be great fun. She used me as something of a symbol of all that was wrong with the world, as I was the representative of that nasty group of culprits known as males.

Around the same time a web site entitled 'Kevin Warwick Watch' and an e-newspaper, *The Register*, became rather vitriolic towards me. The former was a web page that someone had started up to poke some fun at me. It wasn't actually anything to do with me, so I felt quite honoured that anyone would want to spend their time, and money, writing things about me. It was good to know that what I said must be having an impact if someone wanted to criticize me for it – if what I said was rubbish or not noticed by anyone, then such a web site would not exist. But now, because it was known that I would be giving the Royal Institution Christmas Lectures, a group, primarily from Sussex University, decided to grumble about it via those web sites and more generally to the press.

They didn't seem to have any technical reasons for their grumbles, they just appeared to want to call me names and contend that I shouldn't be doing the lectures.

The grumbles continued into September until the *Sunday Telegraph* decided to do a small piece on it. One of the claims had been that I was not academically up to it, which I was surprised by, as I was more academically qualified than any of those grumbling. Thankfully providence provided a solution when, in the middle of September, I was invited over to MIT in Boston to receive the Future of Health Technology Award for 2000. As a result, the *Sunday Telegraph* article, as well as indicating strong support for me from Susan Greenfield, concluded with the fact that I was about to go to MIT to receive an award. The grumbles subsided rather quickly after that.

Irena and I went over to Boston a week early and had a short holiday touring New England, stopping in bed and breakfasts. Our trip concluded with the award ceremony at MIT where I received a bust of Asclepius, the Greek god of medicine. Marvin Minsky had been the previous award holder, which made the award even more special. It meant a great deal in that it came from MIT, one of the top research universities in the United States, and only one or two awards were made each year. It was for the person deemed to be doing most to further the future use of technology for health. It was good to receive an international award and provide academic credibility for the work we were doing at Reading.

November meant many meetings with Carlo Massarella and others at the RI. Carlo was producing the Christmas Lectures for Windfall films, on behalf of Channel 4, and we had met up several times in the last few months. Iain Goodhew often came with me, as he was to be my right hand man for the lectures. At the RI, Bryson Gore had a lot of experience in getting the demonstrations ready while Bippin Palmer actually made things work. We had a good team, but by the end of November 2000 there was still a lot to do.

When you are giving the Christmas Lectures it is certainly a great honour, but you do have to give up the whole of December of that year, and you don't have much of a Christmas yourself. On 24 November we did a pilot lecture at the RI, trying out some of the demonstrations we were hoping to use, getting the Windfall production team used to the run of things and giving ourselves an idea of what we still had to do. If I said that it was a complete shambles I would be heaping praise where it was not due.

For December 2000, the implant work was put on a back burner and my whole life revolved around the Christmas Lectures. The first few days mainly involved working with Carlo, trying to nail down five lectures, which demonstrations would be used and which not. As well as robots from other groups in the UK, we had a team bringing a robot from Japan and a potential live satellite link-up with the NASA Johnson Space Centre in Houston, Texas. The plan was to pre-record the first four lectures but have the fifth lecture, on 30 December, live. This was another first. In the long history of the RI Christmas Lectures no lecture had ever been televised live before.

On 11 December I appeared on Radio 4's *Start the Week* with Jeremy Paxman. My three fellow guests were Callum Brown, who had just published a book entitled *The Death of Christian Britain*, Bonnie Greer, a broadcaster who had just presented a series on black madonnas in Europe, and Niall Ferguson, a tutor in modern history at Jesus College, Oxford. Paxman immediately opened the debate by asking me whether I was a visionary genius or a publicity-crazed lunatic. I answered that perhaps I was somewhere in between. I certainly felt that I was a visionary scientist, looking to the future, but at the same time I liked to let the public know what I was doing in a way that would be easily understood. This in turn generated publicity which was useful in raising the money that allowed me to do the research. I continued by saying that I felt it was better to be open about the research we were doing, rather than to do it behind closed doors. I thought it was better that society knew what we were up to.

But from there it got tougher. Paxman asked why I would want to carry out the cyborg research with implants, as it was not something anyone was ever likely to make practical use of in the future. In this respect, I thought he was being a bit of a stick-in-the-mud, although even I was surprised when all three of the other guests jumped in on my side, firmly asserting that this was just the sort of exciting, futuristic research that should be done. So it was four of us against Paxman, but he stood his ground. He's a great interviewer, even if he can seem rather narrow minded!

On 13 December we rehearsed the first lecture, and rehearsed it twice the next day, the actual programme being recorded at about 4p.m. It was an absolutely brilliant feeling to walk out in the lecture room at the RI to give the Christmas Lectures with the lights, the cameras, and an expectant audience. For a scientist, I suppose it is the equivalent of a cup final in soccer, only with the Christmas Lectures it is just you, on your own. Although I had been extremely nervous beforehand, I need not have feared. It really went well.

The next day we rehearsed lecture two, with two further rehearsals on the 16th before the programme was recorded at 4p.m. This programme featured a robot called Eye-Chan, which had been brought over by Atsuo Takaniski from Waseda University in Tokyo. The robot was brilliant: a robot head which responded rapidly to light, sound, touch and even the smell of alcohol. That night Irena, my daughter Maddi and her friend Anna, all of whom had been at the lecture, went out for a meal with me, then Irena stayed the night in London. I had been staying on my own in London for the past week, so it was good to see the family again.

The 17th and 18th saw lecture three recorded in a similar way to the first two, but included a live satellite link up with Houston. Apparently the link up only came through ten seconds before I started talking to them, but fortunately no one told me at the time. On the 19th and 20th we got lecture four in the can, attended by Irena, Ali Jamous and his son.

Next day Irena and I headed off to Prague for Christmas, which was spent with her mother, her son Petr and daughter Lenka, in her mother's flat in Prague. It was a typical Czech Christmas with carp and potato salad as Christmas dinner on 24 December. The carp swims around in the bath for the two or three days up to Christmas when someone (not me) hits it over the head and it gets fried. It was a nice relaxing time, but I knew I had one more lecture to do – the live one.

On 27 December I flew back to London. We had three days to put the lecture together rather than the two days we had had for the first four lectures, and we certainly needed the time. Not only did I have to present demonstrations for the hour of the lecture, but I also had to make sure that the interviews and demonstrations each came in on time and that we stopped at the right time for adverts. As it was live, if I fell over, or did something stupid, everyone would see. It was all down to me. The lecture was going ahead on the 30th, and, worryingly, the rehearsals on the 29th were a bigger shambles than ever before. That night I went to bed early, with a sleeping tablet. I counted sheep, got up, had a hot bath, tried everything, but I didn't sleep a wink all night. The next morning I felt physically ill, and worried about being sick all over Faraday's table. But I wasn't sick, and didn't do anything to embarrass myself. In fact, apart from a couple of very minor mishaps, everything went wonderfully well. Not only that but my kids, Maddi and James, were there to witness it. Afterwards there was a bit of a party where everyone was congratulating everyone else. Maddi, James and I sneaked out fairly quickly and went for a pizza just off Piccadilly Circus. Then it was back to Reading, where I spent the night.

On New Year's Eve I flew back to Prague to be with Irena and the in-laws for Silvester, the New Year celebrations in the Czech Republic. A few days later and we were back in Reading. As 2001 began I knew it was time for us to get down to some serious work with the new implant experiment. Little did I expect what 2001 would have in store, and the surprises that it would throw up, not only as far as the project was concerned, but also in terms of my personal life. Just when it appeared that my marriage to Irena was nice and secure, in 2001 it was to be tested like never before. Would it hold together?

Chapter 10

ON THE AFTERNOON of Friday 10 March 1876, Tom Watson stood in the bedroom of Alexander Graham Bell with a receiver pressed to his ear. Meanwhile Bell was behind closed doors in his laboratory at the far end of the corridor. Bell spoke into the mouthpiece: 'I then shouted into the mouthpiece the following sentence, 'Mr Watson – Come here – I want to see you.' To my delight he came and declared that he had heard and understood what I said.' When Bell made the world's first telephone call, he altered things for good, but at the time no one guessed just how dramatic that change might be.

The greatest Hollywood storylines simply cannot match the epic proportions of real scientific moments such as this. As 2001 was born I wondered if we would be able to achieve anything like Bell's momentous and historic feat. On the surface it sounds pretentious to try to put yourself in the same frame as scientific geniuses such as Bell, but they were merely human and had success in their endeavours. Any scientist who wishes to change things must believe in themselves and their science, believe that they can achieve, that they can look outside the box. The end result of what we are looking at now could in fact have an even more profound effect than Bell's telephone. But, most likely, we will never know how great an effect, just as Bell, who died in 1922, never knew what effect the telephone would have in 2001, 125 years on from its invention.

I had announced the goal of having an implant connected on to my nerve fibres, making me into a cyborg and thereby moving science forward into a new era. But achieving it was turning out to be quite a task, although it was one I felt that I was equal to and one that I was determined to bring about. I had to dig in and keep going; I simply could not entertain the idea of giving up.

As a scientist trying to change things I had, in 2000, been subject to some attacks, prior to the Christmas Lectures, peaking with the Paxman treatment on *Start the Week* in early December. But as a new January got underway, Tim Sebastian gave me another half-hour onslaught in BBC TV's *Hard Talk*. Firstly he attacked my views that some machines would one day be more intelligent than humans. Then, when I had hit him with quotes from *In the Mind of the Machine*, he tackled me on what I was hoping to achieve with the cyborg experiment. It was tough going at times but largely he stuck to the issues and as a result I felt that I was on home ground. He asked, 'Are we, with these technological advances, still going to be able to control our destiny at the end of the day?' I answered that the cyborg route provided our main hope of staying in control.

Tim also threw at me a quote he had obtained from Dave Clarke, with whom I had worked during my period at Oxford University, and who was now Professor and Head of the Department of Engineering Science there. Dave Clarke had said that I 'use highly emotive language, which is unsuitable, but the media love it'. By this I felt he meant that when talking about my science, I use words that people understand. It probably wasn't intended as such, but I took it as quite a compliment. It really is easy for a scientist to hide behind their subject, but it's not something I want to do. I suppose I will always be accused of using emotive language. I stand guilty as charged, and am proud to do so.

Later in the month I witnessed a more positive incident. Steve Reich, a classical music composer from New York, contacted me and said he wanted to include me in a new digital opera he was putting together. I'd never heard of him so ignored several emails and faxes before his agent contacted me and persuaded me to let Steve visit and do some recording at the end of the month. This duly happened.

—Just before his arrival I contacted the music department at the university and was told by Jonathan Dunsby, the professor there, that Steve Reich was a pretty famous guy, and he described him as a 'minimalist'. A couple of days later John Bowen, one of the lecturers in the Cybernetics Department, heard that Steve Reich was coming and asked if it was possible to meet up. I agreed and asked if John knew Reich's music. John told me he did, and added that he was a 'minimalist'. John lent me a CD of Reich's compositions called 'Hands Clapping'. It consisted of hands clapping. After a few minutes I decided it wasn't quite my scene. Obviously I am not a great fan of 'minimalists', I'm more a Kylie Minogue man I think. Still, I had gained some knowledge of modern classical music and if, in the future, I was ever asked if I had heard of Steve Reich, I would be able to provide a positive response. Steve seemed to be a nice guy, and only spent a couple of hours recording me talking. I am yet to hear what the finished product sounds like.

At the next implant project meeting Brian Andrews, Mark Gasson and I discussed the number of channels we would try to deal with in parallel – i.e. at the same time. Although there were going to be a hundred connections to nerve fibres, it would not be possible to transmit all one hundred signals at the same time. However, we definitely wanted the possibility of transmitting approximately any twenty-five that we cared to choose. Mark was therefore designing a multiplexer to select these twenty-five from the hundred. Unfortunately most commercial chips were designed for four from sixteen or two from twelve, but not twenty-five from a hundred, so Mark had his work cut out. The multiplexer would also need more power and, although we could reprogram it by radio, we agreed that it would be preferable if, during the experiment, we had direct access to the multiplexer from the outside so that we could see how everything was working. From that moment on it was decided that we would move forward with two plans: Plan A was a full implant; Plan B a partial one, with some electronics and the power supply fixed on the *outside* of my arm.

Elma, our six-legged walking robot, relaxing with Happy, one of the 7 Dwarfs.

Rogerr, our half-marathon robot, lined up alongside other (human) competitors at the start of his ordeal.

The 1998 implant, shown next to a two pence piece for scale. The implant was in my arm for nine days.

Presenting the Year 2000 Royal Institution Christmas Lectures in front of the Faraday table.

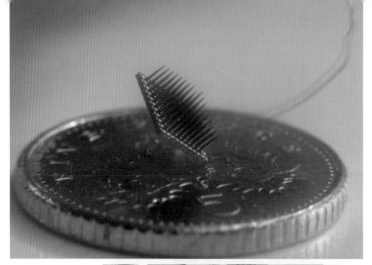

The microelectrode array, which was implanted into my nervous system via the median nerve in my arm for the 2002 experiment. It is shown next to a five pence piece for scale.

Iain Goodhew, Mark Gasson and Ben Hutt in the Madlab at Reading University.

The gauntlet, which held the interface that incorporated a radio transmitter/receiver. Underneath the gauntlet can be seen my operation scar. (© *Mail on Sunday*)

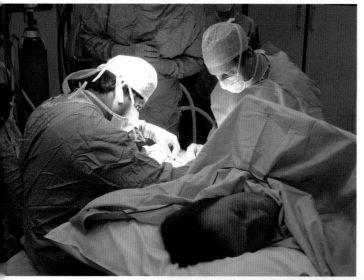

Top neurosurgeons, Amjad Shad (on left) and Peter Teddy during the two-hour implant operation at the Radcliffe Infirmary, Oxford, March 2002.

During the 2002 operation the array was passed down the tube until it reached my wrist, after which the tube was removed. On the right can be seen the connector pad.

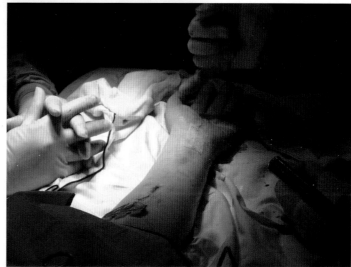

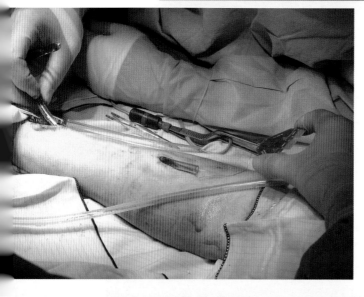

My arm on completion of the operation. The array was positioned in my median nerve just below the wrist.

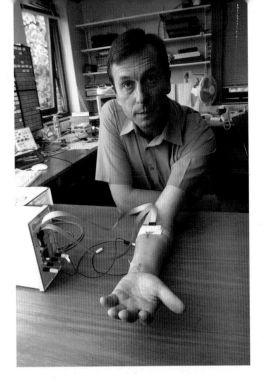

ABOVE LEFT: Attached to my arm is the cable linking my nervous system, via the connector pad, to the computer-monitoring equipment. (© *Mail on Sunday*)

ABOVE RIGHT: With Brian Andrews in the Madlab, searching for some useful sensory signals.

RIGHT: The computer monitor showing some of the signals including neural signals detectable via the array. (© *Mail on Sunday*)

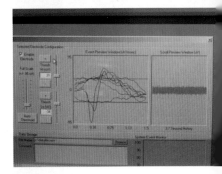

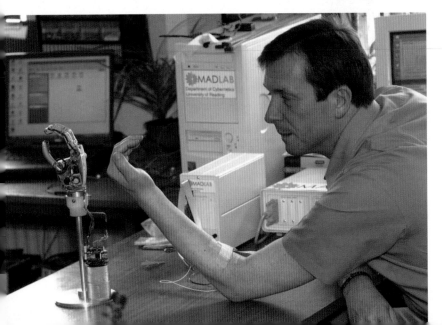

With Peter Kyberd's articulated hand. When I moved my hand, signals from my nervous system made the hand copy the movement. (© *Mail on Sunday*)

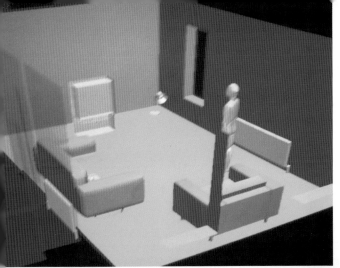

A virtual me in a virtual house. Signals from my nervous system were used to enable the virtual me to move around the house. However, when the virtual coffee maker was selected, a pot of real coffee was brewed.

The Lego robot controlled directly from my nervous system.

The Diddibots can flock together in a friendly way or try and escape as fast as they can from each other. I controlled their mood from my nervous system.

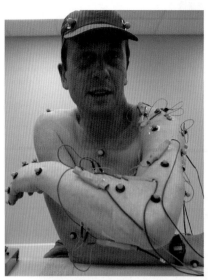

At the Nuffiled Orthopedic Centre's Gait Lab in Oxford. I was connected up with external electrodes to monitor muscle movement and light-sensitive grey balls to visually track my actions.

At Columbia University, New York. Linking my nervous system with the Internet to send signals between the Madlab in Reading and my brain in New York. (© *Mail on Sunday*)

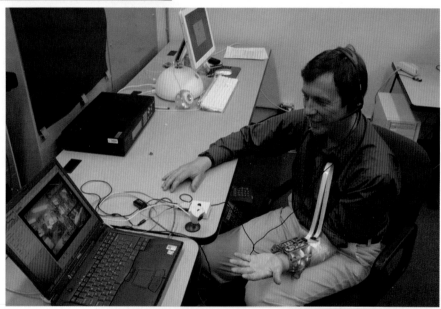

Testing my new-found extra sense. Ultrasonic sensors fitted on my cap are linked directly to my nervous system. My new sixth sense could detect the distance between Iain and myself. (© *Mail on Sunday*)

Different signals coming from my nervous system caused Irena's jewellery to change its colour from red to blue.
(© *Mail on Sunday*)

Mark and Nicoletta attaching electrodes to my newly shaven head. Could we link the signals in my arm to those in my brain? (© *Mail on Sunday*)

Driving a wheelchair around by means of signals from my median nerve. No need for joysticks or steering wheels in the future.

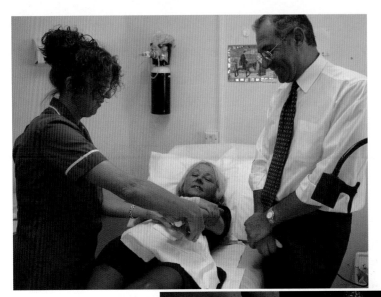

Jacqui and George in the surgery with Irena after a successful microneurography operation.

George using forceps to push the microelectrode needles into Irena's median nerve fibres.

Irena and I. The first married couple ever to experience nervous-system-to-nervous-system communication.

The initial plan of a full implant began to look less likely partly because technically there were good reasons arising for us not to choose this option, but primarily because we felt we needed to learn more before going for a full implant. Scientifically, the main aim was to achieve a radio connection between my nervous system and the computer, and it was this that I kept in mind all along. Whether the implant was full or partial was not so critical. I just wanted to make the link happen in whatever way we could, retaining safety as much as possible, but not at the expense of not going ahead. I knew it was inevitable that there would be changes to the plan, but it was the end goal that was overriddingly important, and achieving it in a reasonable time.

In February, Birmingham Science Museum confirmed that they definitely wanted a group of little interactive robots for their 'Think Tank', which was to be centred at a new building called Millennium Point. As the robots were to be on permanent display, and we only had until September to get everything together, I put Ben Hutt on to it because of his prior success with the London Science Museum robots.

In February I also got a call from Danepak. They had picked up on the IQ studies I reported on in my book *QI*, where I had looked at the effects of elements such as chocolate, peanuts and orange juice on IQ scores. Danepak wanted to know if there were any results showing how eating bacon might affect IQ levels. I didn't know of any, although one school of thought was that from looking at archaeological records, it appeared that a period of rapid development of the human brain may well have occurred when we started eating meat. I asked if they were interested in us carrying out some studies, and told them it would cost them the price of one research assistant for about three months.

Danepak quickly got back to me, agreeing to the project and costing. As a result I brought on board Jane Moore at Thameside School, a junior school in Caversham, just north of the river in Reading, to provide the base for a one-month study, and Danepak agreed to give the school a new computer for their troubles. Fifty children would all take part in IQ tests, both verbal and non-verbal. They would each have a specific regular breakfast for a month, and at the end we would see how each breakfast intake affected their test scores when they took a further test. We decided to look at five groups of ten, with five boys and five girls in each. One group would be given cereals (cornflakes) every morning, another toast and orange juice, another eggs and another bacon sandwiches. The final group of ten would have their normal breakfast, but would act as a control group by undertaking the tests. Danepak supplied the breakfasts. Jane Moore was pleased because it meant all the children had regular breakfast, which, for many of them, was a rarity. May was chosen as the best month to run the experiment.

February's implant meeting was at Stoke Mandeville Hospital. This time, because Ali was present, it took on more of a medical theme. Initially the discussion focused on where we should make the incision – in the upper, fleshy part of the arm where the nerves are a long way in, or just above the wrist where the nerves are not far from the surface? We had discussed these options before, but the wrist position now came out as the favourite because it was much easier from a surgical point of view. However, we would now have problems with the size of the implant and some electronics would therefore have to be mounted on the outside. If this were the case – if we mounted some electronics on the outside – wires from the array and any implanted electronics would have to pass through the skin to connect these electronics. Ali saw the skin hole as a possible site for infection, and Brian saw it as a place that would not heal if the diameter of the wires passing through it were too great. Ali therefore thought it would be best to make one incision in order to implant the array and then a separate incision for the wires to go through; he drew with a black pen on on my left arm to show the positioning of the implant. He was keen to stitch up the original incision and not have wires trailing out of it. But how many wires could we manage coming through the skin? We wanted one hundred from the array, but would this be too much? Would the wound heal? Would the wires be damaged and break if so many passed through a hole in the skin? We needed some answers quickly.

Most of these issues I had to look at and discuss in a detached, scientific way, even though it was my body we were talking about. But I had taken the decision that the operation would happen, and what would be, would be. If there was a chance of infection then that would have to be dealt with, because I was not going back now.

In the meantime I continued to give presentations, which included a public lecture at Reading Town Hall to an audience of about six hundred people. I was slightly miffed when I was told that Susan Greenfield had had an audience which might have been a little bit bigger, but cheered up somewhat when I heard that Lewis Wolpert had only had half as many as either of us. I also gave what had become my annual talk at the Royal College of Defence Studies in London and another at University College, Dublin. In Dublin the lecture was supposed to start at 7.30p.m., but at that time there were only about ten people there. So I waited a few minutes and, sure enough, by 7.40p.m., several hundred were present. Apparently in Ireland the start time of a lecture only means that is the absolute earliest time that you should turn up.

In mid-March I went over to the US for about ten days. My first stop was the University of Kansas in Kansas City, where a team had done quite a bit of work towards the Medtronic Parkinson's disease implant. These implants, as described in Chapter 8, are specifically for the purpose of targeting some of the effects of Parkinson's disease. Apparently many implants were now in place and working well, and it was good to hear that they were gaining long-term success. Clearly the material being used for the implants was relatively inert.

Mary Faith Marshall, the professor there, chairs a biotechnology ethics committee in Washington, and they see the whole cyborg area as something they have to start addressing, covering the general area of people linking up directly with technology in one way or another, but principally through implants. One of her main worries was how the identity of the individual could be changed.

From Kansas I went to Austin, Texas. There they were very much into technology and the body, and had been visited just two weeks before by Stelarc, the man who wires himself up to computers. One thing that shocked me was that on two separate occasions people came up to me on the street and asked me if I was Kevin Warwick. I suppose it was because of the *Wired* cover story, but it had never happened to me in the UK, even in Reading, and was a nice feeling.

On my return, our monthly implant meeting mainly revolved around ethics and how we were going to get our experiment through or past the various ethics committees. Brian had been sounding people out; he had discovered that if we said the implant was potentially for medical purposes we would face all sorts of different committees and it could take us several years before obtaining approval to go ahead with a limited, completely obscure, trial. But Brian's contacts seemed to be aware of what we were trying to do and hinted strongly that if we explained that our experiment was purely for scientific purposes we could then avoid a plethora of medical ethics committees altogether. We would just have to face the ethics committee at the hospital where the operation would take place.

Before carrying out a new surgical operation at a hospital, one must first obtain ethics committee approval, the committee consisting of around a dozen lay people with no particular specialist knowledge. It put a big question mark over the whole experiment. Would our proposal get through the committee or not?

In considering the issue, Ali felt that if we simply told the Stoke Mandeville ethics committee he was going to carry out an operation for scientific purposes only, they would question why it was being done at all, at their hospital, if there was no potential for medical gain. This was clearly a difficult situation. We would have to put a storyline that the main reason for the experiment was scientific but that, if we were lucky, there might be some medical spin-offs – we would see. Coincidently, this tied in very nicely with my own way of thinking. The decision was taken there and then that we would severely limit the amount we said about the experiment in terms of medical results expected, and stick to pushing the scientific side: extra sensory input, nervous system to nervous system communication, etc.

The trouble was that while we could read things one way, the ethics committee might read them in a completely different way. Bringing about computer-controlled movement, inputting extra-sensory information or electronically affecting feelings could be regarded, possibly, as medical. On the other hand, mentioning controlling my movements via the internet or getting the building to say hello when I entered could be seen as flippant and not something with which the hospital would want to be associated. We were at their mercy.

In early April I paid a quick visit to Bologna to take part in a debate. At the event I put forward the case that in the future, becoming a cyborg, with the help of implants, would give individuals much greater powers than those who remained human. Another speaker postulated what might happen if the Pope decreed that we should all remain human and not take on board any implants. My response, perhaps with little feeling for the audience, was that the result would be that all Catholics who obeyed the Pope's wishes would become part of the subspecies human race. I wasn't the most popular person at the meeting from that point on.

While I was in Bologna, Irena was in Prague, visiting her relatives and friends. Despite the fact that we were both outwardly stating that we were looking forward to going ahead with our implants, things had not been too good between us recently. We weren't as close, and Irena was talking about retirement and us buying a house in Prague so that she could be near her relatives and friends. It really made me think, as retirement was certainly not a word that I particularly wanted to hear, and spending my latter years with Irena's relatives popping in and out all the time was not at all to my liking. We would have to see what transpired.

Back at Stoke Mandeville, a few weeks later, I met up with David Tolkien. David is a cousin of J.R.R. Tolkien, author of *The Hobbit* and *The Lord of the Rings* trilogy, and raises money, as a charity, for medical research and equipment at Stoke Mandeville. He works extremely hard for the cause, and between his work and that of Jimmy Saville, enormous sums of money have been raised for the National Spinal Injuries Unit. He was delighted to hear about our cyborg project, and seeing it as a vehicle by which he might be able to raise lots more funds for the unit, he put his full support behind it. I was very much uplifted by this, as I had really, to that point, focused on our project as a scientific experiment. The possibility that what we were doing could also raise more cash for David's charity provided a wonderful extra.

At the technical meeting that followed, sterilization of the implant became the main topic of conversation. One way, it transpired, would be to send it off to Cardiff, as the hospital there was probably the only place anywhere near that might be able to deal with our requirements. Sterilizing the whole implant sufficiently is obviously critical to the experiment, yet Bionic Tech, who were supplying the array, couldn't help us that much. At that point the implant had only been used on animals, where sterilization requirements are far less stringent, so they were not able to provide us with any useful data for use of the array on humans. In fact, at that time, we still didn't want to let them know what we were doing, so we couldn't even ask the question. Alternative suggestions were made regarding different acidic treatments, but that, we felt, was something we would have to look at again, nearer the time.

When exactly we could inform Bionic Tech about the experiment was a very difficult call to make. Most importantly, we knew that we needed to use their technology, and at some stage soon we would need to buy in the actual array to be employed. However, at this stage we hadn't settled on our requirements. Informing them now would be useful in terms of gaining up-to-date information on their own experimentation, but it might also blow the whole ship out of the water. If they knew that we were going for a human trial it was possible that they would clam up altogether, not even letting us have an array. Our plan was to bring them fully into the picture when we had the final array in our hands and were ready to go for the operation.

At that stage, the end of April, we tried to best guess when we would be able to go ahead with the experiment – when we would have the technology in place, but also when we might get the go-ahead from the hospital to carry out the operation. In the *Wired* article of February 2000 I had believed that eighteen months would be a likely preparation time, but it was now clear that we would be very lucky to go ahead within that period. September was put forward as an outside possibility, but it was agreed that we would not realistically be ready before November 2001.

This above all made me feel frustrated. In one sense we seemed to be moving forwards, but our end goal didn't appear to be getting any nearer. While I didn't get too upset as certain technical aspects of the project shifted – how many channels we would use, or how much was to be implanted – the fact that our target date was drifting made me very nervous. Dates have a habit of drifting into the horizon and never actually happening, so I had to make sure that this date became a reality.

After the successful set of RI lectures, I was asked to give the lectures again that summer, firstly in Japan and then in Korea. The Christmas Lectures had been given in Japan for the previous eleven years, but this would be the first time that they would be repeated in Korea. In both cases they would be televised in front of an audience. It sounded quite a daunting task, but one that was extremely exciting. How could I refuse? A week later Irena informed me she was off to Prague again for about ten days. As I saw her on her way, it felt as though I was also waving goodbye to my marriage.

In early June we got the results from our school IQ study. Toast and orange juice turned out to be the winning breakfast, increasing scores by almost three points over the month. This connected nicely with other reported results indicating that regular intake of vitamin C improves IQ and exam scores. Bacon sandwiches seemed to have a positive effect though, which appeared to tie in with the meat-eating theory. Meanwhile, our experiment suggested that cereals had a very slight negative effect, while eggs generally pulled results down for everyone that had them. *New Scientist* published the results, as did one or two papers, the *Daily Mail* in particular, but I was surprised that the media didn't make more of it. This seems to be the type of project that the UK media widely report if it comes from a US university but give little airing to if it comes from the UK – or maybe that's just sour grapes.

Our June implant meeting saw us discussing exactly how much of the implant would be implanted, and how much was going to be on the surface. Ali decided conclusively that, if the full implant version was going to be about the size of a cigarette packet, then there was clearly no way he could implant it all, particularly with a connection just above the wrist. We therefore rejigged our plan. From now on Mark would continue his work on the main electronic transmitter/receiver design, with a clear view that a large proportion of it would be positioned on the surface of my arm rather than under the skin. Obviously the array, which had to connect directly on to my nerves, would be implanted.

At the beginning of July I received some disastrous news. Stewart Bruyn from Nortel Networks, who had been funding Mark's position on the implant project and whose money was vital to us, telephoned to say that, unfortunately, Nortel had had a pretty awful year, lots of staff had been laid off and that as a result they would not be able to continue with their support after the end of the first year. On the one hand I was grateful for the support they had given, but on the other hand I realized that this could mean the end of the project. Mark was central to the implant design and build, and I needed the money to pay him. What was I going to do?

The next day I had to go to Geneva to make a presentation at a meeting called Net Finance 2001. In my presentation I talked about the implant experiment and what we were planning to do. I also mentioned the demise of our Nortel funding, and how we were in desperate need of financial support. About half an hour after my talk I was sitting by the side of the hotel pool with Andrew Liddle from Tumbleweed Communications who were happy to pledge their support on a quarterly basis at least. Not only that, but whereas the Nortel total amounted to £25,000 a year, Tumbleweed were happy to give us £32,000, plus help with security aspects in our internet link-ups. The security aspects were a vital part of the experiment. Sending signals across the internet and down on to the nervous system was dangerous enough and naturally we did not want the signals to be corrupted. It was an element of the experiment that we had been leaving until later, but we were now being handed a ready-made solution. Tumbleweed seemed to be the perfect partners, and within a few days the project was afloat again.

A week later and I was in Orlando, Florida, making an appearance for Computer Associates (CA), our other sponsors at CA World, their annual jamboree. Not only do a lot of CA employees attend this get-together, but so do many people from different companies who work with or are partnered with CA. One such person was Marc Silvester from Fujitsu/ICL. Kate Darby, who runs the TCS Centre at Reading, was also helping me with the CA account. She chatted with Marc about what we were doing and he appeared to be extremely interested in

Fujitsu also providing us with some support, although at that point it was certainly not guaranteed.

A few days after my return from Orlando I had to leave for Tokyo on the first part of the RI lecture series. The custom is for the lecturer's spouse to accompany them, but Irena said that she didn't want to go, and with a similar offer on the table for the Korean lectures to follow, she left it too late and couldn't get the time off work for those either. I was therefore accompanied by Maddi, my daughter, instead. We had a great time in Japan, and were perhaps the closest we had been since I had left Sylvia, her mother, over ten years earlier. Maddi, at nineteen, was now a very different person.

We first went to Toyama and spent a few days rehearsing before giving four lectures over two days in front of a theatre audience and Japanese television. Because of the audience participation in the lectures, one of the most important things was for me to learn how to interact with a Japanese, as opposed to British, audience. I thought this might be problematic, but apart from one or two cultural differences, the kids in the audience soon seemed to be on my side once we started demonstrating robots. Iain Goodhew and Mark Gasson were there to help with the lectures, as was Bippin Palmer from the RI, and it felt good to be working as part of a cohesive team.

After Toyama we moved on to Tokyo and Waseda University. As in London, Atsuo Takanishi and his team at Waseda contributed their Eye-Chan robot to the second of the lectures, so by the time of their last performance we had got to know them all very well.

The highlight of the lectures in Toyama and Tokyo was the chance to work and interact with Honda's Humanoid Asimo robot, a marvellous piece of engineering that walks, dances and moves around just like a little boy. It appeared at the start of the first lecture at both venues in Japan, its entrance being greeted with Jurassic Park sound-alike music. On both occasions the audience gasped in amazement when Asimo started moving. A prize possession of mine is now an Asimo Operations Staff sweatshirt presented to me by the Honda team.

In Tokyo we attended a function involving several Japanese government officials and dignitaries. At this event we were also joined by Susan

Greenfield, Director of the RI, who had by this time become Baroness
Greenfield. Her husband Peter Atkins was with her, and I believe him
to be one of the cleverest guys I have ever met. He also has a very dry
sense of humour which I like. However, his subject is chemistry, but I
suppose nobody's perfect.

At the end of July we moved on from Japan and Maddi returned to
Reading. Iain and I boarded a plane for Shanghai. Mark stayed a while
in Japan and Bippin went directly to Korea. The five days Iain and I had
in Shanghai were spent with the British Council raising the profile of the
UK by making presentations and giving several press interviews, even
making the front page of the *Shanghai Daily* and several Chinese-
language newspapers. We then moved on to Korea, where my first stop
was Seoul. After giving several presentations and press interviews there,
I continued to Daejon where the RI lectures were to be held.

Whereas the Japanese TV people, having seen all of it before, seemed
extremely professional about the whole lecture tour, in Korea it was a
very different story. Iain, Bippin and I had already been through the
lectures in London with Channel 4, then in Toyama and Tokyo with
Japanese TV, so by the time we reached Korea we had a good idea what
we were doing. We ended up doing a lot of the initial directing
ourselves, but by the end of the lectures we were all working well as a
team, and for the 2002 lectures I'm sure the Korean TV people will be
well into it.

It was quite an honour to be the first RI Christmas Lecturer to present
the lectures in Korea and I enjoyed it immensely. After the final
programme was filmed, Iain and I travelled by train back up to Seoul, as
he hadn't had an opportunity to see the place en route to Daejon.
Unfortunately when we arrived it was pouring with rain, so we ended
up heading straight to my hotel, where we went for a swim and played
innumerate games of pool. After losing heavily at pool, Iain had to catch
a plane out on his way back to the UK. That evening saw a formal
dinner at the Paris Grill of the Hyatt Hotel in Seoul. Once again Susan
and Peter turned up and we were joined by several Korean dignitaries.
The next day I flew to Hong Kong where I spent a couple of days at the
Polytechnic University going through research proposals with them.

In some ways the whole set of Christmas Lectures, firstly in London in December 2000 and then in Japan and Korea, was a complete diversion from my main goal, the implant experiment. However, apart from the honour of doing them, they did allow Iain and me time to discuss what we were going to do when the implant was in place. One suggestion that appeared at this time was to remote control one of our robots from my nervous system. The idea was that when I moved my finger the robot would move left, right and so on, as directed by me. Bringing about such a result, which seemed quite possible, would mean that thought-controlled vehicles and other technology should be achievable subsequently. It was an intriguing idea.

When I got back to Reading it really seemed time to sort things out with Irena, one way or another. She had been back to Prague again when I was in the Far East and I felt strongly that she wasn't interested in our marriage anymore. So during the last couple of weeks in August we spent many an hour discussing what we wanted to do, did we want to stay together? At one time Irena said that even if we didn't stay together, she still wanted to be part of the experiment. But just when it looked as though our marriage was over, things took a different turn. Probably the easiest thing imaginable would have been for us to split up and go our separate ways. But once we had made that suggestion, and thought about the consequences seriously, things seemed immediately to be much brighter and we felt a lot closer. We clearly didn't want to lose each other, we had a life together to get on with, and an implant experiment to get back on the rails.

Within a week, Eaglemoss had launched the *Real Robots* magazine with Cybot, our robot, the key feature. Trials had indicated that it was likely to be far more successful than at first expected. Still, I could not believe it when I was told that they printed 650,000 copies of each of the first two issues; this meant that Cybot would be the most prolific robot in the UK. A few days later I found out from *Esquire* magazine that their readers had voted me the forth-fifth Sharpest Man in the UK (whatever that meant!) and I appeared as such in their September issue. I was even more chuffed to find out that people such as Hugh Grant and Tony Blair did not make the top fifty, and that I also seemed to be the only scientist or academic in the list, with most being pop stars, sportsmen and film stars.

On 21 September, Ali, Brian, Mark and I had a get-together to push the implant project on. It was at this meeting that we decided that it would probably take at least another year to put together something small enough to be fully implanted. Given the fact that we wanted to go for the experiment within the next six months, we decided that the array and wires would be implanted but that the electronics that Mark was working on would be placed on the outside on an armband. A key factor was that we would be able to apply test signals to ensure that everything was operating correctly.

During our time in Japan, Mark and I had discussed the full implant issue on a number of occasions and hence when the armband decision arrived, it seemed almost inevitable. In any case, we needed to gain access to the circuitry, which would be impossible with a full implant. Critically, our main drive was for a link on to the human nervous system, for which a full implant was not essential, and we wanted to be the first to do it, whether or not everything was under the skin.

In the first week of October Irena and I went to Montreal to attend a big conference at which I gave the plenary speech. It was surprising how many Americans had been frightened off travelling even the short distance to Montreal following the 11 September terrorist attacks on New York and Washington. On one occasion I was talking to the camera for a news item and held up an identical version of the implant I had used in 1998. It slipped from my fingers, dropping to the ground where it smashed into pieces. It made me realize what might have occurred during the first experiment, and I wondered what would have happened if it had done that inside my arm.

As soon as I got home, I had a big meeting at Stoke Mandeville with Mark, Ali and Brian. The main topic this time seemed to be infection. As we had made the final decision that wires would be coming through the skin for the duration of the experiment, it was important to minimize the possibilities of infection, which might run down the wires into the nerve fibres. Ali stressed that this could be a very serious problem, as if it occurred and wasn't caught quickly enough, there was a possibility that I would end up with a dead hand, i.e. my left hand would be completely useless. As a result Ali felt that it was best if the array came out after one week, or two at most. Both Brian and I were, by now, looking towards a two-month experiment and said so. When I mentioned Irena's implant Ali completely clammed up and indicated strongly that despite what had been said previously, there would only be one implant. This came as a huge shock, as to me, a big part of the experiment was to be the nervous-system communication between Irena and me.

We also discussed pushing everything forward to the ethics committee for approval. However, Ali wasn't prepared to do this until he had seen the array and the electronics, and had had practice at firing the array into an orange at least. It was therefore agreed that an ethics committee submission would wait until we had the circuitry together. This meant Brian had to order the array and the gun from Bionic Tech in Utah as soon as possible. The package was ordered via the Radcliffe Infirmary at Oxford where Brian had a share in an office. This way, the people at Utah would still think, we hoped, that Brian was using it on animals, and so would still be unaware of our experiment. Our reasoning was that if we had ordered the array from a Reading address, Bionic Tech would link it to me and know, from the *Wired* article, what our plans were.

The Radcliffe Infirmary had another plus in that Peter Teddy a consultant neurosurgeon, who was Ali's boss, also had his office there. Brian had been keeping Peter informed of progress and it now seemed to be time to bring him much more firmly on board, particularly as he would be useful in helping with ethics committee approval and would most likely take part, and oversee, the operation itself. We therefore made an agreement to touch base with Peter as soon as possible. Because of the time it would take to get an ethics committee proposal together and submitted, it became clear that a November date for the experiment was out of the question. It looked like things would be delayed until the new year.

After the meeting I talked with Mark and Brian about Ali's opinion on Irena's involvement. Now we were starting to get close to the operation we felt that Ali was getting nervous. He seemed to be making excuses to delay things, and was perhaps beginning to worry about what might happen if things went wrong. It was a shame he seemed to be saying no to the second implant for Irena, despite the fact that he had been in favour of it up to that point. Brian suggested that we see what Peter Teddy made of it all, thinking that maybe he would become much more involved. Brian also felt that, with my implant in place, it might be possible for the communication experiment to take place with just two or three wires inserted through Irena's skin and hence no implant. I knew that Irena was extremely excited about the whole experiment and that such a reduction in her role would disappoint both of us, but we would have to see what Peter Teddy thought.

That day I returned to Reading and went straight into a meeting with Andrew Liddle of Tumbleweed. Andrew had expected the experiment to go ahead in November and Tumbleweed had, because of this, provided funding to cover Mark's salary up to the end of December. I now had to tell Andrew that the experiment would not go ahead until the new year. At the meeting Andrew seemed very disappointed about my news and indicated that the money from Tumbleweed might not be there after the end of December 2001. I tried to convince him otherwise, at the same time realizing that once again funding had become an issue. Fujitsu still hadn't provided us with any money despite assurances from Marc Silvester, and I knew I needed to chase them up.

My role in the project was clear. Firstly I was the main patient and the person with the scientific vision of what we were trying to achieve. But I also had to bring in the money to pay for people to work on the project and, in addition to my own input on implant design and positioning, I had to push things along, get paperwork completed, equipment ordered and delivered, etc. At times it felt as though various people on the project were doing all they could to delay things, although I'm sure that wasn't really the case. I am generally an impatient person and don't like waiting in queues. With the experiment, I knew what we were trying to do, and I knew what a unique group of people was working on it – the best team I am ever likely to work with – but all the time it was taking was very frustrating. However, I reminded myself that we were undertaking a piece of science that had never been done before. We were involved with something that would most likely change the world as we knew it, for good. In achieving that, we were bound to encounter unforeseen problems, and hence experience delays.

Meanwhile Mark and Ben were working on the electronic design, Brian was sorting out the array, and Peter and Ali taking care of the surgery. One point of view might therefore be that I wasn't really doing anything! In the next couple of weeks I gave invited presentations at Durham, Edinburgh and Cambridge universities. Each venue had a really good-sized audience and questions were thrown at me from all angles. There was no doubt that people were interested in the project, and each meeting, in its own way, spurred me on to work harder and make sure it happened. There were plenty of questions, much food for thought. It made me realize that the momentum was building.

On 13 October I was one of a panel of five who met at the Science Museum in London for the Loebner Competition, an annual event sponsored by Hugh Loebner to see if anyone has been able to get a computer to pass the Turing Test. The idea is that the computer should fool those asking it questions into thinking that it is actually a human. If you can't tell the difference it has passed the test. We had nine stations at which to converse with whatever was on the other end of the keyboard connection, and were told to give one mark if we thought it was a machine and five if we thought it was a human, with marks between for uncertainty. Behind two of the nine stations were humans, and machines at the other seven. Three of the five judges, including myself and Hugh Loebner, made a clear distinction between the machines and the two humans. However, one machine fooled two of the judges. Frankly I was amazed, not so much at how good the machine responses were, but rather that two out of five judges couldn't tell the difference.

Then some trouble arose. A seemingly innocuous article about artificial intelligence appeared in the *Guardian* claiming that I would be given senses like those of a bat. Although this was loosely true, it was not so liberal as the article perhaps implied. However, as a result of the article, one of the administrators at Stoke Mandeville, sent a letter round to the high-ups at Stoke asking what on earth was going on. Why hadn't we gone through the ethics committee with this? Why didn't anyone at Stoke Mandeville know about it? The letter went one stage further than the *Guardian*, implying that I was actually to receive a bat's senses. As the article contained a nice photograph and a good mention of the hospital, I had expected it to have a positive effect; that's why I had agreed to be interviewed for the article in the first place. However, here it was being turned into a negative, as alarm bells rang around Stoke. Luckily Brian Gardner, one of the senior consultants at Stoke overseeing things, and who knew generally what was happening, poured some calm on the troubled waters by bringing people up to date with the project. Things got better a few days later when I staged a teleconference with Peter Teddy at Oxford and Brian Andrews at Reading while I was down at the Royal Society in London for a meeting. It was the first time I had spoken to Peter Teddy and I was hugely impressed by his authority. Apart from being extremely excited about what we were trying to do, he suggested that, if there were problems at Stoke Mandeville, we could always do the experiment at the Radcliffe Infirmary instead. While feeling slightly more positive that it would go ahead, my only negative response to this was that Oxford University might end up laying claim to the experiment and getting plaudits for something it had nothing to do with.

On leaving the Royal Society I met up with Moi, my Thai student from the Royal College of Art. At the meeting we linked her jewellery into the implant experiment. The aim was to get her jewellery to change colour in response to signals on the nervous system. I hoped she would be able to get it functioning, as it sounded like a nice, non-medical demonstrator part of the experiment. While Iain Goodhew and Ben Hutt were arranging for my nervous system to control robots as I had discussed with Iain on the Far East tour, Justin Gan was arranging for my nervous system to interact with the Cybernetics building, firstly so that I could switch on the coffee-maker from anywhere in the building and second so that people would be able to track my movements on the web. However, having jewellery that changed its appearance seemed an exciting extra.

As October became November I received three good pieces of news.

Firstly I was asked if I would mind being included in the 2002 edition of *Who's Who*. Naturally I didn't object. Second I discovered that I was already included in the 2002 edition of the *Guiness Book of Records*, for the 1998 implant experiment. Not only that but the robots that Ben Hutt had put together for the London Science Museum were also included, although Reading didn't get a mention. It was nice because I hadn't been in the *Guiness Book of Records* since 1999 when they reported on the robot internet-learning experiment. The third piece of news was a message from Mark that the Utah package had arrived at Oxford.

Brian collected the package and immediately took the array blanks and the gun across to Ali at Stoke Mandeville. But the array itself had not yet shown up. Brian had only ordered one, termed a (uniform) flat array, in which all the pins were the same length. Bionic Tech had claimed that their new slant array would be ready within a few weeks and Brian wanted to hold out for that for the actual experiment. I was more inclined to go for several copies of the flat array, which had at least been tried and tested on animals, unlike the slant array.

On 5 November we were supposed to have a meeting at Stoke involving Mark, Brian, Ali and me, but Ali cancelled at the last minute. A few days later Brian turned up at the department to say that Ali had had the array blanks and the gun for over a week but hadn't actually used them yet. We had all been expecting him to carry out practice firings from the moment the blanks arrived, and we wondered how committed Ali now was to the project.

A week later Brian telephoned to say that it would be better if I increased the medical content of any statements that I made. For the last few months I had been trying to avoid any such content because of the possibility of ethics committee problems. But it now seemed that Stoke wanted to hear much more about the medical side. In the proposal we would need to describe exactly what was going to happen medically in terms of the operation and why we were doing it, and I just hoped that when we put in the ethics proposal they didn't reject it because of too little or too much medical content. Also, as the patient, I had to make a statement saying that I fully consented to the operation and had been made aware of the medical risks. However, a lot of leeway was available in terms of what words were used to describe operational details. I felt that the main problem was that some old codger, who didn't have a clue what was going on, would simply dig his heals in and be awkward. It seemed that pioneering medical research, such as ours, could be thwarted by someone on our ethics committee who didn't have a full understanding of the work we were doing. It was frustrating.

Later that day I met up with Mark, who informed me that technically we were just about ready for the experiment, in that the electronic transmitter/receiver design to go with the array had been completed. We still needed to fit it into an armband of some kind though. Mark said he knew of someone in London who might be able to help and we agreed to meet up as soon as we could arrange a date.

A few days later Brian, Mark, myself and Koye, who was helping Brian at Oxford, met up with Peter Teddy at the Radcliffe Infirmary. It was a momentous meeting. We discussed with Peter the problem of firing the array into the median nerve in my arm, missing (hopefully) a fairly prominent blood vessel positioned in the middle. Peter confirmed that if it was not possible to do the operation at Stoke then we would be able to do it at the Radcliffe. If so it would be Peter, not Ali, who would perform the operation. Peter also said that his registrar, Amjad Shad, also a consultant neurosurgeon, would be very happy to assist with the operation.

We agreed on February 2002 as a potential date for the operation. When Peter said that it would be easiest on a Saturday as the operating theatre would be free, I suggested Saturday 9 February, my birthday, and nobody objected. We realized that some sort of frame would have to be built for the mechanism from which the implant would be fired into the nervous fibres, and that it would have to sit on a table by the operating table, so we all walked quickly downstairs, Peter leading the way, in order to see one of these tables in an operating theatre. This meeting really moved the whole project on a pace, and with Peter on board it looked good. But what about Ali? He had been the neuro-surgeon concerned with things until now. When we got back to Reading later that day, Brian and I both tried to arrange a meeting with him, at which point we discovered he had gone on holiday and wouldn't be back until 19 December.

On 26 November I made a presentation at the Oxford Union. Throughout history this has been one of the famous places for new ideas to be presented – for example Charles Darwin got into major arguments there over his evolutionary theory. Now here I was telling the students about wanting to be a cyborg. Two days later Irena and I appeared on Richard and Judy's new television afternoon chat show. We talked about what we were hoping to do with the implants, and I even got in plugs both for Stoke Mandeville Hospital and the David Tolkien Trust. It seemed like a good idea to indicate that we were also doing the experiment for charity purposes.

It was patently obvious from both the Oxford Union and *Richard and Judy* events that there was great interest in Irena's role in the experiment. As well as the nervous system to nervous system signalling, which stimulated me scientifically, the possibility of transmitting signals associated with pain, shock and excitement really seemed to set people's imagination racing. Irena was very upbeat and keen to be involved, and I was very happy about this.

The day after our appearance on *Richard and Judy*, Kate Darby and I went out to see Marc Silvester at Fujitsu. He spent several minutes telling us how difficult it was for him to give us any money to help with the implant experiment, then said we could have £50,000 from April 2002 for the next year, but £10,000 immediately. This latter bit was great news as it meant that I now had enough to pay for all the researchers involved, Mark Gasson in particular, until Easter 2002.

As November played its own endgame, I reflected on the eleven months just gone. I thought about how close I had come to separating from Irena, but even when our marriage had seemed doomed, she had said that she still wanted to go ahead with the experiment. What a brave and wonderful woman I was married to. I owed it to her to make sure she was part of it. One evening, when Irena was in Prague, Maddi and I had a drink together. She asked me why I was doing the experiment – I didn't have to, it was highly dangerous and there was a possibility that I might have mental problems or even die because of it. When I told her that I was a scientist, that this was my life and what I was all about, she cried openly.

Maddi's tears made me more aware than ever that I was not only a scientist, but that I was also a husband and a father, with the plethora of responsibilities attached to those roles. I felt deeply for Maddi, and tried to comfort her. In doing so it raised questions in my own mind about how important the experiment had become in my life. I was throwing everything into it, my reputation, my career and even my family. There was no way that I could stop now. But was the experiment so important that I would give my life for it? I didn't have to think twice about that one, I knew that I would. But as the build-up to the experiment got under way, I had no idea how close a call it would turn out to be.

CHAPTER 11

By DECEMBER 2001, there were a significant number of people on the team working on the experiment. I had six paid research assistants on the project and half a dozen research students and academic visitors. My research assistants were concerned with the implant electronics design and putting the experiment together while the research students carried out subsequent analysis of the data collected to provide a more in-depth understanding of the results. Department faculty members were also involved, as were a number of medical people at Stoke Mandeville and the Radcliffe Infirmary. For the operation we would have a further team. The total number involved was well over thirty, not including secretaries and administrative staff.

The experiment now began to take over my life. Not only did all my daylight hours focus on making it happen, but I would frequently wake up at night and find myself going over different aspects of the experiment, planning and scheming, and trying to make sure all angles were covered. The operation was of prime importance, and I had to make sure I put my all into making it happen. I could worry about the rest of the experiment later. I still gave my lectures and set examination questions but everything else – the presentations, trips, reviews of academic papers, research – was put on hold.

In the first week in December we had a visit from Sylak Ravenspine, from Sylak Special Effects, the man who was putting the 'gauntlet', as the arm band had become known, together. He was very much an artist and had previously produced armbands of one type or another more for artistic effect than practical purposes. Mark Gasson and I had looked at what the medical world could offer us and we weren't happy. We needed to have our own designed, and in came Sylak. With his long black hair he looked like Ozzy Ozbourne, and he spoke as though he was doing a screen test for the film *Easy Rider*, reminding me very much of my motorcycle days back in Coventry many years before. I liked him straightaway. At the meeting, he talked about what he could do, and we said what we wanted, with a hope that we could meet somewhere in the middle.

We knew that if the array was connected on to the nervous fibres near my wrist, the wires linked to it would come out of my skin in a bundle some distance up my forearm. They would then need to be bent back round and joined to an external connector, which would act as a pad of electrical terminals, linked on one side to the wires in my arm, and with our own electronic interface unit plugged into the other. This connector needed to be fixed to my arm as much as was possible because any movement or slack might pull my nerves around, or even dislodge the array.

It was clear that we first needed a bracket around my arm that would firmly fix the external connector. But we also needed a housing for the electronics that would link up to it. I only needed to be linked to the computer when we were experimenting, so it was sensible for the vast bulk of the electronics to be readily detachable. The parameters agreed, Sylak left to work on the initial design. We wanted it to be functional, but we also wanted it to look good, as it was likely that the housing would be photographed extensively.

I was concentrating on short-term goals, and I hoped my colleagues were, too. I found that as a result of the short-term planning, my mind sometimes drifted from the big picture, and I forgot the reasons *why* I was doing the experiment at all. Talking to Sylak, Mark and I had to explain, from first principles, exactly what we were doing and why. Sylak seemed astonished that I would be willing to have my body cut open by some serious surgery and face various dangers, with a few unknowns, in order to carry out the experiment. All this combined made me think deeply about my convictions, so much so that I couldn't get to sleep that night – I wanted to sort things out in my own mind. I wasn't scared about the operation, although maybe I would be nearer the time. Instead I felt incredibly excited about the whole investigation, especially now that it all seemed to be going ahead. There were three main reasons for taking the risks involved. There was also a host of smaller ones, such as putting both the University and Stoke Mandeville more firmly on the map, and raising money for the David Tolkien Trust.

The most important of my reasons was my science, cybernetics. I wanted to find out. I was curious, I *had* to find out what it was like and nothing was going to stop me. I think that if this had been my only reason it would have been strong enough anyway, as the implant experiment and experience was central to the main purpose of my research. What would it be like to be connected up to a computer in this way? Might it be possible for humans to have extra capabilities, particularly mental attributes, and become super humans or, as some regard it, post humans? Not only was I interested in how the implant would change my feelings when I was a cyborg, but also how I would react when the implant was removed and I returned to the ranks of humanity.

At the same time there were a number of technical questions that needed to be examined. What would be the effects if different electrical currents were played down on to my nervous system? In carrying out the experiment, would we discover any signals or feeling that we would not be able to understand, quite simply because no one had witnessed anything like them before? We had our initial agenda of scientific research that we wanted to carry out, but how much of it would we actually be able to do when the implant was in place?

I think that there is a drive, a passion, in any true scientist to investigate the unknown, to see what's around the corner, to find answers to the question 'Is it possible . . . ?' Certainly such a force exists in me. I am not content, not happy to relax and accept that, scientifically, we have gone as far as we will ever go. Life would not be worth living if that was the case.

The least important of the three reasons was my desire to be the first cyborg, to be the pioneer. Reading about the exploits of Scott and Lindbergh had thrilled me as a child and stories such as Jekyll and Hyde were fascinating. Now I was in a similar position. I could go where no one had ever been before. How could I refuse? There is something incredibly exciting about the possibility of treading a path that no one has trodden before – the chance to be the first to witness an event, to discover a phenomena or scientific relationship previously unencountered, to get to a place on earth or in science and be the first one there, despite the dangers or problems that may stand in the way. It is a challenge, which you cannot be sure can be met until it is; a hill to climb, where you don't know how steep it is, or if you have the energy to climb it, or if you are choosing the best route to the summit.

It is wonderful that there are opportunities such as these in life. There is an air of mystery about it all as you have no idea what you will find, simply a best guess or hunch about how things might be. You have to trust in your own abilities and the help of those around you to reach the goal, to stretch understanding and knowledge beyond its present position.

Coming in closely in second place was what I felt we might achieve with the experiment. Maybe we could help to get people with a break in their nervous system moving again. Maybe we could give different senses to those who are blind. Maybe we could help to remove pain electronically from those permanently afflicted. Maybe we could help many more people in ways we simply couldn't imagine. Because of this, taking part in a little operation seemed a trivial price to pay. I had the wonderful opportunity to help maybe thousands of others by taking a relatively small risk myself.

The next day Brian Andrews and I had a review meeting in Reading. It was the beginning of December and we wanted the operation to go ahead in the middle of February – in about ten or eleven weeks' time. What did we still have to do and what were priority items?

The first issue was the ethics committee approval. We had decided to put forward two ethics proposals – one to Stoke Mandeville and one to the Radcliffe Infirmary. The operation would then take place at whichever hospital gave us the fewest problems. Peter Teddy was consultant surgeon at both, so he would be in charge on the medical side regardless of which one we went for. As Ali Jamous seemed to be drifting out of the picture, it looked more likely that Peter Teddy would do the operation. Both ethics committees had a submission deadline of 16 January, so all the forms had to be ready by then.

A problem arose when we discovered that we wouldn't hear back from the ethics committees until the first week in February. Even if it was good news and we were given the go-ahead, we felt that we would still have to satisfy the committee chairman on a number of points, which might take a few extra days. Our operation date of 9 February suddenly looked impossible, so we set our sights on the 16th or 23rd instead. Whether the operation was carried out at the Radcliffe or Stoke we would need to get the implant sterilized. It now seemed that we wouldn't have to send it off to Cardiff as the unit in the Radcliffe would be able to look after the process for us by sending it off to a lab in Surrey. Unfortunately they usually took around two weeks to complete the process, with a fair amount of this time taken up with transport and bureaucracy. With an operation date of 16 February, this would mean we would need the actual implant by the end of January at the latest. All we had at the beginning of December was one test flat array which just about everyone in the team was playing with.

To ensure we got the order through in time, we had until around 16 January to decide which array and wires we wanted to order from Bionic Tech in Utah. However, even then, it was likely that one of us would have to go over to Utah to collect it. We particularly wanted the slant array, despite the fact that to the best of our knowledge it hadn't been fully tested on animals. The benefit of the slant array was that it might provide us with more information. Unfortunately Bionic Tech were still being extremely cagey about whether or not they could supply it.

It was clear from the meeting with Brian that there were still a lot of things to be done, but there was very little time in which to do them. Funding for the six researchers working on the project – namely Mark,

Ben, Iain and Justin along with John Newland and Mohammad Arshad – was scheduled to run out at the end of March or mid-April. Computer Associates, Tumbleweed and, more recently, Fujitsu had all been very good at providing the money to allow us to get on with the project, but it was now getting critical. If the operation hadn't been done by the end of March at the very latest, we would not be able to get any money from them, the six researchers would be out of a job and the whole project would come to an abrupt halt. If the operation went ahead, I felt confident that the three companies concerned would continue the funding.

December flew by, taken up with the fiddly things, including filling in forms, sending emails, telephoning, and trying to make sure that we hit the February schedule. However, I did go on two small trips, one of which was to Lancaster University for a conference on ethics. This was extremely useful, as it helped considerably in nailing down ideas for our own ethics proposals. It was clear that directing the cyborg project towards the goal of helping those with a disability received a positive reception in general. On the other hand, when mentioning the up-grading of humans and the realization of the superhuman being, there was a mixed response. Some people were definitely in favour of this concept, while other were hesitant.

After the Christmas break, I was back in the department again on the 28th for a meeting with Brian Andrews and Andrew Williams from the David Tolkien Trust. Andrew wanted the Trust to be clearly associated with the project, and we shared the worry that, because it was only connected with Stoke Mandeville, if the operation went ahead at the Radcliffe in Oxford, the link with the Trust would be too obscure. It was therefore agreed that shortly after the operation, a press conference would be held at Stoke Mandeville regardless of which hospital the operation had actually taken place at. David could be there as well as, we hoped, Jimmy Saville, and maybe even Lord Carrington, the Chancellor of Reading University, and a number of David's board. Andrew would coordinate the press session, and before he left he took some photos of Brian and me with the old microelectrode array we already had from Utah.

A week or so later it all became very hectic, with two things taking centre stage. Firstly there were the two ethics committee submissions. The deadline of 16 January was close, and all the finishing touches needed to be put in place. We were helped considerably when we found out that indemnity issues could be dealt with separately, as this meant we could concentrate strictly on ethics paperwork. A fair volume of this was involved with making sure that the patient(s) understood the risks involved and knowingly consented to the operation. I therefore wrote a letter of consent, while George Boulos – who was both my GP, and the man who carried out the first operation in 1998, put a letter together saying that I was in good health, of sound mind and knew exactly what I was doing.

On 11 January Brian, Mark, Peter Teddy, Amjad Shad and I met at the Radcliffe. Peter had a few modifications to suggest with regard to the ethics submissions, but apart from that they seemed ready to go in. Peter was also keen to carry out a dry run of the operation so that we could go through all the necessary elements first. That way, when the actual operation took place, everything should be in place.

Amjad was keen to practise firing the array, so Peter suggested he buy some pork chops from the local butcher first, then move on to testing on cadavers. For some reason lots of legs were available from the deep freeze at Oxford, but very few arms. Amjad therefore took it upon himself to find an arm, and hence a median nerve, for practice. A discussion also ensued as to whether they would have to cut away the outer sheath of my nerve fibres in order for the array to make good contact. I didn't like the sound of that and was much relieved when Amjad stated that simply stretching the nerve would be sufficient.

A notable absence from the Radcliffe meeting was Ali Jamous. I emailed him again, but got no reply. This was a great shame, as Ali's advice had been invaluable in the earlier stages of the project. It now looked as if Peter Teddy would handle the operation instead and that Amjad Shad would assist.

The following week the ethics proposals were submitted. All we could do now was wait until early February and hope for the best. It was agreed that Brian would order the microelectrode array, along with a back-up in case something went wrong with the first. Brian ordered it because he could use his Oxford address, as we still hadn't told Bionic Tech what we were up to at this point. However, reading between the lines on their very helpful emails, we all suspected they were aware what was going on. Nonetheless, until we got the arrays in our hands, we wanted to avoid all potential problems.

But when Brian put the order through, he was told that the slant array would not be available until the beginning of April at the very earliest. Even though Brian and I had our hearts set on going for the slant array, the dates we were working to meant we would have to go for the flat array after all. A uniform array was therefore ordered, with 20 centimetres of wire to ensure it would come out well up my arm, hopefully thereby reducing the possibility of any infection getting down on to the nerves. The theory was that the further any infection had to travel, the less likely it was to set in.

When Mark and I met with Sylak, we were shocked at what he proposed for the gauntlet design. We had expected him to design something futuristic, and our worry had been that it would look too much like something from a science-fiction film. However, what he showed us was a design based around the idea of bones, with electronic circuit boards intermingled with what looked like bony structures. It was certainly a cybernetic idea, human and machine in harmony, but it wasn't quite what we were expecting. Although we had not wanted it to look too much like something from a sci-fi film, we had hoped for a certain element of that style to feature in the design.

When Sylak had gone, a group of us discussed the designs and realized we all felt much the same. Anna Bradbrook, a secretary in the department, sketched out some new ideas and we agreed that they were more what we were looking for – a combination of Sylak's ideas with a much more sci-fi appearance to them. We sent the ideas off to Sylak and he agreed to incorporate them. We needed to make some measurements, but otherwise agreed to go forward with the design and planned to meet up again at the end of January to finalize everything.

The following day I received a couple of unexpected emails. The first was from Channel 4 to say that the *Self-Experimenters* Equinox programme we had filmed two years before was scheduled to be shown on Sunday 3 March. I was surprised that they had left it this long before airing it, and wondered if they had heard the experiment was taking place and wanted to tie their programme into it. Their timing was absolutely perfect, as the implant would probably be put in place around the time that the Equinox programme went out.

The second email was from Sue Nelson of the BBC, enquiring about a *Los Angeles Times* story on cyborgs which mentioned me a number of times. Sue also asked when the new experiment was likely to go ahead, and when I told her it was only a few week away and that TV news coverage had not been finalized, she was extremely interested. Sue had done the story on the previous implant in 1998, so it seemed a good idea that we worked with her again. She suggested that the story went out on TV on the Monday morning after the operation, at the same time the news appeared in the papers. It seemed an excellent idea, and we agreed that she would come to Oxford when we did the dry run, so she could see the lie of the land.

On Friday 18th Brian Hatt from Bionic Tech let us know that although the slant array was not scheduled to go into production for a while, they would be able to wire up a couple to our specifications. We not only quickly agreed on an order but also arranged for Brian Andrews to go over to Salt Lake City to collect them in the first week of February. Brian Hatt told us that Brian Andrews could inform him of our intentions in an off-the-record way while he was there. It seemed a perfect way to go about things, as we would then find out if Bionic Tech were happy with our plans. Even at this stage none of us were really sure how they would respond.

That day I was also informed by Ben Hutt, who, with Mark Gasson, had been working for several months now on the radio transmitter/ receiver circuitry, that it was now working successfully and the final printed circuit board was being designed. This meant that technically we could be ready to carry out the experiment in the next couple of weeks. Although 16 February was not out of the question, it seemed that the 23rd was more realistic.

But not everything was happening so smoothly. Although it looked as though the operation could go ahead in February, it had to have been done by the end of March at the latest, otherwise we were out of money. On top of that, there was a whole list of potential problems that kept me awake each night, including the fear that both the hospitals' ethics committees could say 'no', or at least cause us so many problems as to make the experiment impossible; that both hospitals could stop us going ahead; that Bionic Tech might say 'no way' and bring about a legal injunction (we still had to get hold of the array anyway); that there could be an immediate problem, the University of Reading might wash its hand of the experiment; and that there could be all sorts of technical problems, even now. On the last point, we really were not sure if the array, once hammered into position, would make reasonable contact with the nerves. We had no real idea if we would get any signals at all. At our last meeting at Oxford it had been agreed that during the operation, once the implant was in place (with my arm still exhibiting an open wound), Mark would connect up his box of tricks and see if the array was transmitting any signals. With a gaping wound in my arm, in the middle of the operation, I would therefore have to start wriggling my fingers about in the hope that Mark would get a positive result. If we were successful, Peter Teddy would stitch me up and the experiment would begin. If we didn't get any signals, the array would be pulled out and fired in again in the hope that better contact would be made. We didn't discuss how many attempts would be made before we gave up.

I wasn't particularly happy at the prospect of the length of the operation being extended in that way, but I didn't see that I had much choice. However, Peter hadn't really contributed to that conversation, so I wasn't sure of his feelings, and ultimately it was his decision as to whether it happened that way or not.

Another worry was perhaps self-inflicted. Having read how Charles Darwin's *Origin of Species* had sold out before it hit the shelves, I wanted to maximize publicity. Yet stating that we would go ahead with the operation on 16 or 23 February would immediately raise media expectations. The fears increased the more enquiries came in from around the world. For example, I received an email from David Akin representing Canadian National TV and two Toronto newspapers, stating that he had heard from the BBC that the operation would be going ahead and wanted to book his flights to make sure he was there for everything. What was I supposed to say? I still wasn't totally sure about the date, and having a reporter buy tickets and fly across the Atlantic only to find that the experiment had been delayed did not seem fair.

Back in the department, quite a few people had already expressed an interest in contributing to the series of experiments we wanted to carry out. So on 23 January I called a meeting of all those interested, to ensure that everyone knew what was happening, as well as allowing us to coordinate interest. Mark and I also sent round a description of exactly what we were up to:

A micro electrode array consisting of 100 individual electrodes will be implanted in the median nerve. The radius of each electrode tip is 1–3mm, the active region being 50–80mm long.

This technique should provide highly selective recording and stimulation of sensory and/or motor neurons within the nerve fascicles. The number of channels that provide useful information could be anything from 1 to 100!

The 25-Channel Neural Signal Amplifier amplifies the signal from each electrode by a factor of 5,000 and filters the signals with corner frequencies of 250Hz and 7.5KHz. The amplified and filtered electrode signals are then delivered to the Neural Signal Processor where they are digitized at 30,000 samples/second/electrode and scanned online for neural spike events. This means that only 25 of the total 100 channels can be viewed at any one time.

Neural spike events are detected by comparing the instantaneous electrode signal to level thresholds set for each data channel. When a supra-threshold event occurs, the signal window surrounding the event is time stamped and stored for later, offline analysis. The neural stimulator allows for any of the 25 monitored channels to be electrically stimulated with a chosen repetition frequency.

The meeting attracted about twenty people, which was more than we anticipated. Brian Andrews indicated that we would have to spend a fair amount of time doing clinical trials, which involved recording the output from one of the pins while pricking my hand and wrist at many different points. This was what could, literally, be described as painstaking research. Several people volunteered to help with this, Virginie Ruiz and Will Browne, both lecturers in the department, among them. In return they would gain much unique data that they could use for their own research using signal-processing techniques to obtain a deeper understanding of what was taking place. At the same time we would be making an enormous contribution to the mapping of the nervous system.

We also decided on a number of experiments:

1. Ultrasonic extra-sensory input.
2. Controlling a robot from my nervous system.
3. Exciting my nerves remotely over the internet.
4. Interacting with the network in the Cybernetics building.
5. Mimicking my hand movements on a 'third' (artificial) hand made by Peter Kyberd, one of the lecturers.
6. Interactive jewellery, if Moi had it ready in time.

Directly after the meeting, Mark and I spoke with Brian Andrews. We agreed that even though there were several unknowns, especially the results of the ethics committees, we needed to settle on a date for the operation. Given the time-scales involved, and what still had to be done, we decided on Saturday 23 February. We had exactly one month to go.

I felt glad that we had an actual date to work to, even though I realized that, while being realistic, it was still quite a challenge. Without a date I felt things would drift, that something that could be put off until the next day. But with a clear date in everyone's mind we had a specific target. It was surprising how it galvanized everyone into action, concentrating our efforts. We had been waiting for ages for Amjad – and Ali if he was still on board – to start firing arrays into whatever they could, preferably nerves, but even pork chops would suffice. Practice firings now occurred frequently and, perhaps most importantly, on 24 January Peter Teddy booked an operating theatre at the Radcliffe Infirmary for the agreed date. I had decided to opt for the Radcliffe because there seemed to be far more unknowns about having the operation at Stoke Mandeville. A bonus was that we would hear from the Radcliffe ethics committee just after 1 February, and if everything was okay then it would be all systems go.

On 24 January, apart from possible ethics committee problems, the only blot on the horizon was getting hold of the array from Utah. The previous information we had received had been incorrect, as it now appeared that we would have to use the uniform array after all, as it turned out that they had not yet been successful in making a slant array. But they were unclear about how soon could they get a uniform array ready for us, which left me frustrated and on edge. This was coupled with the fact that someone had decided to have the Winter Olympics in Salt Lake City at the same time we needed to pick up the array. Despite Brian Andrew's eagerness to zip over the pond and back again, getting a flight appeared to be impossible. But we had to find a way of getting the array over to Reading – as long as Bionic Tech could produce it in time.

On Saturday 26th Irena and I went into the Cybernetics Department to meet with Mark and Sylak. Again, Sylak's gauntlet designs looked very different from what we had expected. He had taken the ideas from the claws of a hermit crab: the gauntlet was in the shape of a crab's claw and looked rather strange.

A plaster-cast of my arm was made by putting my arm in a makeshift mould box, then pouring in some cold blue liquid. After fifteen minutes or so it had set into a thick jelly and I was able to remove my arm. Sylak would then use the cast to mould the device to my shape.

On the way back home from the university I had a surge of excitement and felt the tingling of butterflies in my stomach. Although there were still a lot of things that could go wrong, everything seemed to be moving forward. As 23 February came ever closer we were working entirely towards making *my* operation happen. Irena's operation had been put very much on the back burner. This was a great shame, as I knew Irena was looking forward to being part of things, part of the experiment. I was therefore determined that, once my operation had taken place, I would do all I could to make it happen for Irena too.

On the Monday I emailed my GP, George Boulos. Once the implant was in place it seemed much more sensible if I dropped in and saw George on a regular, possibly daily, basis so he could check for any signs of infection. This made more sense than driving over to the Radcliffe for ten minutes with Amjad – a good two-hour round trip at the least. With the experiment work to do, I would have enough to fill my time, and I felt that one trip up to Oxford every week would be sufficient. In addition to the time factor, it was also possible that someone would have to drive me, as I had no idea if I would be able to drive myself. George said he would be delighted to assist, which pleased me immensely. Not only would I save quite a bit of time, but George had been involved at the start of the implant work, and it was good that he would be a part of the next stage.

That week my excitement continued as Sylak emailed us some new, and much better, designs for armbands. I also did some functional hand testing with Peter Kyberd. Peter, in preparation for the 'third hand' element of the implant experiment, got me to go through various routines with my left hand and then again with my right hand. I had to pick up a card with my fingers and then put it down again, grip a block, lift it and put it down again, pick up coins one after the other, and put them into a jar. It took about twenty-five minutes for each hand and every movement was timed. The plan was to try these functional tests again every so often once the implant was in place, as it would be a good way of monitoring if my left hand was affected at all, and if so in what way.

As the week drew to a close, my feelings shifted from excitement to worry, and sleeping became more difficult and erratic. I am generally a positive and optimistic person, but I had come to realize that one or two things could stop the project. Firstly getting the array from Utah might delay the operation for a week or so – not too bad a prospect. The second was the real possibility that the ethics committees at both Stoke Mandeville and the Radcliffe Infirmary might say no to the operation, and therefore the whole experiment. Many years of work, half a million pounds or more in sponsorship and several PhDs could all be blown out of the water.

On Friday the 1st, I gave two of my weekly lectures to the undergraduate students. Luckily this took my mind off the fact that the ethics committee were at that point meeting at the Radcliffe. I emailed Peter Teddy to ask if he had any idea when he might hear something from the committee about our experiment. His reply was a simple 'No'. I took the hint.

I received an email from Sue Nelson at the BBC asking me to confirm the date for the operation. Another email came from David Akin in Toronto, who needed to book tickets. In the afternoon I talked to David Tolkien, who also needed to know a definite date so a press meeting could be arranged at Stoke Mandeville. How could he be expected to invite Lord Carrington to a press meeting when we weren't sure of the date? I saw his point. Jimmy Saville had said he would come – good old Jim.

When I talked to Brian Andrews about the situation, he felt that it wasn't really appropriate to get in touch with the committee chairperson or try to find out about the decision until they were ready to tell us. He didn't want us to upset them in any way. So Friday came and went. That weekend was sheer hell. The previous weekend had been great, everything had been under way. This weekend was quite the opposite. What if the committee said no? What would happen to my research team? Right now, my life was centred around the implant experiment – if it didn't happen, what then?

On Sunday Irena and I went for a run along the River Thames at Purley, near Pangbourne, partly to try and keep fit but partly to clear my mind. In the afternoon we went ten pin bowling, but whatever we did the experiment and the ethics committee remained in my mind. The Monday and Tuesday went much the same way. Meetings, lectures and discussions happened, but my mind was on the ethics committee and its possible outcome. On Wednesday morning I could wait no longer. I didn't care about protocol, I had to find out: I telephoned Diana Street, the secretary to the Oxford ethics committee. When she asked me for a reference number I had no idea what it was but luckily she remembered the project and told me all I needed to know. As far as the committee was concerned, there were two issues: firstly we needed to satisfy Mike Chapman, the ethics committee chairman, on the reasons for using the median nerve, as it was pretty dangerous in comparison with other nerves in the arm; secondly we needed to sort out indemnity insurance, etc., but basically the committee had passed it. We had no need to go back to them, and as long as we could satisfy the chairman, it was all systems go. I whooped and hollered. Carole, my secretary, came rushing in at the commotion. I kissed her, lifted her up and spun her round. The show was on the road.

For the next few days I was just about insufferable because of my enthusiasm. When I discussed the ethics committee response with Brian, he tried to be much more down to earth about it, pointing out that we still had a lot to do, and that much could still go wrong. But I had just about convinced myself that we were going to get turned down by the ethics committee, and the fact that their response was very positive had given me a tremendous lift.

On Monday 11th we had only twelve days to go until the scheduled operation and it was all looking good. Ben and Mark informed me that the electronic design was complete and that the PCB layout had been sent off to Quick Circuits in Reading, a company who would manufacture the boards overnight. In addition to that, Moi turned up with her latest jewellery designs and spent the day working with Iain. It looked as if she would have two or three designs that could be used with the implant, the nicest of which was a necklace with long plastic tubules that lit up in red and blue light-emitting diodes, the actual shade of which would depend on my mood – or so we hoped.

With regard to the media coverage of the experiment, the BBC confirmed they wanted to do a news piece on the operation, and CBS in the US confirmed that they would film a documentary, with RTL in tow for Germany. The biggest surprise of all was when I found out that the *Mail on Sunday* wanted to serialize the book. I was delighted with this for a number of reasons: with the BBC covering the operation I felt certain that they would present to a good-sized audience a well-balanced view of what we were doing and what it might mean. While international coverage is important, serialization of scientific work in the national press is a rarity, and I knew that the *Mail on Sunday* would also be excellent at putting forward the project in a straightforward way.

Later on that Monday, all those in the department interested in the project got together. Once again I was delighted at the turn-out and the way people were all chipping in together. For example, William Harwin said he wanted to do some experimental work with ultrasonic inputs, to take measurements and see how well my brain could discriminate between ultrasonic signals corresponding to objects at different distances. As no one had done anything like this before, we would be in a unique position to carry out such an experiment, and it was extremely exciting.

More good news was that Brian had found a place in Birmingham that could turn the array sterilization around in three days rather than the two weeks we had been quoted previously. Now the only thing that remained to be finalized was getting the array from Utah. We had expected it to arrive by the 9th, but as yet it hadn't appeared, so I asked Brian to email Bionic Tech to check that it had been posted. Even if we didn't get it until the end of the week, it would be okay. Everything was going really well; a 23 February date looked set to go and I went home a happy man.

The next morning, Tuesday 12 February, the following email arrived from Almut Branner in Utah:

> The 10 x 10 electrode array with 20 active electrodes should be
> done by next week.
>   Almut

I was shocked. If we were very lucky the array would arrive in Reading a few days after the date of the operation – a slight mismatch in timing. Not only that, but why were only twenty electrodes going to be wired up? I had understood that it was to be a hundred.

Although the time-scale was a shock, the wiring up of only twenty electrodes – ten on one edge and ten on the opposite edge – hit me even harder. While it did not mean the end of the experiment, it did mean that the chances of discovering the sensory signals we were looking for, and our chances of stimulating muscles were very much reduced. It was very disappointing.

About five minutes later, the post arrived, including a letter from the University Pro-Vice-Chancellor, Peter Gregory. The letter said that many questions had been raised as a result of my bacon IQ studies, and went on to say, 'I must insist that all future research involving human subjects, including yourself, must be submitted in the required form, to the University ethics committee for approval.' With eleven days to go before the operation I was now being asked to apply for university ethics approval on forms that could not be submitted before 1 March, for the committee to consider several weeks later. If this committee had not liked me giving breakfast to malnourished children or giving computers to a school, it seemed unlikely that they would pass the implant experiment without comment. Not just that, I would only be informed of their objections around the end of March, when all my research assistants would be out of a job. I couldn't believe it.

I immediately telephoned Brian Andrews and grilled him over the twenty electrodes. His reasoning was that the array would be wired up much more quickly if we only asked for twenty of the one hundred to be connected. I calmed my nerves and persuaded him to try and instil in them some sense of urgency. Surely it wouldn't take them another two weeks to put the array together? Brian considered and said he would see what he could do.

I then called Peter Gregory. His mood on the phone was not as fierce as his letter. He eased off when I informed him that we had just about obtained ethics approval from the Radcliffe Infirmary, and he said that the Radcliffe approval would be fine on its own. Things were suddenly looking better, although the experiment was turning out to be an emotional rollercoaster. One minute everything was ready to go, the next we were experiencing problems.

The next morning an email arrived back from Almut. Bionic Tech realized that there was a rush on, although they still weren't sure why. However, they had agreed to get the array finished off quickly and get it shipped over by express delivery, arriving in Reading on Monday 18th.

With three days for the sterilization, the timing was looking manageable again, although I still had worries about going ahead without Bionic Tech's definite knowledge.

I then received an email from Peter Teddy. He had had a conversation with Brian and had come to the conclusion that, because we still had to sort things out with Mike Chapman, the Radcliffe ethics committee chairman, and because the array was yet to arrive, we should therefore wait until the slant array was ready and hold the operation until early March. My spirits sank. It seemed that while the team at Reading were trying to get the operation to happen, everyone else was putting it off and delaying as best they could. I urged Peter to hold tight, for the moment at least, with the original date we had scheduled, pointing out that Mike Chapman had only requested a few paragraphs of information substantiating why the median nerve had been selected, and that this shouldn't take too long to do. I also indicated that if all things were equal, we would all have preferred to go ahead with the slant array, but it was still an untried technology, and that speaking from recent experiences, it was unlikely that we would get a slant array from Utah, even if we delayed until Christmas. It had to be the uniform array, and it had already been shipped.

The following Monday, the 18th, turned out to be a very positive day. At a meeting I had with Brian, it transpired that the previous Friday he and Amjad had had considerable success firing a blank array into the nerves of dead sheep, and that Amjad was very happy with the results. They had, however, experienced a slight problem when firing the array into a rubber glove – intended to simulate my own nerves – in that it seemed impossible to get the array back out again without the spikes breaking off. If that happened in my nerves, it could lead to permanent damage and pain, possibly with the loss of some movement and feeling. The discussion quickly moved on to Michael Rogers, a patient at Stoke Mandeville, whom Brian wanted to bring aboard as the next implant recipient. Michael had almost no movement in his hand and was extremely willing to participate. I mentioned Irena and her willingness to be included, and we came to a compromise that as long as everything was going well with me, there was no reason why both of them should not receive an implant. This was good news – subject to Peter Teddy agreeing, Irena was very much in the picture again.

When the array arrived from Utah Brian immediately took it to Birmingham for sterilization. A little later Peter Teddy telephoned me. The chairman of the Radcliffe ethics committee had asked him to sign Annex D and Annex E of our application, which required details of project costings and information about us. It seemed that all that was required was a signature or two and they wouldn't cause us any problems. Peter also agreed that satisfying the chairman on the reasons for our going for the median nerve would only require a paragraph or so. On the whole, he seemed to dismiss it as being something relatively minor, which I was very happy about.

I went home on the night of Monday 18th knowing that there was little left to do. We had the array, the ethics approval was just about tied up, the electronics were completed and we had an operating theatre booked for Saturday the 23rd, only five days away. What could possibly go wrong? The only negative was that although we were pretty confident about putting the array in, getting it out again was not as clear cut. However, it was too late to turn back now. That night for the first time I started to get nervous at the prospect of the forthcoming operation. I thought about what would be involved as I lay on the operating table for an hour or more.

I knew that my left arm would be dead because of the regional anaesthetic, and that I would not be able to move for an hour. Would I see what was going on? I hoped not. Amjad had sent an email describing how he would use a plastic bodger – a long rod with a handle on one end – to create a pathway down my arm, from the point where the wires would exit, to the carpel tunnel in my median nerve where the array would be fired in.

The array would be fed down the bodger to the firing point and then the bodger would be removed. They had decided to use a plastic bodger so as not to break the spikes on the array. The positioning for firing in the array was going to be just above the wrist because of the ease with which the median nerve could be located at that point. The main incision would extend for about two inches down my wrist. I wasn't looking forward to that part, and when I thought about it all I felt a bit sick. But of course I would go through with it. Amjad's initial estimate was that the whole operation, if it went without any hitches, would be completed within the hour.

On Tuesday morning I told my regular class that I would not be able to give them a lecture the following week because of the operation, and instead of my normal lecture I talked to the students about what was happening. They were very excited about it and had many questions, including 'How long will the operation take?', 'Do you think you will be part of a Borg, as in a *Star Trek* story?' and 'Does this mean you are likely to win the Nobel Prize?' To the last question I answered truthfully that I wasn't interested.

When I returned to my office just before lunchtime I saw that Brian had forwarded me an email from Peter Teddy. It read as follows:

> Brian
>
> Kevin is still pushing tirelessly for next Saturday.
>
> Whatever else this must NOT go ahead without a practice run, and if I am to be responsible for it, without a practice application of the electrode [array] by me on an animal preparation. To do otherwise would be irresponsible in the extreme and would undoubtedly incur the wrath of the Ethic Committee if something went wrong. As I have massive operating and outpatient commitments for the remainder of this week, I don't think I can fit any more into my schedule and I really feel it would be sensible to delay by a fixed period of, say, no more than 2 weeks. I can then let theatres know and the entire procedure can be properly organized and not rushed.
>
> Peter

So the operation was to be delayed. While it was fully understandable given Peter's commitments, I was, to say the least, bitterly disappointed. Perhaps I could be called a pessimist after all, but I felt that once the operation was delayed for one reason, it could be delayed for others, and no doubt even more reasons to delay would appear before long.

On Wednesday morning I emailed round to Peter, Brian and Amjad, accepting and understanding the reason for the delay. However, I also suggested formally settling the dry run for Saturday 2 March, with the operation taking place a week later, on Saturday 9 March. I was not convinced that Peter would agree, as I felt that he was under pressure and had relieved some of this pressure by delaying the operation. Accepting new dates would only mean putting him under pressure again. He didn't reply. We had gone from having a firm date for the operation to being in the ether, with nothing fixed, not even a date for the dry run. I felt down and found it difficult to get motivated.

For the rest of the next week I was generally pretty low in morale. I spent some time trying to tidy up the ethics paperwork with Diana Street, as we still needed indemnity letters from both the University of Reading and Stoke Mandeville Hospital, which essentially covered people's backs, insurancewise, if something went wrong. Diana was very helpful, as indeed was everyone else. But now there wasn't such a rush to get everything completed, and Peter Teddy still needed to sign Annexes D and E.

The array was to be ready, fully sterilized, on Friday 22 February, but Mark and I moved the delivery to the following week. We also gave Sylak a bit more time to finish the gauntlet.

Sue Nelson at the BBC had to be put on hold, as did the Press Association. It was a truly depressing time just putting everyone off and introducing an unknown delay into the system.

Amjad contacted me about the operation, indicating that he felt it best if it was not stopped halfway through to test for signals, but that the array would be fired into position and the wound would be stitched up at once. His experience of firing in blank arrays indicated that he would only get one shot at it, and he would just have to make it a good one. I was happy with this, as it meant that the operation would be quite a bit shorter. However, I just hoped that when we tested afterwards, we would at least discover *some* signals. It was difficult to get excited over the news though, when we still didn't have a date even for the dry run.

On Friday 22nd a telephone conference call was arranged. Peter Teddy and Ali Jamous were supposed to take part, but didn't. So it was me, Brian Andrews, David Tolkien and Brian Gardener from Stoke Mandeville. The date of the operation was top of the agenda but we couldn't talk about that because it was completely in Peter Teddy's hands. The reasons for Ali Jamous seemingly taking no further part were discussed. It was a shame, but his choice.

During the call it was generally agreed that everything was pretty much ready to go for the operation. We didn't really feel that the remaining ethics paperwork presented much of a problem, and all the technology was just about in place, as was all the paperwork. It was simply down to Peter to set two dates – one for the dry run and one for the operation. The conversation then went on to the publicity that might surround the operation, when we should tell people and what we should say. Although I took part in the conversation, I wasn't very interested. It seemed that because of the delay everyone had started worrying themselves about lots of other issues that were not really their concern. Quite simply, everyone was ready to go for the operation, and it was now down to Peter. I knew that he had my best interests at heart and needed to be sure about the operation, but this didn't stop me feeling frustrated, particularly when I had to cancel a presentation meeting because of the uncertainty.

Maybe it was just me. I have always been rather impatient, and this situation was no exception. The operation meant the world to me and everything was now in place. The one person left to make a decision was the one person without whom we could not go ahead. I felt so uptight that we couldn't forge on. It was the same feeling, a hundredfold, that you have when you're driving along and someone in front is driving at 10mph and you cannot overtake them. But I respected Peter immensely, and knew that he would call as soon as he could.

That Friday night, the 22nd, should have been my last night as a human before becoming a cyborg. Instead Irena and I comforted ourselves with a meal from the local takeaway. They gave us a fortune cookie each and after the meal I opened mine: 'All good things come to you if you wait.' But how long did I have to wait? In fact it was the next week that I got my answer.

CHAPTER 12

ON 1 MARCH Brian sent me the following e-mail:

> Peter, Amjad and I are now happy with the insertion/
> extraction procedure. A dry run involving Peter and Amjad
> will take place next week. The operation is now scheduled for
> Thursday 14th March at 8.30a.m.

So there we had it, a new date. But would it be the final one? Each time
the date was pushed back I worried that the extra time would allow further
problems to crop up, thus pushing the date even further into the distance.
But I knew that Peter wanted to be certain about how the operation would
proceed, and that waiting that bit longer wouldn't actually matter a great
deal in the long run. Yet with most communication being via email, I was,
in some sense, at arm's length from Peter and so simply had to accept the
situation. In addition to this, the situation meant that I was having to
cancel a number of presentations, many of which I had agreed to do quite
some time in advance. Although the operation was by far the most
important item on my agenda, taking precedence over everything else, I
felt bad about letting people down at short notice.

By the beginning of March everything was just about in place for the operation. There were still a few points to be sorted out to put the ethics and indemnity issues to bed once and for all. Mike Chapman had to be completely satisfied and a few forms had to be signed, but nothing that would take more than a day or two. Medically and technically everything appeared to be in hand, and Sylak would be delivering the gauntlet on Wednesday 6th. Unfortunately, our finances were not looking good, and it was difficult to see how much longer we could go on without the operation taking place. Because the whole research team was focused on the implant experiment, morale started to dip and the researchers became unsettled. Rallying the troops became a serious issue. Peter Kyberd suggested that the reason for the delay was not really due to the surgeon asking for more time, but rather that a Terminator-style robot had travelled back in time to stop the first cyborg – me – from being created and was threatening Peter Teddy not to carry out the operation. It was comforting to realize that I was not the only crazy member of the Cybernetics Department.

In truth I found the delays extremely upsetting. Just like the others in the research team, I found it difficult to get on with anything else. Most days I dealt with the incessant stream of paperwork trivia that confronts a professor in today's universities; apart from this, it seemed that all I could do was wait.

On 4 March I travelled up to Durham to give the annual Gordon Higginson Lecture, in which I talked about our implant project and the potential future for cyborgs. Once again there was a good audience who seemed amazed at what was about to happen. At the end of the lecture, one of the questioners raised some ethical points, suggesting it was highly dangerous to bring about technology that could enable certain humans to remote-control the movements and actions of others. I agreed, but pointed out the enormous positive possibilities, particularly in helping those with nervous-system problems to regain control over their movements. At the end of the lecture one student, with a partial paraplegia of the entire left side of his body, said he would be only too willing to volunteer to help with the project if there was a possibility that his full range of movements and control might be restored. His comments acted as a spur for me, and renewed my drive.

By Thursday the 7th, although things were nearly in place, we still needed to agree on a press information pack, we still hadn't had a dry run of the operation and, most importantly of all, we still hadn't got final ethical approval in order for the operation to go ahead at the Radcliffe Infirmary. I therefore spent much of the day trying to finalize indemnity issues and was very productive. However, towards the end of the day I discovered that the paragraph to the committee chairman explaining why we were using the median nerve still hadn't been written. I think Brian had been focusing on the press pack. I flooded him with emails and telephone calls, but by 5p.m. it still hadn't been done. I felt agitated and annoyed as I was worried that this might mean yet another delay to the operation. However, at around 10.30 that evening, Brian telephoned to say that he had sent the paragraph off to the chairman. It was a huge relief.

On the afternoon of Friday 8 March I was informed that the Radcliffe ethics committee chairman had reviewed and approved our application. I was delighted. My excitement levels rose as the operation date of 14 March looked more and more positive.

That day I also received an email from Frank Kech, who worked for a company called Stakklek in Texas. He suggested that, as part of the project, we might be able to investigate whether we could simulate Braille using 8-bit code to represent different letters of the alphabet. The idea was to map the code to individual sensory nerves in order to see if I could distinguish and learn the letters. Pulses would be sent directly on to the nervous system by a form of Morse code – dots and dashes – using electronic signals of different strengths for different lengths of time. Frank felt that although it might be awkward at first, I should be able to 'feel' the letters after a few hours of training, and it would be interesting to witness what my brain made of it all. It seemed a very good, and potentially useful, idea. I discussed the suggestion with Iain Goodhew and we immediately put it on our list of experiments to try once the implant was in place. As long as we could stimulate at least two distinguishable sensory nerves we thought we would be able to achieve something.

By the weekend it really looked as though in the next week the operation would go ahead. On Sunday morning I felt myself starting to get excited, nervous and worried. Not so much worried about the operation anymore, but worried that a problem would occur which would delay things yet again.

On Monday 11th, Sue Nelson contacted me, saying that she would like to come to the university on the Tuesday to do some pre-recording for the piece that BBC News would be putting together on the operation. It had been agreed that Sue and a cameraman would be there for the operation; Sue had not been well during the 1998 operation and I wondered how long she would last this time. For the pre-record Mark and I needed to get hold of some monitoring equipment that Brian had taken over to Stoke Mandeville a couple of weeks before, so we made the one-hour trip and made the collection. On the journey, Mark commented that, with less than three days to go to the operation, at long last everything seemed to be coming together nicely. 'What can possibly go wrong now?' he asked.

When we arrived in the entrance foyer of Stoke's National Spinal Injuries Centre we were greeted by a duo of smiling Brians, Brian Andrews furiously waving a piece of white paper over his head. This was a letter from Mike Webley, the chairman of the Stoke Mandeville ethics committee, stating that they had unconditionally granted us ethical approval for the operation to go ahead at Stoke Mandeville Hospital. The two Brians were absolutely delighted and, rather akin to the Thompson Twins in *Tin Tin*, they uttered in unison that the operation need not go ahead at the Radcliffe Infirmary, but could be carried out at Stoke Mandeville instead. Brian Andrews had therefore emailed Peter Teddy to make him aware of the situation.

My mood changed in a split second. It had taken a month or so to sort out indemnity issues at the Radcliffe, and it had taken several weeks for Peter to book an operating theatre and assemble the appropriate staff for my operation. Now, with less than three days to go, the two Brians seemed delighted at the prospect that the operation could be carried out at Stoke Mandeville. I tried to plead common sense with them, but they would have none of it. I even suggested that my operation with the uniform array go ahead at the Radcliffe Infirmary, and then perhaps Irena's operation could be done at Stoke, using the slant array. This didn't seem to impress them very much.

The implant operation was a team effort and both Brian Andrews and Brian Gardner were very much part of the team. Stoke Mandeville was the hospital originally in the frame to host the operation and I could see that it was important for both Brians, given their respective positions at Stoke, that the operation go ahead there rather than at the Radcliffe. Yet I felt that they seemed to be trying to impose their own agenda on the project, without considering my own feelings. But I knew that it was Peter who was in the driving seat as far as the operation was concerned, and that he alone would make the decision.

Mark and I picked up the equipment and headed back to Reading. I didn't want to email Peter Teddy to plead with him not to switch venues, in case I alerted his attention to the possibility. So I went home, only to have another sleepless night. I didn't know for how much longer I would be able to cope with this roller-coaster.

On Tuesday morning, and with only forty-eight hours to go, I emailed Peter asking him to confirm that everything was on for Thursday morning at 8.30a.m. He replied, saying that we were all set, and that he wished to have the dry run at the Radcliffe that afternoon, after 3p.m. I confirmed that Mark and I would be there.

Sue Nelson and a BBC cameraman turned up at the university at 10a.m., setting themselves up in the Madlab where Ben and Mark's interface design and construction was laid out alongside the equipment we had picked up from Stoke the night before. With this we were able to show examples of the type of signals we were likely to see on my nervous system. Sue filmed a lot of footage around the lab and then interviewed me.

Mark and I drove over to the Radcliffe for the dry run that afternoon. We met up with Brian Andrews and Amjad, then went to the laboratory next to Amjad's office so we could check that everything was in order. The laboratory also occasionally doubled as a meeting room, and several chairs and tables were scattered in the middle. Around the outside were a number of computers and various pieces of medical equipment, intermingled with the odd half-built and distorted piece of electric circuitry. It was quite dark, even with the lights on full, smelled rather musty and didn't look as though it was used on a regular basis. I felt a little nervous yet at the same time excited that we were actually taking an important step forward in science. An air of expectancy smothered everything else. A few minutes later Peter joined us, immediately taking charge of the proceedings. After a few jokey words between us, perhaps to relieve the tension a bit, Peter sat me down on a chair and then sat down next to me. The other three huddled around, all looking on: Mark sitting on a table, Amjad on a chair, with Brian standing to the side.

Peter asked me to roll up the shirtsleeve on my left arm, then got a biro ready to draw on it. Firstly he told me that I would only be having a local anaesthetic, although this would be fairly regional in that it would numb the whole of my left arm below the elbow, but would allow me to move my fingers. Chris Kearnes, the neuroanaesthetist, would be there to check things, and if I was feeling any pain when they started operating, he would give me a general anaesthetic. However, it was agreed that he would only do this if it was completely necessary.

Peter described in detail how the median nerve surfaces from beneath muscles and tendons about halfway down the lower left arm as it heads towards the wrist. He would therefore make an incision approximately two inches long below the wrist, and have a look for my median nerve. He referred to all the different muscles by their medical names, which didn't mean a lot to me although I clearly got the picture. He then started to talk about the bodger. This would have to tunnel up my inner arm from the incision to a point about fifteen centimetres from the elbow in order that the microelectrode array, with attached wires, could be passed down in the opposite direction. I wasn't particularly looking forward to this part of the operation, but accepted that it was necessary. Amjad had brought along a number of bodgers of different diameters for Peter to try, along with various lengths of plastic tubing to go round them. Once the tunnel was made, the bodger would be removed, leaving behind the tube through which the array would be passed. It had to be done this way because the wires from the array were attached to a large pad of connectors, which had to remain outside at all times.

The array was a 3mm by 3mm square, and each electrode spike was 1.5mm long. Unfortunately, none of the tubes Peter tried were of sufficient diameter to allow the array to pass down freely. He tried pinching at my skin and saw that it was fairly floppy, and decided that a bodger normally employed for chest operations would have to be used, as my skin would clearly give a fair bit. As with all other equipment needed for the operation, it was Amjad's responsibility to make sure that it went into an autoclave the next day, so it would be sterilized in time for Thursday morning's operation.

Peter then discussed the method of inserting the array in the median nerve, which was to be done by hammering the array of a hundred electrodes directly into my nerve fibres. He, Brian and Amjad had all now had insertion practice, mainly on sheep's nerves. However, none had been able to practise on human nerves in cadavers. Peter felt that the sheep nerves they were able to use had been sufficiently like those of a human as to make no difference.

It was funny. Peter normally rushed around at top speed and, when we had discussed the project before, had talked in quite a clinical and detached way. But as he loosely held my elbow with one hand and deftly indicated different points and regions on my lower arm with his pen, his voice was gentle and caring. He gave me a look of great empathy as he tried to make sure I understood exactly what would happen surgically, yet he was not condescending, or belittling. I knew that Peter had an excellent reputation as a neurosurgeon and for the first time I was witnessing why this was so. I felt comfortable and relaxed, and very confident to hand my arm over to Peter, one of the top surgeons in the world, for the period of the operation.

When I asked how long the operation was going to take, both Peter and Amjad said it was not likely to be over an hour. I also asked what I would need to do after the operation – would I have to stay in Oxford on Thursday night in order to take antibiotics, or would I be able to go home fairly soon afterwards? Amjad said I should be able to go home as he would give me some oral antibiotics that I could take myself. This cheered me a lot. I knew Irena would be with me, but I much preferred the idea of being able to recover at home, particularly if my arm was going to be extremely painful for a while.

And that was it. We had completed the dry run. Mark, Brian and I walked out of the hospital to our cars. It was then that Brian told us that he still hadn't told Bionic Tech's Brian Hatt that the operation was going ahead, but said that he would do so that evening.

On the way back to Reading, Mark and I wondered what Brian Hatt would say when he heard the news. Now the dry run had taken place, it seemed a certainty that the operation would go ahead on Thursday, and we hoped that Hatt's response would not change this. One blot on the horizon was that the press pack was now causing some problems. We had been working on a press pack in the department for some time now so that we could give out material in response to progress requests. Brian, David Tolkien and Peter had not contributed to this until recently, but now seemed to be trying to take the pack's contents in a medical direction, with no mention of cyborgs at all, and were also trying to be incredibly conservative in what was said.

I wondered if they had recently started to think about how the media would present the project if it had an emphasis on cyborgs and super-humans. They seemed to want the experiment to appear to be primarily a medical investigation, with me a volunteer patient. However, even in that sense they had to be very careful about what was said because of the criticism they might receive from colleagues. Conversely, I believed the press pack should reflect all interests, particularly as the whole project had started in the Cybernetics Department at Reading University with cyborgs as a key aspect. Nevertheless, I had been giving into their wishes in the last week or so, to ensure that they were happy and that the operation would go ahead without any further problems. Still, Mark and I knew that as soon as the story was released, the press would focus on the cyborg storyline regardless of what was said in a press pack, and expected that Brian, Peter and David would be annoyed when the newspapers' printed the story when it broke. It was a difficult situation, and we tried not to let it dampen our spirits.

I spent most of Wednesday in my office getting bits of paperwork done, seeing students and answering emails. Part of the time I was also trying to come up with some wording for the press pack that would satisfy everyone on the medical side, but would also be reasonably exciting for a press person to read. Fortunately, the main newspaper story was to be pushed out by Robert Westhead at the Press Association. At about 1.30p.m. he visited me at the university. We made final arrangements for his photographer to be at the hospital the next day, and also took the storyline on further. It was clear that he was disappointed that we couldn't really say much about Irena's potential involvement, as we still weren't sure whether she would have her own implant or not. However, it was also obvious that he was producing what appeared to be a good, balanced article, which included liberal sprinklings of what it all might mean medically and the potential bonuses for those with spinal injuries, but also addressed the cyborg issue head-on. His first line read: 'Surgeons have carried out a ground breaking operation on a cybernetics professor so that his nervous system can be wired up to a computer.' This sounded great to me. The storyline still needed to be added to after the operation, but it looked good as far as it went. Because the operation had originally been scheduled for a Saturday, we had hoped that the story would appear in the following Monday's papers. However, two things had altered that. Firstly the operation was now scheduled for a Thursday, and secondly Peter Teddy wanted to be sure that everything appeared to be going well medically before the story was released. So Robert, along with Sue at the BBC, would have to hold all copy until Peter gave the word.

That night, the night before the operation, I was involved in a two-hour conference call with David Tolkien, Brian Andrews and Brian Gardner. Sheer panic seemed to have set in with regard to the press pack and the storyline that the press might put out. Brian Andrews had supplied a six-page medical background report on the array and spinal injuries. However, it didn't contain information on the forthcoming operation, such as where, what and when, which to me seemed a bit strange, as the event *was* the operation and the press pack was supposed to support that. This was to replace an earlier piece by me what was part-medical and part-cybernetics.

During the call, Brian Andrews made it clear that he felt the press pack should only reflect medical aspects. David Tolkien was annoyed that he had sent us eleven pages about the David Tolkien Trust, yet we had only included three. By contrast, I was keen to ensure that the cyborg element of the experiment was clear. It was an extremely stressful call. I was only a few hours away from the operation and everyone was pulling in different directions. Before the call I was quite relaxed, but afterwards I was nervous. Nevertheless, I tried to put it behind me. I knew that I should try to understand the position of the two Brians and David. We were about to experience an operation that would probably receive a great deal of publicity. In each case their position demanded that the experiment should be seen mainly in a medical light rather than them being regarded as having links with cyborg investigations and all the science-fiction concepts conjured up by that. However, my own interests were mainly on the scientific, cyborg side of things, and it was therefore a very difficult balance to achieve. On the one hand I wanted the David Tolkien Trust to raise lots of money, as I knew this would help a large number of people and I had a lot of respect for David and his work. But on the other hand, how much could I squash my own cyborg interest? As a result my mind was in a turmoil by the end of the call.

I was in bed by 10.30p.m. I took some hot milk and read a little of Jean-Paul Sartre's *The Age of Reason*, hoping that it would help me get to sleep. I knew clearly that this was very unlikely. As I lay in bed, the events of the day just gone went round and round in my head, particularly the problems that had arisen in the conference call earlier in the evening. My emotions were pulled every which way. In theory, lying in bed should have given me time to relax, but in practice my mind raced. I was excited that the operation was about to start and I looked forward to the experimentation we would be able to carry out. But I was also tense about the operation itself. I was expectant about the publicity we might attract, yet I was worried about how it would be received by David, Peter and the two Brians. The adrenalin had kicked in far too early. Common sense told me to go to sleep but my body said no way.

We had set the alarm for 5.30a.m. but actually got up at about 5.20. I had been awake all night and Irena for most of it. I watched Irena enjoy her early morning cup of coffee, knowing that I couldn't have one in case I needed to have a general anaesthetic later. I don't think a cup of coffee has ever looked or smelled as nice as Irena's did that morning.

By 6.20 I was washed, dressed and shaved. Mark arrived at the house in a taxi, and soon afterwards the three of us got in my car and drove off into the half-light towards Oxford. There wasn't much traffic on the roads so we made good time. The conversation was fairly jolly although we did have a grumble at the way the press pack had gone. However, we were all a little nervous, and certainly I felt slightly sick – not surprising, given that I hadn't slept all night and that the experiment we had been working towards for the last few years was only a couple of hours away from starting. Mark had brought a video recorder with him and as I drove he recorded my feelings about what lay ahead. Apparently I used the word nervous several times. I can't really remember as I was too nervous to care.

We arrived at the Radcliffe at 7.30a.m., parked, and went to the restaurant so Mark and Irena could have coffee. Brian arrived shortly afterwards and started talking about the press pack once more, but I let it all wash over me. A few minutes later it was agreed that we should concentrate on the operation.

Just before 8.00 we left the restaurant and headed along the grey-walled corridor towards Block 5, Neurosurgery Pre-admissions. One or two doors to the outside were open, so as we walked along we were occasionally struck by a chill wind. Halfway along the corridor we turned up one flight of stairs and walked along the first-floor corridor towards the Admissions area, also known as the Lichfield Suite. Tim, the photographer from the Press Association, was already there. We checked that the secretary knew that I had arrived and then settled into one of the comfy old-fashioned green padded armchairs. We didn't have to wait long before Sue from the BBC, her husband Richard representing the *Today* radio programme, and Sue's cameraman arrived.

We sat around talking for a while. It was the sort of talk that is jokey and flippant on the surface but hides the excitement, nervousness and uncertainty underneath. We were all slightly tense. Sue didn't look particularly bright, and I asked her if she would do any better than she had in the 1998 operation. She said she would try but that we shouldn't hold out too much hope for her.

At about 8.20 Peter Teddy arrived and asked the two cameramen to accompany him to the operating theatre so that they could get ready. Sue and Richard were disappointed, as they had thought that they would be able to be in the operating theatre as well. Soon after that my name was called and a porter arrived to whisk me away. We walked to the lift and went up two floors. Once we were out of the lift the porter took me into the reception room adjacent to Operating Theatre 1, the main and largest operating theatre in the hospital. The room was bright and smelled quite fresh, not at all how I expected a hospital room to smell. It contained cabinets and drawers full of equipment and material to support the operating theatre; quite a few nurses and technicians were milling around making sure that final preparations were carried out. The atmosphere was pleasant, the chat friendly and light-hearted. It was very relaxing. It was there that I met up with Amjad, who asked me to sign a consent form allowing them to carry out the operation.

Chris Kearns, the anaesthetist, was also in the room, already dressed in a light-blue surgical outfit. I had always thought that green was the colour. He went over what was going to happen in terms of anaesthetics and checked with me that I had not had anything to eat or drink for some time. I took my sweater off and left it with my keys and watch in the corner of the room although I kept on my shirt and trousers. Chris asked me if I wanted to remove my shirt, as it might get a little bloody, which I took in a businesslike way, as a side product of the job to be done. It was comforting that all aspects of the operation were being dealt with very professionally, but with considerable care for me as an individual. I remembered that a lot of surgeons like to work in a very cold operating theatre. I wasn't sure about Peter Teddy, so thought it best to keep my shirt on just in case.

Amjad then took me through into theatre, which wasn't especially cold, and asked me to lie down on the operating table and make myself at home. There were four, possibly five, female nurses in attendance, one of whom put a cushion under my feet and generally tried to make sure I was comfortable. I looked around theatre. It was very large, perhaps more than ten metres square, with several TV monitors, a few computers and a very large microscope connected to a TV. The theatre was well lit, bright and modern and, as with the reception room, it didn't have the sort of depressing smell that is often associated with hospitals. In fact it smelled like a recently cleaned house and was quite pleasant. The atmosphere was still fairly light although it was clear that everyone knew there was a serious job to be done.

As I lay there, the nurses set out sterile equipment, including lots of forceps, scissors and knives. They chatted with me as they worked, trying to ensure that I relaxed, but I also felt confident that everyone seemed to know what they were doing. Amjad and one of the nurses got to work on a small sterile table that my arm could rest on. They had quite a bit of trouble clipping it into place and adjusting it to the correct height, which wasn't surprising, as Amjad had arranged the table specially for this operation. Chris then pushed a needle/drip arrangement into the back of my right hand and taped it into place, explaining how he would now flush in a huge dose of antibiotics and would then leave the connection in place in case I needed a general anaesthetic. As he pumped home the antibiotic I checked the time on a large clock on my right in the ante-room: 8.35a.m. I was delighted that we were under way, but was a little apprehensive as to how the next hour or so would pan out.

As soon as Chris had finished, my left sleeve was rolled up and two nurses began sterilizing the whole of my lower arm with a variety of brown, sticky concoctions which were sponged on one after another. It felt quite cold on my arm but didn't smell particularly bad. I had to keep my arm in mid-air as the concoctions dried, but was then told to lie on my back, as a metal bar was positioned above me, across my body just down from my chin. Surgical drapes were placed over me and over the bar so that my head remained uncovered and I could see clearly to my right. However, I could no longer see what was going on on the small side table to my left, where my left arm lay exposed. I was pleased about that, as I didn't particularly want to see everything that was going on close up.

Peter Teddy appeared in his blue operating gown, fully scrubbed, and checked that everything was okay and that I was happy. He instantly made me feel full of confidence at what lay ahead. I realized, not for the first time, that there was no one I would trust more in the circumstances. Shortly afterwards Amjad returned, also fully scrubbed, along with a smiling Brian Andrews, who seemed a lot happier and more relaxed than he had been in the restaurant an hour or so earlier. A crowd of around sixteen or seventeen had now gathered, including the two cameramen, all gowned up, Richard and Sue smiling at me from behind masked faces, Peter having given them permission to attend. The atmosphere was tense but expectant. I felt excited and deeply interested in what was going to happen in the operation, but at the same time was looking ahead to when it would be over.

Peter and Amjad settled themselves down to my left on either side of my outstretched arm, Peter on the side nearest my feet, and Amjad quite near my head.

On my right was Chris, with Richard (microphone in hand) and one of the nurses just behind him. Chris was peering intently over to my left arm as Peter explained about the anaesthetic he was shortly to apply, which would numb the lower part of my arm, but leave my hand free. As he did so, several of the TV monitors flickered into life, all of which were showing a close-up of the operation site.

I glanced at the clock again, it was still only 8.45. I felt fairly relaxed, even though I had not been given any medication to help me wind down. I couldn't see Peter or Amjad as they spoke to me, but I smiled up at Chris who smiled back from behind his mask. I lay back on the table, quite comfortable with a pillow under my head. I thought of Irena waiting downstairs in the Lichfield Suite. She would have liked to have been there, but was too worried that she would be sick and have to be carried out of the theatre.

Peter said that I would feel some pinpricks, and asked if I could feel this and that. He then told me that we were under way, by which he meant that he had made the first incision. I could feel someone mopping and padding around the wound, but I couldn't actually feel anything at the wound site. Chris kept me closely informed as the work began.

Peter worked steadily and started to look for my median nerve. It appeared that everything was going well when he suddenly announced that there was a haematoma – a swelling of clotted blood. He had to deal with it fast, which he did, skilfully, finding the root cause and stopping it in its tracks, partly by repositioning a blood vessel, therefore allowing blood to flow freely within the vessel. It was an incredibly tense moment, and as I lay there the nurses set out sterile equipment, including forceps, scissors and knives. They chatted to me as they worked – kindly and light-heartedly. It relaxed me considerably, but at the same time I felt confident that everyone seemed to know what they were doing.

As he operated, Peter explained that although there was a model anatomy in books, everyone was different and nerves and blood vessels appear in different places and in different orders in different people. He explained that I had a fairly large blood vessel partly obscuring my median nerve and that this was getting in the way.

Suddenly as he was talking, I was jolted by what felt like an enormous bolt of electricity blasting down every finger of my left hand at the same time. It was an incredible feeling, as though someone had connected my left hand to a power supply. I flinched and swore at the top of my voice. Richard was instantly in with his microphone for an on-the-spot interview for Radio 4. I spoke with incredulous excitement as it was brought home to me in an instant how the human body, just like a robot, operates by means of electricity.

By touching nerve fibres an electric charge can be released. The median nerve serves much of the hand, and a large charge had just shot down the nerves in each of the fingers of my left hand. I certainly hadn't been expecting it at all. Just like any electric shock it was extremely painful, but for only a very short period, after which my feeling was immediately back to normal. It was apparently at this point that Sue left the operating theatre. She had looked pretty pale anyway, but me shouting out in that way was the last straw for her.

Peter apologized and said that he had accidentally caught hold of the nerve while he was trying to get the tricky blood vessel out of the way. He was now very happy, in response to the extent of my shout, that he had tracked down the correct nerve. He asked me to wiggle my fingers and thumb around, which I did furiously. He also touched each of them in turn and I was able to confirm that everything felt perfectly okay. It was then that Mark appeared in his blue gown. He was obviously delighted to be party to the operation and gave me an exaggerated thumbs up. I smiled back. There wasn't much else I could do. Although still excited about the electric shock, from a scientific point of view I was comfortable about how things were progressing.

Peter made sure that I was happy to proceed, and then started with the first bodger, warning me beforehand what he was about to do. Initially he made an incision further up my inside arm, with the aim to tunnel up from the original incision where he had discovered my median nerve, to the new one. I hoped his aim was a little better than the channel tunnel constructors and that he managed to point his bodger in the right direction. As he got under way my arm was liberally doused with more local anaesthetic. It was difficult at times to decide what was local anaesthetic and what was simply water to wash it all clean.

Peter began his burrowing. At first I didn't feel much, but as he reached further up my arm it started to feel slightly uncomfortable. Not really painful, but just what it was, something extra on the inside of my arm. More local anaesthetic was used and I became less aware of the bodger. Peter was very careful with what he was doing though and took his time, checking occasionally that I was all right and happy with the way the operation was going. From time to time Richard poked his *Today*-programme microphone in my direction to get an up-to-date account of how I was feeling. Generally I was very pleased with the way it was progressing. Someone else was doing all the work and I just had to lie there. Any earlier sick feelings that I had had were very soon gone as the adrenalin kicked in, and were swiftly replaced by sheer excitement as the operation progressed.

The first bodger was not making a big enough tunnel, so Peter called for the 'Roberts', which I presumed was a larger bodger. I sensed a certain amount of nervousness, particularly in Brian and Mark, yet at the same time Peter exuded such an aura of confidence that everyone there, including myself, felt that he was totally in control. I asked who Roberts was, but nobody seemed to know, the only suggestion being a surgeon who had first used this particular bodger. Peter then proceeded with the Roberts, again checking that I was all right. The operation was taking longer than we had anticipated. When the Roberts broke through, completing the tunnelling, everyone sighed with relief. I checked on the clock: 9.30 – we had been going for an hour already and there was still a fair amount to do.

Peter then removed the Roberts, leaving a plastic tube in place as a tunnel down my arm. He then took the sterilized microelectrode array from its sealed packaging and carefully fed the array down the tubing from the end nearest my elbow. He pushed the array down by means of the platinum-titanium connecting wires, trying to be as delicate as he could. Pushing too hard or fast could easily snap the wires and make the whole operation instantly worthless. However, it soon became apparent that the wires were doubling back on themselves. As Peter pushed, they did not seem to want to go further down the tube. It was clear that the array had become stuck halfway down. No one had expected this problem but there was no sign of panic, and the team responded quickly.

Amjad immediately suggested trying suction on the end of the tube nearest my wrist. This was quickly attempted, but to no avail: it appeared to be stuck fast. Peter tried pulling back on it a bit, but it didn't seem to want to come back either. Suggestions flew thick and fast from all corners. Although we seemed to be in a bit of a mess, it was great the way that everyone worked together as a team. I felt a bit left out because I couldn't see exactly what the problem was. I was merely the guy with the tube in his arm and a microelectrode array stuck halfway down it. Would this be the end of the experiment, meaning that all we could report was that the array had become stuck in the tube?

To my left I heard one of the nurses suggest that Peter could try flushing it down with water. Chris Kearns immediately seized on the idea and connected up some further tubing that would force water into the gap. I could feel water gushing through the tube into the open wound below my wrist, and was delighted when I heard Peter exclaim that it had been successful, that the array was through. A wave of relief spread around theatre.

Peter removed the tube that had been in my arm through the site where the median nerve was still exposed. The array of wires were now in position and all we had to do was fire the array into my nervous system. Although a lot of surgery had already taken place, I was aware that until now it was all reversible. Peter could simply pull things out, stitch me up, and in a few weeks' time I would be back to normal. But the insertion into my nerves was not reversible. This was an area we didn't know about. This had never happened to a human before. This was the dangerous bit. To say that I was nervous would be wrong. I was a little apprehensive about what was to happen and what the effects might be, but I was eager to proceed and find out. We had come this far and there was no going back.

It was now 10.10a.m. I thought about Irena, still downstairs in the Lichfield Suite. She must by worrying. Before the operation, all the smart money was on it lasting about one hour, meaning I would have been back downstairs by 9.45. Yet we still had plenty to do. I think it was tremendously exciting for everyone in Operating Theatre 1 – no one knew exactly what was going to happen, and getting over the jammed array problem was something I couldn't believe any fiction writer would even think about, less still the water-torrent solution.

Peter called for the large microscope, which was wheeled forward and rotated into position over my arm. Out of the corner of my eye I could see that one of the monitors flicked channels to display the view through the microscope. If I had turned my head slightly I could have seen the monitor clearly, but I wasn't sure that I wanted to. Mark said that you could clearly see both the array and the exposed median nerve and they looked just as we had expected them to. Carefully and painstakingly, Peter manoeuvred the array head into position over the radial side of my median nerve. Brian suggested moving it slightly and Amjad commented on how it would be best positioned for the impactor to make contact.

Peter doused my median nerve with more local anaesthetic. I could feel it swishing around, probably as it touched parts of my arm that were not fully anaesthetized until then. Next the impactor unit was switched on and it was brought into position. The impactor is actually a fancy name for a pneumatic hammer. We had had to bring it across from the US. The unit charges up with compressed air, the head of the impactor is sucked up and is then forced down, just like a hammer. The head had to hit the array in order to force the pins through the outer nerve membrane so they could make contact with the nerves. It is just like hammering a nail into a piece of wood.

The array was poised over my nerve and Peter and Amjad held the impactor head just above, only a few millimetres away.

'Kevin, can you wiggle your fingers?' asked Peter. I tried and found that I could. 'Right then, are you ready to go for it?' As Peter asked the second question I knew this was it. This could easily be the last time I would be able to move some, or all, of my fingers. It could be the last time I would be able to feel with some, or all, of my fingers. But this was what I was here for. 'Let's go for it,' I replied. Peter nodded. 'Brian, please would you charge the impactor unit?' A few moments later, Brian said it was ready. There was a sense of hush and expectancy in the operating theatre. All eyes, except my own, were either on the impactor or the TV monitor.

'Okay, here we go,' said Peter. I heard a loud click as the impactor fired, and I felt a ping of electricity in my thumb, but nothing too much. Brian asked if the array was in okay. Peter looked at it carefully and said that the corner of the array had not gone in. Then he said that the array had not gone in at all. 'Let's try again,' he said. So Brian charged up the impactor unit once more. Peter checked that I was ready, and fired it again, a loud click echoing around theatre as the impactor fired for the second time. But yet again the array had not gone in. Peter asked me to move my fingers, which I did. Everything was still okay. He tried once more but to no avail.

Brian and Amjad checked for leaky pipes. The impactor unit and all its pipes had had to go to the autoclave the day before and Brian wondered if the autoclave procedure had affected things. However, all seemed to be in order. Peter tried again. Still no good. And once more. Still no good. Each time I felt a bit of a twang in my thumb or middle finger, but nothing serious. Once again the equipment was checked, and deemed to be in working order. Peter tried seven or eight times to force in the array, but it wouldn't work. There was nothing I could do though, and I felt tremendously sad. We had come so far. It had taken a lot of people so much time and effort to get everything together, and here we were, falling at the final hurdle. All that was left was to pull out the array of wires, stitch me up, and we might as well go home.

Brian then spotted that the two connecting tubes on the impactor unit had been connected up the wrong way around so the unit had been sucking instead of blowing. The impactor head was being sucked up with considerable force, then merely dropping on to the array head by means of gravity. The effect was about the same as trying to crack open a coconut with a teaspoon. Brian changed over the connectors and he and Amjad tried a practice run. Then Peter tried a practice firing on another part of my skin just to check if it was working, lined it all up for real once more, and asked Brian to charge the impactor unit. Once again everyone heaved a great sigh of relief. Just as it looked as though one problem too many had been encountered, so the solution had been found.

'Okay, Kevin, are you ready?' asked Peter once more.

'Go for it,' I replied. Peter then fired the impactor. This time the click was much louder and I felt a bolt of electricity down the inside of my thumb – zap! Peter checked once more that I could move my fingers and had not lost feeling and announced that the array had gone in successfully. Relief poured in abundance from everyone there. To make sure that we really had a connection, Peter used the impactor to hit the array twice more. Each time I felt a large zap on the inside of my thumb. At last the array was sitting comfortably, and the incision could be closed up. At this point the tension that had infused the whole operation seemed to dissolve into thin air. It felt like the end of term, time to wind down.

Almost directly afterwards, Peter started stitching. I could see the very neat, very well rehearsed stitches on the TV monitor. The connector had been dangling from the end of the fine wires protruding through my skin further up my arm, so when Peter had finished the stitching Amjad taped the connector securely to the skin. My lower arm was then bandaged up and I was swiftly lifted from the operating table on to a trolley. I checked once more on the clock – it was now 10.45. The operation had lasted for over two hours.

I was wheeled into the adjacent recovery room although I felt fine. I was brought a bag of bandages and other goodies, such as plasters and liniment, to use in the weeks ahead, and my watch and keys appeared in a kidney bowl at my side, while my sweater was put over my feet. After about ten minutes I was wheeled back to the lift and thence downstairs and into the Lichfield Suite where Irena, Sue and others were waiting for me. Irena was delighted to see that I was okay. Tim took some photos of me and Irena, Sue did a further interview for the BBC and then they were gone.

Amjad came to make sure I was all right. He seemed very pleased with the way the operation had gone, saying that when it was repeated, it would probably only take half an hour as we now knew what to do. This pleased me, as it meant that at the very least, whatever else happened, by acting as a guinea pig I might have helped operating procedures a little. Amjad prescribed my antibiotics and took the tube out of my right hand. We hadn't needed general anaesthetic after all. Peter also arrived. He looked a little tired, and less of an authoritative figure than he had been in theatre. He looked me over and said that I was free to go as soon as I wished.

The array pins now directly linked my nerves to the fine wires which came through my skin and on to the connecting pad outside my body. Although I was wired up, nothing was working yet. Once Peter was happy that the operation had gone well and the incision was healing, we could plug in Mark and Ben's interface unit to the connecting pad and see if we could measure any signals from my nervous system, then try and stimulate my nervous system from the unit. However, it was likely that the interfacing would not be done for well over a week. Meanwhile, we had to get our priorities sorted out. I needed some painkillers as my arm was likely to be sore in the hours ahead. I also needed some gel to touch on the wound, to reduce the possibility of infection. But most of all, before Irena drove Mark and me back to Reading, I needed a cup of coffee.

CHAPTER 13

THANKFULLY, MY ARM wasn't too painful after the operation. My thumb was quite numb for several hours which did make me worry, however as the anaesthetic wore off, all feeling returned. At 6p.m. I took one cephradine antibiotic tablet and a painkiller to ease things a bit, but was then challenged to a game of Monopoly by Irena, which completely took my mind off any pain. As usual Irena won easily. I think it should be a warning to all: never play Monopoly against former socialists – they are by far the worst capitalists.

Later in the day Brian phoned to see how I was, followed soon after by Amjad, then George Boulos. It was nice to hear from all of them. I was extremely relieved that the operation had gone so well and that I seemed to have come through it unscathed. I don't know that I felt any different in myself, other than the fact that I now had the potential to be different: I had an array connected into my nervous system, wires running up my arm and a terminal-connector pad waiting to be plugged in. It was as though I was still a human but with a cyborg socket. How well it would work when I was plugged in – and what I would feel like – remained to be seen.

I thought Friday would to be more relaxing. As it turned out I was on the telephone just about all day, helping to get the press pack finalized. We had to make sure that, even though the operation had taken place at the Radcliffe Infirmary, Stoke Mandeville Hospital and the National Spinal Injuries Centre obtained good coverage in every newspaper story and TV item on the operation; after all, they had both been part of the project for quite some time, and I had to make sure that the two Brians and David Tolkien were happy with the coverage.

On the morning of Monday 18th, Irena and I went to see Peter at the Radcliffe so that I could have my check-up. We were both very pleased with my progress. There was no sign of swelling and bruising appeared minimal, with just a slight yellowing in places. Peter decided that he didn't want the story pushed out to the press just yet, but wanted to see me again on Thursday morning, exactly one week after the operation, and would decide then. I could understand that Peter needed to be certain that everything was going well before the story went to the press, yet it meant that I had to keep a very low profile in case someone leaked the story before the BBC put it out. So I couldn't breathe a word about it. It was frustrating, as I was keen to get going with the experimentation in order to find out how well the implant actually worked.

Thursday duly came around and I headed up to Oxford for a 9a.m. appointment. When I arrived it felt quite strange that only one week before I had been lying on an operating table in the same building. This time round Peter was especially delighted with my progress as both wounds in my arm were healing up nicely. As a result he handed me over to the nurse for a further wound dressing and gave us the all clear to release the story of the operation to the press. That afternoon the story went out. After a week of silence, it felt good to be able to talk about the operation as an event that had actually happened, rather than as something that might or could happen in the future. However, I was worried that some parts of the media would lean exclusively on the cyborg issues and neglect any medical positives, which would upset the hospitals involved. I needn't have worried.

A busy few days with the press followed the announcement. The next morning I was down in London to do a live interview on the BBC's *Breakfast* followed by radio interviews for the *Today* programme, Radio

5 Live and Radio Scotland. Back in Reading, the interviews continued later in the day, with Reuters and the INS News Agency, and so it went on. In each case I was pleased to find that a fairly balanced story was reported, although some of them were more interested in me and why I had subjected myself to the operation. For the most part though, as well as indicating some of the longer-term cyborg possibilities, good coverage was given of how the project might help those with spinal injuries and other medical issues. Both Brian Andrews and David Tolkien appeared in some of the TV coverage, so I hoped they were happy with things.

On Monday 25th I was back in Oxford for the nurse to take the stitches out of the two wounds in my arm. Because they had healed up very well, this task probably proved to be a little more difficult than expected. As I sat there with the nurse picking away at the stitches, I reflected on how well it had all gone so far. My left hand really gave me no pain at all. However, two or three times a day I felt the odd 'zing' (an electric impulse) down my thumb or finger. These were not painful in any way, and actually gave me confidence that when we started testing we were very likely to get some signals in and out. There was a possibility that they were due to the pins settling down in my nerves, or simply the nerves calming down after the operation. Alternatively, they might have been due to some static electrical pick-up on the connector-pad terminals outside my arm. I tended to forget that I had a direct electronic link from the pad outside my arm, down to my nerve and then on to my brain.

After the stitches were out I waited at the Radcliffe for a while in order to meet up with Brian Andrews. We wanted to use the Bionic Tech monitoring equipment for our first check on the signals in my arm, but we needed several cables to connect the pad on my arm to the equipment. Brian had kept hold of these connectors, but now brought them to the hospital so that I could take them back to Reading. When we met he told me that the night before he had informed Brian Hatt and his team at Utah that the operation had gone ahead. He needn't have done so, as they were already well aware of it from the publicity they had seen. Fortunately it appeared that they were very happy about it. Perhaps our previous worries about them finding out what we were up to had been unfounded. However, that was with hindsight, and if we had told them what we were doing before the operation, it might have been a very different story.

Publicity about the operation had sparked a variety of reactions. Predictably, one or two academics in the UK grumbled that I had only done it for the publicity. This was something I had expected. Naturally there was bound to be a certain amount of jealousy around, and if they couldn't make any technical comment, that was about all they could say. As it happened, it did actually help the publicity, in that a few articles appeared because of the controversy. Professor Steve McMahon of King's College, London, commented that the implant I had received 'leads us nowhere'. I was surprised by this, and felt that it was extremely narrow-minded. How can anyone tell where something like this can lead us until it has actually been tried out and we have some results?

On the other hand, I received many emails congratulating me and asking for more information on what we were doing. It amazed me that of all the emails I received – at least a thousand within a week – not one was negative or derogatory. Several came in from the US, in particular one from Ray Kurzweil who, as a guru, had predicted such implants; it delighted me in the way it was extremely supportive. I also received emails and letters from a number of people who felt that what we were doing might actually help them, if not instantly, then possibly in the future. I felt like forwarding them all to Steve McMahon, but of course I didn't. I have picked out one, as an example, from Kevan Llewellyn of Eastbourne. When I first read it I sat in my study crying. It went like this:

Dear Professor Warwick,

After reading, with great interest, about your implant experiment, I would like to put myself forward for further experiments.

In 1963, at the age of 3 years, I was hit by a drunk driver. I was standing at the side of a kerb in Middlesbrough, when his van ran out of control and I was hit by it. This left me paralysed in my left side. Throughout my life, like so many others, I have struggled with the injury, to find work to suit my disability. But I can say that I've tried, taking up keep fit, road running, entering marathons etc. I would dearly love to have feeling in my left side. I was told by a surgeon that it is like having a Novocain injection that can never wear off. Please contact me if you are interested

Yours sincerely Kevan Llewellyn.

This letter spurred me on considerably. We had to do this research. If, in the future, we could help someone such as Kevan, then it would be fantastic. I wrote back to him telling him that it was early days in our research, but that we hoped it might prove fruitful in the future.

Kevan's letter emphasized the importance of my research. However, even though my body hadn't rejected the implant and there was no sign of infection, we had still not tested it to see if it was actually working. Although the operation had gone well, the array could have worked loose from the median nerve and even now be floating around in my arm. Failing that, the wires might have broken, as they appeared to be fairly delicate. There was also the possibility that, even if the array was still in place, the signals might not be clear. If Steve McMahon was to be believed, we would only obtain rough, average signals, which would be fairly meaningless – containing an amalgamation of the signals on the nerve fibres. So what should I do at this stage? Believe a senior, eminent academic and give up? Not likely. And yet inside I knew that Steve McMahon might turn out to be correct. Maybe something had gone wrong with the array. Maybe it just wouldn't work as we hoped. But deep down I felt confident that we would be successful. Everything appeared to have gone well so far, so why shouldn't we witness some useful, meaningful signals?

On Wednesday afternoon, thirteen days after the operation, a group of around ten of us collected together in the Madlab. I sat down next to the Bionic Tech monitoring equipment which was linked to the computer. The equipment consisted of a couple of fairly bland joined boxes with connector points on the outside. The second box was linked to the computer, on the screen of which the signals picked up on any electrode would be displayed as they happened. Mark and Iain helped with the technical proceedings, Mark connecting a cable between the pad on my arm and the monitoring equipment. The computer allowed us to select and display any one of the one hundred channels although we only had twenty wired up. One of the first jobs was therefore to flick through the channels and see if we could find any signals at all. We were all very tense. This was a make-or-break point in the project, and we didn't know what to expect. Maybe some of the critics would be proved right. Everyone looked on fixedly with the eagerness and incredulity of a child as a Christmas present is unwrapped. This is what science is all about, I told myself.

The first three channels we tried did not look hopeful. As Mark selected each one in turn, all we could see was a mass of signals – clearly only noise was being picked up, as all that was being displayed was a plethora of typical high-frequency signals. An image suddenly flashed through my mind: a picture from almost two weeks before, when it appeared that the impactor was not firing the array into the nerve. Then, I felt we had come so far only to stumble at one of the last fences. Now, here we were again, everything was going well but we didn't have any signals.

Mark then switched channels, where we found a very different picture. Certainly there was what looked like noise, but it was at a very low amplitude. I tried wiggling my finger around, and much larger, clear and distinct signals appeared. I stopped and the picture returned to one of low-amplitude noise. I tried again and the same thing happened. We could see two distinct types of signal which completely overpowered the noise: one was very slow, of high amplitude, looping over the top and bottom of the screen, while the second was not quite so strong in magnitude and looked very similar to a heartbeat. Not only that but the signals were sharp. It seemed to be movement of my index (first) finger that was actually causing it. When I made a movement with the finger repeatedly, the picture on the screen repeated the signals almost identically. When I stopped, the picture returned to low-amplitude noise. At least we had one channel working. Through the array we were now able to witness signals on my nervous system that were directly linked with specific movement.

It took a while to hunt through all one hundred channels. However, we were delighted to find that we had twenty working channels, each one connected to the electrodes in the array. Different movements, mainly with my thumb and index finger, caused different signals to appear on the twenty channels in turn. One type of movement would cause signals of a certain amplitude via one electrode, but they would be at a different amplitude or not exist at all via a different electrode. We therefore concluded that different movements caused signals of different amplitude via different electrodes. It was certainly true that there was an amount of overlap between the channels, but there were also considerable variations in the signals, all of which could be repeated as desired. For a brief moment I felt happy that we had proved Steve McMahon completely wrong. But more strongly I felt a considerable warmth and hope in terms of what, in the years ahead, this result could actually mean to the numerous people who, at present, were unable to control or even move large sections of their body. Although it was early days, these results showed us that, with further research, it should be possible to connect directly into the nervous system of an individual and bridge over any gaps due to broken nerve fibres in order to feed signals down to the hands or legs, thereby bringing them back to life by restoring at least some movement. Bringing back movement was not something we could do for many of them straightaway, but it now looked to be very possible that it could be done in the years ahead.

For most of the next two weeks I camped down in the Madlab. Most of the testing was done with Mark, Iain and Ben in attendance, as we tried to make a start in understanding the signals we were obtaining. Although we could obtain distinct signals on a particular channel when I moved my finger, it was another matter to try and put some sense into those signals. Even moving one finger meant that a number of muscles became operational. Which signals related to which muscles was a question that we quickly realized would take a lot of research to answer. Within a few days it was evident that we had opened up a whole new view of the operation of the human body, a new line of research that was as exciting as it was daunting. While we were hopefully going to gather a lot of data in the time the implant was in place, it was clearly going to take a long time afterwards, and much research, to give us a deeper understanding of what we were witnessing.

Publicity about the experiment seemed to hit home more in the US than anywhere else. Apart from getting a front-page story on the *Toronto Globe and Mail*, I had to travel down to London one day for a live satellite broadcast to Canada AM TV, and a few days later for a live appearance on CNN Headline News. Soon after came a three-hour radio interview for Art Bell's *Coast to Coast* radio programme, listened to by upwards of ten million people in North America. While the magnitude of interest was roughly similar to that in the UK, the tone was quite different. There weren't any questions about why the implant was in place, and certainly no criticism that it wasn't going to work. Instead the emphasis was on how it could help people in the short term and what it might mean in the long term – the cyborg issue.

On 4 April, five of us headed over to Stoke Mandeville in a van. Firstly we needed to check out the safety aspects of the interface unit on which Mark and Ben had been working. Essentially it consisted of a populated, flat, printed circuit board, not much bigger than a credit card, that was attached to four small batteries and a little aerial, which was about the size of a couple of cigarettes. The unit was designed not only to transmit signals from my nervous system by radio, but also to receive signals and to stimulate my nervous system accordingly. It meant that I could move around when the interface unit was connected to the connector pad on my arm. In comparison, the Bionic Tech equipment, which was for monitoring rather than stimulating, consisted of two boxes, each about the size of a video recorder, with no radio transmission capabilities. Our own interface unit had been ultimately designed as a prototype for a complete implant. We therefore needed to be sure that when the unit was connected to my nervous system, it didn't send in any strange, unwanted signals that might stimulate my nerves in indescribable ways. The unit passed with flying colours.

The second reason for our trip to Stoke was to pick up a couple of electrically-operated wheelchairs. One demonstration we wanted to do was for me to control the movements of a wheelchair by means of my nervous system. We felt that this would bring home to people exactly what we were up to in an extremely visual way.

As soon as we returned to Reading we went to the lab to try out the interface unit. We were still not ready at this time to send signals down on to my nervous system to bring about movement; we merely wanted to use the unit to record signals in the same way that we had been doing with the Bionic Tech equipment. Once Ben, Mark and Iain had connected me up, we switched on the interface unit and at first everything seemed fine. However, within a few seconds I started to feel a multitude of small electrical currents scurrying down my arm from the terminal pad in the direction of the array. We disconnected immediately. Mark had put several light-emitting diodes (LEDs) on the unit, and we wondered if they were creating the sensation by intermittently causing false signals to be transmitted into my arm. The feeling hadn't been painful, but it was not something I wanted to feel every time my nervous system was linked to the computer. Clearly Mark would have to take the LEDs off and we would try again in a few days' time. I was a little worried that it might turn out to be something more serious than the LEDs, but they did appear to be a likely source.

To make sure everything was still all right, I was connected up again to the Bionic Tech equipment. This involved a cable being run from the terminal pad on my arm, to the equipment, and from there to the computer. Basically, my nervous system was hard-wired to the computer. At first everything still seemed to be in order. But then the signals went berserk, shooting around the screen in front of us, far in excess of any of the signals I could generate by moving one of my fingers. What could have caused such a reaction?

The answer was clear: Mark had left his mobile phone switched on and a text message was coming through. As Mark rushed out of the lab with his phone, the signals on the screen returned to normal. It was fascinating to see how the signals we were witnessing directly from my nervous system were completely swamped by those of the phone when it was brought to life. It might have been the Bionic Tech equipment or the computer that was being affected, but it was just as likely that the signals were being recorded from my nervous system. It was impossible for us to conclude anything directly from this event, but it most definitely made me think twice about using a mobile phone in the future.

While I tried to catch up with my backlog of university paperwork, Mark and Ben put in some time over the weekend of the 6/7 April so that we could have another go with the interface on Monday morning. I was a little wary that I might feel the same tingling sensation as before, but the removal of the LEDs had done the trick. The interface was connected and I was still in one piece.

Getting signals from my nervous system through the interface was quite another story. The interface's electronic characteristics had been set up to attempt to filter out noise, yet readily pass through what the books said would be the type of signals we were likely to expect. With the Bionic Tech equipment, when I moved my fingers we were able to monitor signals that were very large in comparison to any noise that was apparent – 250 micro volts peak-to-peak magnitude was recorded. Yet with the interface these signals were not coming through. It was evident that the larger signals were occurring at a lower frequency than predicted, which meant that Mark and Ben would have to alter some of the resistors and capacitors on the interface in order to allow the appropriate signals through. In hindsight it would have been better to design the interface unit to have the same cut-off frequency as that of the Bionic Tech equipment, rather than trust in what the books said we would probably discover. But it was only by experimenting, with the implant in place, that we could find that out. It seemed that we kept taking one step forward only to discover another problem that we hadn't expected – but such is the nature of research. It really made me think about what would have happened if we had gone for a full implant in the first instance. The implant, including the interface unit, would have been put in place and we would not have been able to get any stronger signals out. The only result would have been that I felt constant tingling in my arm. We would not even have been able to wire me up to the Bionic Tech monitoring equipment. Clearly it had been the right decision to have the interface on the outside of my body, even if it had been partly forced on us because we couldn't make the interface small enough.

The next day I paid my weekly visit to Jacqui Saunders and George

Boulos at Tilehurst Surgery in Reading, so they could check me for any infection. The plan was that Jacqui, the nurse, would look at the two wounds in my arm and put a fresh bandage around the connector pad – the aim mainly being to stop it catching on anything. In actual fact my arm seemed to be healing up nicely; there was still no indications of infection and no side effects. My body appeared to have accepted the implant completely.

After that it was back into the department and straight into the lab for more testing. The interface was now working well, and signals were coming through clearly. Mark selected the different channels one by one and adjusted the software in order to clip out the noise that was different on each channel. So not for the first or last time, I spent several hours twiddling my fingers around.

Iain had rigged up the computer so that when I kept my hand at rest the screen showed 'red', and when I moved my fingers the screen went 'green'. We spent quite some time adjusting the thresholds in order to get it operating reliably, and by the end of the session it was working very well. This simple set up was to be the starter for a number of cybernetic projects in the weeks ahead. Although it sounds relatively straight-forward – if I moved my fingers the screen would change colour – it is important to remember that these signals were coming from my nervous system, I wasn't pressing a button or operating a switch. I could now change the colour of a computer screen, as I desired, by means of signals from my nervous system. Quite simply, neural signals of the heartbeat type which we could now associate with closing my fingers, were transmitted to the computer, where we could identify them in order to switch the screen to green. Conversely when open-hand neural signals were witnessed, so the screen switched to red.

On Wednesday Brian Andrews came in to see how things were going. He was pleased and intrigued by the extent of the signals being achieved. Obtaining different signals via each of the electrodes was a big bonus, but although we were able to record motor signals quite clearly, we still needed to do some work as far as sensory input was concerned. We needed to look more closely at the signals now being collected. Our combined feeling was that this wasn't something we could achieve the next day, but that it might take months or even years fully to understand what was going on. Yet again it was a case of collecting as much data as we could while the implant was in place, and hope that subsequent analysis of the information gained would lead to a deeper understanding of what was being witnessed. Not for the first time, it felt as though the project was turning up far more questions than it was answering.

When we left the lab, I took the opportunity to chat to Brian about Irena's involvement. It turned out that we both felt much the same: we realized that we had a lot of work to do to learn more about the functioning of the array and the meaning of the signals we were seeing, and that putting Irena through the dangers of a full operation to implant an experimental piece of equipment simply wasn't warranted. We knew it would be a challenge to obtain ethical approval and talk Peter into carrying out the operation when we ourselves were not convinced of the benefit of such an undertaking.

Yet this was a wonderful opportunity and both Brian and I wanted to witness the effects of passing signals from one nervous system to another in order to communicate. We agreed there and then that a single electrode, passed into the median nerve through the skin, would be a reasonable way to proceed. This could be done in a day or two and, while having certain dangers associated with it, it was nowhere near as risky as a full implant. I telephoned Irena immediately and she was absolutely delighted, although slightly disappointed that it was not going to be the full implant. She had been asking about her inclusion in the project every day since my implant went in, and now it was confirmed.

We knew that we could pick up neural signals associated with movement in my hand via the electrode array. The idea was therefore to position a single electrode in Irena's nervous system, by means of which we could witness a similar thing. We then hoped to pick up a signal from my nervous system and transmit this, via the computer, down on to Irena's nervous system. As a result, if I moved my finger twice, Irena would feel two pulses, three movements on my part and Irena should feel three pulses. The further hope was that we would also be able to do the whole experiment in the reverse direction, from Irena back to me, in exactly the same way. We would therefore be able to communicate with each other, in a very basic way, nervous system to nervous system. Anything more than that would be a tremendous bonus.

Irena was following the whole project as closely as she could and every night I reported back to her on what was going on. Some days she popped in to the lab for a while to have a look at what was happening. She had remained extremely excited about taking part herself and, like me, she saw the possibility of communication from nervous system to nervous system as a major scientific step, something that she definitely wanted to be a part of – whatever it took. Yet even having chosen that route for Irena, it was not going to be a trivial exercise. We still needed ethical approval and we still needed to get the stimulation part of the interface working in order to transmit signals successfully down on to my nervous system. We would also have to sort out the appropriate electrode and method of insertion. All of that would take time.

Before leaving that day I went back down to the lab to do a bit more testing. We were trying to distinguish between different movements. Iain had wired up a sound card so that, as I moved my fingers, the movement – in terms of an electrical signal appearing on my nervous system – was converted into a sound signal. If I moved my fingers back and forth in a regular pattern, it sounded a bit like an old steam train. The faster I went, the faster the train chuffed, the stronger my movements were the louder the train chuffed.

Suddenly, from the other side of the lab, Ben called that there was some-thing else coming through. I had to stay where I was because I was all wired up, but Mark and Iain crowded round the amplifier alongside Ben, listen-ing intently. They all shouted at me to move my arm around, then stand up. I did so, and wondered what was going on. When Mark came and unplugged me, Ben shouted that what they were listening to had stopped. Mark plugged me in once more, which resulted in Ben reporting that it was coming through clearly again. The three of them walked towards me beam-ing inanely, as though they had just heard their first naughty joke. 'Guess what?' said Ben, 'You're picking up Virgin Radio loud and clear.' Iain sug-gested that it was probably the Wycombe transmitter, and that my nervous system was acting as an aerial. We had discovered that with standard tech-nology, we could turn the signals into sound.

This means that, with a piece of technology similar to the one we had developed, people in the future would no longer need an external radio: a single wire could be run from the implant to the person's ear, and, acting as their own aerial, they could listen to whichever station they chose on their personal human radio. It was a fascinating thought – never mind Trevor Baylis and his clockwork radio, the energy to become a human radio would be supplied directly by you.

With everything seeming to go so well I was able to attend a function that I had agreed to do about a year earlier – a keynote conference address at the University of Arizona in Tucson. On 11 April I left Reading armed with reams of paperwork explaining all about the implant, and including a letter from George Boulos to help me get past the X-ray scanning process. It was also my first opportunity to check that it was safe to fly with the implant in place.

My trip started from Heathrow and involved a change at Chicago in order to get to Tucson. At Heathrow I got all my paperwork ready, and when I was told to walk through the scanner, I expected to hear it beeping loudly. However, there was not a sound, possibly because the amount of metal involved in the implant was not only relatively small, but was also spread in the wires up my arm. But didn't they realize that I had just smuggled a human radio out of the country? At Chicago I had little time to change planes, and I was worried because many people had warned me that security had been increased considerably in US airports since the September 11 terrorist attacks in New York. Surely I wouldn't get past the Chicago scanning process so easily? I knew it would be difficult to explain what the implant experiment was all about.

Again I needn't have worried, as I just walked through the scanning, with no alarms. In fact, the whole trip to Tucson turned out to be well worthwhile. My presentation was very well received by a big audience, and questions at the end revealed that quite a few artists were in attendance. They wanted to know how I could use the signals obtained through the implant to produce different visual effects to represent the state of my body. It was interesting that this linked in nicely with what Moi was trying to do, and I was surprised but pleased to realize that the project was receiving interest from sectors that I hadn't imagined it would attract.

On the morning of Sunday 14th, just before my return trip, I sat on the veranda of the guest-house at Tucson, looking over the desert, and reflected on the weeks gone by. It was now one month since the operation, one month of being a cyborg. Medically everything seemed to have gone well. Every so often I felt a pain in my arm that was similar to cramp, which I assumed to be mainly muscular, but other than that I was fine.

It was awkward taking off and putting on the bandage around the connector pad on my arm, which had to be done every time for testing in the lab, but the bandage was still required to stop me catching the pad, and pulling on the wires in my arm. I was a little disappointed that things had not moved on more quickly, however this was due to discovering a few technical problems, which you have to expect. I was really looking forward to getting on with the cybernetic demonstrations though. Changing the computer screen from red to green was all well and good, but being able to operate different pieces of technology from my nervous system would be much more impressive and meaningful.

Over the month we had experienced a steep learning curve: first, trying to get to grips with, and form, an initial understanding of the signals we were able to record; and second, finding out what type of interface would be best suited to those signals. Even though I knew we were already going as fast as we could, my impatience meant that I was keen to forge ahead, to link my nervous system directly with technology. I wanted to feel much more what it was like to be a cyborg.

On the return journey from Tucson airport I had to go through the rigours of screening once more. This time it would be much stiffer because of the military-level standards imposed there. I had to take off my shoes and belt. I even took off my watch and wedding ring for good measure. Once again I sailed through the scanner. On the other side I was greeted by a uniformed official who reeled off a pre-programmed set of instructions telling me that I had been randomly selected for detailed screening. I had to stand with my legs splayed and arms stretched out by my side while he ran a hand-held scanner all around my body. When he got to my left arm I knew the game was up, that the scanner would start beeping and I would have some explaining to do. I held my breath.

To my amazement, nothing happened. The second time round there was still nothing. Then once more for good measure from behind, but there were no beeps. He told me I was clear to go. I had been through possibly the strictest airport screening process in operation and nothing had been picked up. I had never before been through such an elaborate procedure and felt pretty confident from then on that I wouldn't have any trouble at airports. From Chicago the plane was packed and it was impossible to get comfortable. As a result I suffered more muscle cramps, but there was nothing I could do to relieve them and it was an extremely painful return trip. I couldn't wait to get back to Reading and get on with our first cybernetic demonstration.

On Thursday 18 April several of us grouped together in the Madlab to try out four key demonstrations. We were joined by Sarah Oliver and a photographer from the *Mail on Sunday* who were there to witness and report on our findings. The day before, we had managed to try a few things out and, as a result, felt some of what we were trying would probably work. Although the team had worked overnight on a couple of the demonstrations, we hadn't actually had a chance to test them at all beforehand. Sarah was not warned about how successful we were likely to be, and you could feel the tension in the room.

I sat on the control desk at the top end of the Madlab while Iain fitted the cable from the connector pad on my arm and linked it to the computer. At the same time, Mark switched on the video camera in order to record the proceedings. Then, as everyone stood back, I fully extended my left hand, then clenched it. Everyone stared at the computer monitor. In the grey box in the top right-hand corner the signals being picked up by the array were displayed in graphic form. We were able to witness two types of signal. Firstly, large and slow signals, probably due to muscular movement (emg) and secondly, what we took to be neural signals, peaking and dipping, akin to those on a heart monitor, changing in unison with my hand movement. We cheered. The signals confirmed that the array was still functioning fully.

So the first step had been successful. Now Peter Kyberd's articulated, metallic hand, consisting of two fingers and a thumb, was connected to the computer. Would we be able to pick up and send messages from my nervous system, via the array, through the computer to the hand? Again, the tension in the room mounted.

Iain made the connections between the hand and the computer and stood back. The lab was deadly silent. I straightened my hand once more then formed a fist. My movement was immediately mimicked by the metallic hand. I laughed. It was a fantastic feeling. As I moved my fingers in and out, so the hand copied my movements. I was now able to control another hand remotely, through the array in my arm. At once this opened up all sorts of possibilities for amputees. Some success had previously been obtained by others, by connecting externally to muscles, but nothing like this.

For an amputee it would mean connecting up to the nerves in their stump – possibly using a form of the array that I currently had embedded in my nervous system – then using the neural signals picked up by the array to control an artificial hand or foot, positioned on their stump, as if it were their own. Obviously it would take a lot more research before this could be done effectively and practically; but these were the first steps. In our case we were simply looking at the extreme movements, detecting hand-closed and hand-open neural signals, so I could control a remote hand. We had not yet considered feeding signals back, as might be obtained in fingertips, in order to allow me to judge how much pressure the articulated hand was applying to an object – that would come later.

We had witnessed the first experiment to prove that the array in my median nerve was capable of transferring the signals from my brain to a computer and then on to a robot. I now felt very much part-man, part-machine: a cyborg. My mind flashed back to the research in which the neural signals of owl monkeys had been used to control a robot, but in those experiments the monkeys were not aware of what they were doing. In my case I could witness the movements of the robot hand and control them directly myself. I felt extremely powerful. Although the robot hand was roughly the same size as my own, we could have made one much bigger and stronger, in which case I would have been like the six-million-dollar man from the science-fiction series. The articulated hand felt like a part of me, yet, because it was remote, in another sense it didn't. It reminded me of my first implant and how I felt close to the computer it was linked to. I now felt close to the robot hand and was reluctant for it to be disconnected. But we had other experiments to do.

Justin had worked overnight on a graphic display on another computer screen that displayed a virtual man (me) inside a virtual house. He now connected this to the computer displaying the nervous-system signals. A menu appeared in the corner of the virtual house, allowing me to select from a range of domestic functions. By clenching and unclenching my fist I was able to move the cursor in response to signals from my nervous system. In each room a menu of options appeared. By closing and opening my hand quickly once, the neural signals created were interpreted by the computer and then used to move the cursor through the menu. If I did the same movement twice, so the cursor stopped and that option – for example, switching on the light – was selected and carried out. By keeping my fist clenched, the virtual me moved from one room to another around the house.

Without moving from the control desk I switched on an anglepoise lamp in the far corner of the Madlab. I then activated and deactivated an alarm, turned up the heating and finally switched on the coffee maker.

I could have gone on to turn on an oven, answer the door and lock various windows, all by picking them off the menu. In particular, by selecting the keyboard option, I could have spelled out words and sent an email, all from my nervous system. The overall effect was very similar to using a TV remote, except that I was the remote control. For someone who was bedridden or was unable to move around for some reason, clearly the possibilities of controlling their environment were endless.

The majority of the selections I was able to accomplish first time, which I found absolutely amazing. I occasionally had to repeat a command in order to make the correct choice, but it was more a case of me learning how to use the technology rather than anything else. However, I picked it up quickly, and within a few minutes I was reasonably competent. With a little bit of practice, I knew I could become extremely proficient.

'Anyone for a cup of cyber coffee?' said Ben. The coffee was ready. Several of us took him up on the offer, and raised our cups in celebration. Sarah astutely spotted great pleasure, tinged with a certain amount of relief, on our faces. So far so good. Both the demonstrations we had tried had worked very well. When you decide to demonstrate something for the first time, something is bound to go wrong – take Rogerr, the half-marathon robot, for example. But we had not only been successful twice on this occasion, we had also clearly demonstrated some of the potential powers of a cyborg, when human and machine are neurally linked together. It was exhilarating.

The next experiment involved a little Lego robot, with big beady eyes. The signals from my median nerve were converted into infrared signals which were then passed down from the computer to the robot, enabling me to drive it around the floor. I hadn't realized that Iain had already connected things up, so I was taken by surprise when the robot suddenly burst into life. Iain had already programmed the robot to change direction as it recognized the signals it received. So, with my hand open the robot stopped, but by clenching and unclenching my hand I was able to activate simple commands – right, left, forwards, backwards – and even a u-turn, which caused the robot to spin round on its axis. In fact the conversion of my neural signals into instructions was similar to that used on two previous demonstrations, although the end product – this time a mobile robot – was completely different. My learning process to control it in the way that I wanted was therefore different. Just like a baby has to learn how to send signals from their brain to move fingers, legs and so on, I had to learn how to send signals from my brain to move the mobile robot around.

Surprisingly, I was able to achieve near-perfect control within a few seconds of starting. Everyone, including myself, was astonished at how well this experiment seemed to be working. I told everyone that this would ultimately mean that, in the future, we should be able to drive a car around by picking up the signals directly from the brain, and change direction just by thinking about it, right, left and so on. Ben and Iain groaned. They realized that I half meant it. They could envisage hours of extra work ahead of them kitting out a car with a suitable computer, so that I could drive around the picturesque university campus, wreaking havoc without turning the steering wheel or putting my foot on the accelerator peddle. But in the meantime we already had a lot of experiments to be getting on with.

The final experiment we wanted to do on the 18th involved Nibbler, a robot that made an appearance in the Christmas Lectures, sixteen months before. In this case Nibbler was surrounded by four smaller robots that Ben had been working on. He called them his mood robots, and referred to them as Diddybots. Nibbler had two moods, either passive or aggressive. Each mood transmitted an infrared signal, which could be received and recognized by the Diddybots. When Nibbler's mood was passive, the Diddybots tried to flock around Nibbler, whereas when they received the alternative, aggressive signals, they tried to escape as fast as they could. I was able to determine Nibbler's mood with the nerve signals generated when I clenched my fist, thereby directly governing the response of the Diddybots in the Madlab's corral, an area about nine metres square. In the weeks ahead, it was hoped that I would be able to control Nibbler's mood, not by movements, but in relation to my own mood. For the experiments at hand, however, motor actions would suffice.

This experiment showed how the behaviour of robots towards each other could be altered simply by transmitting neural-control signals so the robots understood them as an order. In a similar way the behaviour of a robot towards a human could be altered from the same sort of signals to act as a friend or foe. Signals originated on my nervous system that were associated with my movement were dictating the mood and reactions of a group of robots. In the future, with a brain implant, the same control might be possible merely by thinking the command.

All four experiments were over in the space of a couple of hours and had worked far better than we could have possibly expected. I was elated. Beforehand I had worried that although the implant had been in position for over a month, we still didn't have any witnessed demonstrations in the bag. If something had gone wrong with the array, resulting in a halt being called to our work, we would have been left with very little to show for it, except a lot of recorded data and a smattering of unsubstantiated claims. But at least we now had some success under our belt.

After two hours of exercising my left hand I felt that I needed a break, so before lunch Sarah and I wandered down to my office so that she could flesh out her article with the whys and wherefores of the whole project. We hadn't been talking long when she was much taken by the handwritten quote from the French playwright Molière that I have pinned on my wall. It reads, 'We are responsible not only for what we do but also for what we do not do.' It is this seventeenth-century imperative that I hold dear to. So, when there are days when I consider taking a break and putting my feet up, I think about what I could be getting on with and realize that I will be the only one to blame if I don't do it. As a result I very rarely put my feet up.

In reference to the experiments she had just witnessed, and her interview with me, Sarah concluded her article in the *Mail on Sunday* with, 'Some may say his work sounds like tomfoolery and others will find it dehumanizing or even downright terrifying. Yet when the history of cybernetics comes to be written, the first moment of oneness between living, breathing human beings and the machines we have built might just be traced to the Madlab in April 2002.'

Although I thought that Sarah's final line was something of an over-statement, I was also aware that we had achieved a target and that it might at least get a mention in the history of cybernetics. Of course we would have our critics, but what we had done was not simple theory or idle spec-ulation, we had actually realized an aim. I hoped that it would at least make people think about what we had done, and felt a sense of deep satisfaction.

That weekend I was brought sharply back to the realities of academic life with one of the great banes of the university calendar – marking exam papers. This is certainly a wonderful way of bringing you back down to earth from the heights of a successful research project. Several of the exam questions I had set were analytical in nature. One, however, was very much centred around some of the issues raised in this book:

(a) It has been argued that wearable computers allow humans to become cyborgs. Give some examples of wearable computers and indicate whether you agree, disagree or otherwise with this claim.

(b) Implant technology can be used in a number of ways to help those people who have a disability. Give some examples of more traditional methods and then discuss achievements now and in the future using electronic stimulation.

(c) Connecting the human nervous system and brain to a computer can allow for the possibility of enhancing human capabilities. In what ways could this be possible?

(d) Research into cyborgs, particularly those in (c), raises numerous ethical and moral questions for society. What are some of the key issues? What role should scientists play in the debate? Should, for example, scientists stop work in the field until the debate has been conducted?

Almost two hundred students answered the questions, and fortunately most gave very good answers.

In part (b) many students put forward pacemakers, cochlea implants and artificial legs as more traditional methods of implant, suggesting several of the techniques discussed in Chapter 8, especially the Parkinson's Disease solution, as being more for now and the future. Part (c) saw discussion on memory upgrades, extra-sensory perception and thought communication in reference to enhancing human capabilities. Obviously some of the students had actually stayed awake during my lectures through the year.

Part (a) gave rise to some interesting answers. Only one or two students, out of the two hundred, considered people with wearable computers to be cyborgs. The vast majority felt it was the same sort of thing as driving a car or even wearing a hat, and that to take the definition that far meant that everyone was a cyborg, which made nonsense of it all. Quite a few saw wearables as easily removable at any time and therefore not actually *part* of the person.

Some very good answers also appeared as to what exactly constitutes a cyborg. For example, one student wrote, 'Technology must be integrated into the human biological existence, to provide humans with abilities they do not have without technology.' Another regarded a cyborg as being 'Symbiotic – you cannot think of one without the other.' But perhaps my favourite definition was one that described a cyborg as being an 'integrally augmented human'. It seemed to sum up the issue in a brief, all-encompassing statement.

I was also delighted, albeit a little surprised, by the deeply thought out answers to the ethical issues raised in the last part of the question. A number of students raised sensitivity to religious issues as a concern. Others felt that the research was fine unless there was an obvious threat to human life or if it was likely to harm people. As a counter many pointed to the potential positive results that could be achieved in tackling a range of disabilities. One worried about the 'potential dangers to the brain – can it cope?'.

Between them, the students raised the most important of the moral issues faced by the development of cyborgs. Historically, religion has often acted as a bane to science, in some cases halting progress by imprisoning or even killing the scientists involved. Where morality and basic rights are injected into the argument from a religious perspective, then this can act as a sensible rudder to steer scientific advances on an appropriate course. However, I believe that blind religious bigotry – that fortunately only a few hold to – should not be allowed to influence science, or even religion for that matter.

The possibility of a threat to human life was raised by several students which, for me, is *the* big issue. If cyborgs are created with superhuman capabilities from a normal human start point, then it certainly brings about a threat to humanity itself. Perhaps the development of direct, military-style cyborgs might be possible to avoid. After all, when cyborgs exhibiting an intelligence that far surpasses that of humans are brought about, it will surely be the cyborgs themselves that make any decisions about how they treat humans. This certainly is a moral issue that humans need to address in the near future.

There are undoubtedly many ways in which cyborg technology can be employed to help those with a disability, and morally this will almost always be seen in a positive light. If it is possible, then it should be allowed to progress. The problem rears its head when the same technology is employed for superhuman cyborg purposes. As for potential dangers to the brain, there's only one way we will find out – through practical scientific experimentation.

With regard to the question of scientists stopping their research, I don't recall one student who agreed with such a stance. In fact, most were vociferous in their support. One wrote, 'Scientists should continue at all cost, otherwise there would not be a debate in the first place.' Another said that it is a 'scientist's duty to do research', while several commented that 'the debate will never be settled.' A number pointed out that if scientists stopped research because of potential negatives, 'fire would have not been invented because it could burn things and destroy them.' One feature of many of the answers given that I was particularly pleased by was the statement that in order to fuel the debate, 'scientists should be more open to the public.' This is always something I have strongly advocated, yet many scientists prefer to make their research incomprehensible to the public, while, at the same time, grumbling about scientists who are more open about what they do, particularly when trying to make their research accessible and understandable.

Even though many of the answers were of considerable interest to me, by Monday morning I was almost brain dead from the sheer volume. One upturn over the weekend was that it saw the end of the muscular cramps I had been getting in my left arm. They had started about a week before my trip to Tucson, possibly partly due to having to change gear when I was driving. As a result, since that time, I had proceeded to drive my Vectra using gears 1, 3 and 5 only

Back in the lab, Mark set to work getting the stimulator operational. As soon as we could we wanted to try sending signals down the array to bring about movement, the simplest being to inject electrical current directly on to the nerve fibres. However on Monday 22nd Brian Andrews was in the department, and we spent much of the time searching for the sensory signals associated with touch. Ben and Mark had developed a filter to try and remove from the computer any signals associated with movement, and by prodding at various points on my hand we were hoping to see something appear on the computer screen that we could link directly to sensory input.

Unfortunately, for most of the twenty channels related to the electrodes in the array, the noise picked up was of the order of 20 micro volts, peak to peak, of varying frequencies. While this was much smaller than the voltage swings we were able to obtain related to movement, it was of the same sort of magnitude as that expected from sensory input. Hence, even if we brought about a sensory signal that we could pick up via an electrode, by touching a point on a finger, we concluded that the signal would most likely be swamped by noise and would therefore be undetectable.

But this was by no means the biggest problem. We still didn't know what points on which finger might be able to send sensory signals via the array. The median nerve associates closely with the thumb and the first two fingers, but we were not yet aware exactly which nerve fibres, and hence which finger areas, the electrodes were linked to for sensory information. As a result, we weren't sure where on each finger we should be prodding. Coupled with that, we weren't really sure what sort of signals we were likely to witness, as with the motor signals we had seen many signals that we hadn't expected at all, for example a signal that suddenly shot up and then rapidly came to rest again.

It was likely to be the same with sensory input. We were, in essence, looking for a needle in a haystack, although we didn't know what the needle looked like and in reality there were quite a few haystacks. We therefore spent a fairly futile afternoon searching. It was a little disappointing, but in research you have to accept that some of the time you will not get instant results. It's a case of digging in, trying something different, looking at the problem in an alternative way, and then hopefully making a breakthrough. Usually, for every success reported, there have been hours and hours of hard work and graft to achieve it.

Thursday 25 April marked the six-week anniversary of the operation at the Radcliffe Infirmary. In that time we had got the motor signal side of the experiment working well and had carried out a number of successful demonstrations reported by the *Mail on Sunday*. Meanwhile, we were yet to gain some success in locating sensory input and had not yet tried stimulating my system by pushing signals in, though hopefully that would be tested in the coming week.

We had a number of other demonstrations to try out; several

depended on us getting the stimulator working. It appeared that we would be able to control the movement of a wheelchair from my nervous system in the same sort of way that we had controlled the Lego robot, but we were not now sure whether Brian Gardner wanted such a demonstration to take place at Stoke Mandeville.

On the positive side, not only were there still no signs of infection or rejection, but my body appeared to have fully accepted the implant, and I frequently forgot that it was there. However, when I was linked up to the computer and able to move technology around from my nervous system, that was a different matter. It was those times that I found most exciting. It was then that I felt I was a cyborg.

Sylak was due to come in on Saturday with his completed gauntlet, and we would have that to fit nicely alongside Moi's jewellery, which seemed to be functioning well by changing colour as desired. In addition to this, I had started work on the ethics application necessary to bring Irena into the project. This was something I needed to get completed and submitted as soon as possible if we were to try person-to-person nervous-system signalling before the end of the project.

As well as reflecting on what we had achieved since the implant was put in position, I also looked forward to what we had set ourselves to do. We were perhaps a little behind schedule, but not much considering the number of unforeseen problems that had been encountered. For the first time I also started to look ahead to the operation to remove the implant. After all, it was only six or seven weeks away. Considering the number of hiccups there had been for setting the date for the initial implant operation, we would probably have to start touting a date for its removal shortly. But that wasn't a subject I wanted to think about just yet.

Irena, Maddi and James were all being tremendously supportive, showing interest in the project and giving me the encouragement to push forward with it. It was very difficult to show just how much I appreciated this. The guys in the lab, Mark, Iain, Ben and Justin, were also proving to be absolutely fantastic. It was a tremendous team, working all hours to get things functioning correctly, and with a wonderful camaraderie. It was like having another family in the university. Overall I felt delighted, and even relaxed, that the project had gone as well as it had, and I pondered that the best, the most exciting bits, were still to come.

But as is often the case, just when it looks like being a nice, sunny day, a dark cloud wafts into view, blocks out the sun and starts throwing buckets full of rain on those below. In my case, I received a call from Chris Miller, at Computer Associates, to say that they would not be able to fund our researchers in the lab in the forthcoming year. This came as quite a blow, but I thanked him for supporting us over the last three years, calmly put the phone down, and tried to gather my thoughts. Their present funding was due to run out at the end of April, only one week away. Clearly I had another job on my hands.

First of all I decided to phone round just to make sure that the other sponsors were still on board. Sarah Evans at Tumbleweed Communications said that although things were fine from July onwards, they wouldn't be able to help in the quarter year from April to June. So that was another research position down the tubes. Finally I tried Marc Sylvester at Fujitsu. He told me that they would be able to contribute something, but it wasn't what I was expecting. So, bang in the middle of the implant project we were suddenly put in a position where, in a few weeks' time, we would be without any money with which to pay the researchers. Without any prior indication from the sponsors, the project had gone from an expected annual income of around £180,000 to one of no more than £10,000. I sat in my office, deliberated at length about the predicament and came to the profound conclusion: 'Damn.'

CHAPTER 14

ON TUESDAY 30th April, Iain, Mark and I gathered expectantly in the Madlab. We were ready to try injecting current on to my nervous system to see if we could stimulate some movement. If I said that I wasn't just a little bit scared I would be lying. But at the same time it was tremendously exciting. It was one thing simply to monitor the signals on my nervous system, but it was quite another to force current in. What would my brain make of it all? Would it be able to cope?

It was really a step into the unknown. We didn't know exactly which nerve fibres the electrodes in the array were making contact with. On top of that, we didn't have much of an idea how much current we were supposed to be applying. Too little and I probably wouldn't feel anything, too much we might fry my nerves.

We had done as much homework as we could, checking on all the academic papers that gave us some sort of an idea as to the amount of current that might be needed. But it was a real shot in the dark. Experiments using the array to stimulate a cat's sciatic nerve indicated that maybe around 20 micro amps would be sufficient, but other results indicated that we might need more than this. Further research that had used electrodes externally applied to the skin indicated that even a level of around 10 milliamps (500 times more than the 20 micro amps) would be necessary and, even at the very last moment, a new paper by John Chapin on his rat research pointed to a figure of 80 micro amps as being sufficient when supplied directly to the brain of a rat. But how much are the human median nerve fibres like those in a rat's brain?

We decided to try a relatively safe figure of 10 micro amps first. We suspected that we wouldn't see any results at this level, but we needed to check it just in case. Our plan was to try several signals on each of the twenty electrodes in turn, both between electrodes and between each electrode and a big earth patch, stuck to the outside of my arm. Once the implant in my left arm was connected up to our interface unit, I sat, rather nervously, with my right hand on a deadman's switch. If it turned out to be extremely painful when the current was injected, all I had to do was let go of the deadman's switch and the power would be disconnected. For some reason the deadman's switch (not a particularly nice name I admit) was made of Lego!

I felt quite warm in the lab, partly because the sun was out and blasting through the lab windows, but partly, I suspected, because I was nervous. We opened a couple of windows and prepared to send the first current. I cupped my right hand over the deadman's switch, ready to let go the instant I felt my left hand in excruciating pain.

I looked at the monitor as Mark pressed the button for the first time. A nice sawtooth wave form appeared, which indicated that not only was the current being injected, but that my nerves were accepting the charge via the first pin we tried. I felt nothing. We moved to the next pin, with the same result. The magnitude of the charge was slightly different, but still I felt nothing. We laboriously worked through all twenty electrodes with no success. From time to time I felt slight tingling on my fingertips, at which point we tried to inject the current again, but at no time was there a repeatable sensation. Clearly 10 micro amps was below the threshold for my nervous system.

One discovery we made was that several of the twenty electrodes on one side of the array seemed to be meeting a much higher resistance than the other electrodes. Essentially we were injecting the same amount of current through each electrode in turn, and could witness the actual voltage being applied on an oscilloscope. According to Ohm's Law, the higher the level of voltage shown, the higher the resistance to the flow of current through the electrodes down on to my nerve fibres. It looked as though one edge of the array was probably not making such good contact, hence the higher resistance, whereas the vast majority of the electrodes were nicely positioned in the nerve fibres.

The next day we went through the whole procedure again, this time applying a current of 15 micro amps through each of the electrodes in turn, to see what effect this had. On one or two occasions we thought that I might be feeling something, but nothing was conclusive. Although we needed to increase the current steadily in each electrode, it appeared that we still had a long way to go. It was most likely that we would increase the current to a certain level, at which point one or two of the electrodes would stimulate some feeling or movement. However, by increasing the current further, most of the electrodes would show some sort of effect. We felt it was likely that some of the electrodes – particularly those facing a higher resistance – would need to have a much higher current applied to them to show any effect. This meant that at each current level, we needed to apply that current laboriously to each electrode to see what would happen. It was an extremely time-consuming process.

At the end of the second day of testing, from what we had learned, Mark and Iain decided to push the current higher. The printed circuit board they had designed and populated with numerous chips, capacitors, resistors, etc., needed some different components to allow higher currents to be applied. The new components were duly ordered, but as they wouldn't arrive until the following week, we had to put off testing for a few days. I was frustrated that we weren't able to move along more quickly, but knew it was better to be safe than sorry. As it turned out, I was able to bring together a few more aspects of the project during this hiatus.

William Harwin took the opportunity to do another round of his testing. He was interested in how the array had impaired the sense of discrimination in my fingers, if at all. He was using a device with two sharp pin-like points at its tip. He was able to adjust the distance between the points finely in order to see if, with my eyes closed, when he pushed the pins against various parts of my fingers I would regard it as being two points being applied or merely one. Despite the array, my left hand appeared to be discriminating as well as my right. As expected, much finer discrimination was achieved at the fingertips than on the palm or lower down my fingers. It surprised me how difficult it was to detect whether William was applying one point or two, the lower down my fingers he tested.

The next day Sylak appeared with the final version of his gauntlet. We had been expecting him several weeks earlier, but he had faced a few delays which had pushed things back. I had been worried that the part of the gauntlet the connector pad needed to fit on to would sit too high on my arm, such that the wires sticking out would neither be long enough, nor have the flexibility, to fit the connector pad on to it. However, I needn't have worried – it fitted together perfectly, the interface slotted in well and it looked excellent.

We had initially planned that I would wear part of the gauntlet – the section holding the connector pad – almost all the time, only clipping on the main body, with the interface unit, when we were doing some testing. But we were now over six weeks into the investigation, which was more than halfway through, and I had got used to working with the connector pad taped down to the inside of my lower left arm. I would certainly use the gauntlet from time to time, but it wouldn't be the regular accessory that we had first thought. At the same time I recognized that while it was nice to have an artistic side to what we were doing, by far the main thrust was a scientific one, and I wanted to ensure that that message came across clearly. I did not want someone with little information on the project to get the idea that it was just a bizarre fashion show.

On Saturday 4 May, Mark and I headed back to Oxford again. This time the trip was to the Gait Lab at the Nuffield Hospital Orthopaedic Centre where they had some very expensive camera equipment for monitoring actions and movements, and a bank of computers for collecting electromiograph (emg) muscular movement information. The idea was to link visually located movements with muscular data and the neural information we could collect from our own equipment.

We wanted to stick further electrodes on the outside of my left arm and position some light-sensitive grey balls along it. (See plate section.) With these in place, as I moved my arm and fingers, we hoped to be able to record muscular movements using the external electrodes, while at the same time visually recording my specific movements, with the help of the grey balls. This information would then be linked to the corresponding neural signals that we would obtain via the implant and the monitoring equipment we took along ourselves.

It wasn't particularly warm in the lab, but I still had to go topless and was kitted out with external electrodes all over my left arm. As well as these I had small, light-sensitive grey balls positioned over the top half of my body, which would be detected by the cameras. One final element to the wiring-up occurred when, by means of an injection into the fleshy lower part of my palm, two electrodes were positioned into the thumb muscle of my left hand. On top of all this, of course, I had the implant and wires in place inside my arm, which was now a mass of colourful wires and electrodes.

First of all, small movements of my thumb were initiated by passing a current into my thumb muscle. It was funny looking at my thumb as it twitched around through no action of my own, feeling perhaps as a nervous twitch would. I thought it might be useful in connection with our work in Reading, and might give me an idea of what I would feel in a few days' time returning to the other experiment.

Unfortunately, the day was not a great success. Our own neural-monitoring equipment was extremely sensitive and there appeared to be quite a lot of electrical noise generated by the lab's expensive lighting system. In the Madlab at Reading, neural signals had appeared to be of much larger magnitude than any noise present. However, in the Gait Lab there was a lot more noise around and it was extremely difficult to distinguish it from neural signals. As a result, although a lot of data was collected as I moved around little boxes, poured water into jars and turned keys in a lock, only time will tell if we can accurately correlate it all. What was supposed to be an experiment lasting a couple of hours turned out to be a full day's work before we eventually called a halt to the proceedings, getting back to Reading as night fell.

It had been an extremely frustrating day. An analysis of the correlation between muscular (emg) signals, the associated neural signals, and the visual tracking of the grey balls could have been useful in the future to help those with movement difficulties. The theory was that having this information would allow future doctors to assess the incorrect orders being sent by the brain. We had achieved only very limited success, just because the electrical noise from the lighting system caused problems with our own delicate monitoring equipment.

A couple of days later the interface allowing us to vary the stimulation current – possibly up to around 200 micro amps – still wasn't ready. Components had been ordered in good time, but were late arriving. I was therefore able to complete most of the work necessary for the ethics application for Irena's involvement. We had settled on micro-neurography, in which Irena would not receive an implant, but rather an electrode that would be inserted from the outside down on to her nerve fibres. Apart from filling in a plethora of forms, I ensured that the university insurance office were happy with things, and brought George Boulos, who would actually insert the electrode, back on to the project. All that was left was for Irena to sign the consent form which, as she had been pushing incessantly to be included, I didn't expect to be a problem.

On the same day I received an email from Brian Gardner, saying that because we weren't yet sure about the exact nature of the neural signals we were obtaining from my nervous system, he felt it would not be sensible to go ahead with a demonstration at Stoke Mandeville, where I planned to control the wheelchair with the signals we were obtaining. Although at that point we were witnessing both emg and neural signals in response to my hand movements, we still didn't know exactly which particular muscles related to which neural signals. All we knew was that when I moved my fingers, certain signals appeared. To me the important thing was that we *could* pick up signals from my nervous system, and that I could generate and use these signals to control a wheelchair. I felt that it didn't so much matter exactly what the signals were ordinarily doing, as long as I could produce them at will. But Brian didn't want us to go ahead with a Stoke demonstration without a much deeper understanding.

I was both disappointed and surprised. Disappointed because Ben had worked hard to get it operating effectively, and because I had done some practice on a couple of quieter afternoons and felt it indicated clearly how what we were doing could help those with a spinal injury. We had really gone ahead with the wheelchair project so that we could demonstrate it at Stoke Mandeville, reinforcing why they were involved in the whole implant investigation. Still, it was Brian's choice, so I didn't argue the point. In any case we could use the wheelchair demonstration ourselves.

I was also telephoned by Sarah Oliver from the *Mail on Sunday*, who told me that following the previous article they had published two weeks earlier on our project, someone had left a telephone message at the newspaper's offices claiming to be me. In the message they had said that the implant project had gone horribly wrong, the implant was no longer working and, as a result, we would not be going ahead with any further demonstrations in Sarah's presence. She was very much relieved when I was able to confirm that, on the contrary, everything was going well and that as soon as we got the stimulation finalized we would be sorting out the next set of demonstrations for her. I was absolutely astounded that someone would take the time and effort to try to sabotage what we were doing in such a way. However, it also brought a wry smile to my face as I realized that our work must be of some importance and interest to this person, otherwise they would not have gone to such pains.

On 9 May I received a visit from Elena Kokurina and her daughter, Daria. Elena was the scientific correspondant for the Russian newspaper *Obschaya Gazeta*, and since she had translated *March of the Machines* into Russian, Elena and I had been good friends. She had flown over from Moscow to see exactly what we were doing. As soon as she arrived in my office she sat down eagerly and told me that she had a strange story to relate.

A couple of weeks earlier, she had been at a party in Moscow, talking to a doctor from a mental hospital in the centre of the city. Elena told him that she was coming over to the UK to see me with my implant and two-inch scar just below my wrist. The doctor looked at her in disbelief and asked Elena if she could be certain that I had actually had an implant. Elena told him that of course she could, and that reports had been on TV and in the newspapers. But she was keen to know why the doctor should question her thus. Before she could ask him, he asked Elena when my operation had taken place. When she told him 14 March, the doctor replied that she had just solved a complex mystery that had been baffling him and his colleagues. He had not been aware that my operation had taken place, yet since the middle of March he had been faced with eleven cases in which he had been confronted by patients with a two-inch scar, just below the wrist, claiming that they had received an implant which was doing all sorts of strange things to the body.

I had hoped, perhaps rather big-headedly, that our experiment might affect how people thought all around the world. But this wasn't quite what I had expected. I did feel some warmth though in that we had had such an effect as far afield as Moscow.

We showed Elena what we had been doing with regard to the monitoring of signals on my nervous system. In doing so we learnt a rather sobering lesson. The six electrodes that we had thought were merely exhibiting a high resistance when trying to push current down them to stimulate my nerve fibres a few days earlier now appeared to be picking up only noise. They were no longer picking up neural signals. Maybe the connecting wires in my body had come adrift, or perhaps the array had started to lift out of my nervous system? We checked the connections between the pad on the outside of my arm and the computer and everything else was fine. From the twenty original electrodes, we were now down to fourteen. I was somewhat worried that we might lose some more of the electrodes before long, but we just had to hope that this wouldn't be the case.

Up until now we still had not had much success in monitoring sensory signals. We had been witnessing motor signals for some time – the signals that travel from the brain to bring about muscle movement, each one looking something like a heartbeat, increasing rapidly then decreasing rapidly in the negative direction, then back up to where it had started from – and we had expected to see something similar for the sensory signals but on a much smaller scale, perhaps only one-tenth of the size. However, we didn't know where on my hand to touch with a pinprick to stimulate the particular nerve fibres that would send out the signals to be picked up by the array. Perhaps the array wasn't positioned near any such fibres, maybe we would only be able to pick up motor signals. Tracking down the correct sensory input was important if we wanted to try to fool my brain electronically by inputting the same sort of signal, rather than from a pinprick.

Elena helped in trying to obtain some sensory signals, and prodded around on my left hand, trying to produce some neural-signal traces on the computer screen. At first it looked like another 'no' result. But when she stroked the top of my palm and the inside of my left index finger in a rather curious way, a sort of half-neural signal appeared on the screen. It suddenly rose dramatically and then went swiftly back to its original level, looking like a heartbeat signal, but only deviating in one direction: it didn't become a negative signal at all. Elena repeated the action and an almost identical signal appeared on the computer screen. After more than twenty such strokes and resultant signals, all exactly the same, we were pretty much convinced that we had a repeatable signal of some sort, but what was it? Was it simply a signal heading off to my brain in response to her touch, or was it a signal coming back down from my brain because of what was happening? It certainly wasn't anything like a movement's motor signal, as it was at a completely different frequency. It was the same size and shape as a neural signal, but it didn't look like a textbook example. Clearly, our investigations were raising far more questions than they were answering.

In fact, since our first fruitless attempt at finding sensory signals, we had had a number of follow-up tests. When I had an hour or so free, I would pop down to the lab and work with whoever was available, usually Mark, to see if we could find anything. Most days we could not find anything at all, but on some days we did record signals, usually due to touching my fingertips, particularly on my left index finger. Sensory signals are generally of a relatively low magnitude, often smaller than the surrounding noise, and are therefore tricky to measure. Part of the trouble was that, although the signals looked distinctly neural, they were not readily repeatable, so we weren't able to find a particular point on my finger that we could prod such that a repeated identical signal would appear on the computer. As a result, no external witness had ever seen any of the sensory signals – until Elena arrived.

In carrying out the stimulation trials so far, we had found that the electrical resistance recorded on different electrodes changed from day to day. In some cases only slight changes occurred, while in others changes could be more distinct. Coupling this with the sensory results that we obtained, which seemed to vary enormously, I tried to understand what it all meant. More questions! Perhaps the array was moving around, thereby changing the connection between the electrodes and the nerve fibres? Or more likely, my body and my nervous system were adapting and adjusting to the silicon pins which had been inserted. The conclusion drawn from this would have to be that the electrical properties of the human nervous system are not like those of an electrical wire, which are the same today, tomorrow and the next day, but, instead, the nervous system differs in its makeup, even over short periods. This presents something of a problem for scientist, because repeatable results are required.

Elena and her daughter left at lunchtime on the 9th, so in the afternoon, Mark, Iain and I got together in the Madlab in order to take the stimulation current higher. Ben and Mark had redesigned the interface to allow us to take the current up in steps and we were now ready to go for it. When we sat down to start work, I felt a sense of excitement well up inside me. We began with 20 micro amps again, just to check our result from before. The bad news we discovered straight-away was that now only ten of the electrodes were working. Whatever had caused the electrodes to go out of commission was still afoot. Clearly our time left for experimentation was limited; if we got to the stage where no electrodes remained, the implant would have to come out at once.

That afternoon we increased the current steadily, in 5 micro-amp steps. At each new value we tested all the electrodes in turn to see if we could obtain a response. It was tedious; there was an air of expectancy at each new current level tried. I was perhaps waiting for a feeling similar to that when my thumb muscle was stimulated at the Gait Lab, but wasn't really sure what to expect. By the end of the day we had got up to 50 micro amps, and I still wasn't feeling a thing.

The next morning we started early. We went up to 60, then 70, micro amps, without any success and it looked as though we were going to be out of luck. Perhaps the electrodes were not making contact with the right sort of nerves? Perhaps it didn't matter what current we injected, we wouldn't get a result. We wondered if we should call it a day and not go any further. After all, it might turn out to be extremely dangerous, as we might harm my nerves. But then came a 'Eureka' moment. As we were polling round the electrodes at 80 micro amps, I suddenly felt my left index finger pull inwards as the muscles tightened.

It was not as distinct a movement as that of my thumb in the Gait Lab. Rather, it was a tightening of the muscles on the inside of my left index finger. Mark injected the current again, and the same thing happened. I wasn't feeling the pull at a particular point on my finger, instead it felt like a wave travelling up my finger from the base to its tip. It reminded me very much of the operation, almost two months earlier, when Peter Teddy had caught hold of my median nerve. Then it was as if my whole hand had been electrocuted, with the charge running from my palm to my fingertips, but this was just a small version of the same thing. When it happened in the operation I was shocked and excited at the same time. Now I was euphoric.

We tried the same current on the other nine electrodes. On some it worked in a similar way, although sometimes the feeling running up my index finger felt broader, not as sharp, but always along the inside of the finger. However, on other electrodes it didn't seem to have any effect at all. Perhaps not all of them were making such good contact? Perhaps they were positioned differently in the median nerve? That night it was difficult to sleep, even though I was delighted and relieved that we were beginning to achieve what we had set out to do: we could send a signal from the computer which would cause my finger to move. I was very excited, perhaps over-excited, and the events of the day kept spinning through my mind.

The next day, Saturday 11th, saw us increase the current further. As each new level was attempted I felt a wave of apprehension gripping my body, as I knew it could hurt. We first polled round the ten remaining electrodes, only to find that only seven were now functioning. Time really did seem to be running out. We would have to get our next set of experiments together quickly, before we had no electrodes left. I was being very careful with my left arm so as not to upset any more electrodes, yet they were still decreasing in number. I even cancelled my appointment with Jacqui, in case the weekly check-up and clean up was having a detrimental effect.

We took the level up to 100 micro amps, then to 120, but it didn't seem to make much difference. The 80 micro-amp mark seemed to be the level at which the neurons were pushed over their firing threshold. We then tried increasing the frequency of the signal, until we were firing 100 current pulses within one second. Each pulse consisted of a positive current of, say, 120 micro amps, and then a negative one, of the same magnitude, with 100 of these per second. The aim was to apply the same sort of charge as a neural signal – the type of which was suggested in a number of text books. That certainly made the feeling a little stronger. However, even with this we found that my finger wasn't triggered every time. Sometimes there was a very strong pull, while at other times it was difficult to detect much of a pull at all. One might think that by injecting an identical current on to the nervous system it would have the same effect every time, but this clearly wasn't the case. By the end of the day, after we had tried twiddling with both the current and frequency, we seemed to be obtaining a 70 to 80 per cent success rate. The human body is indeed a strange entity.

On Sunday I started to plan our next set of experiments, the first of which would involve a trip to New York City for Iain and me. We needed to book our flights, find somewhere to stay and, most important of all, finalize a venue in New York so that we could fix up an internet connection between there and Reading. Sarah Oliver was to come along with us in order to witness what happened. If we wanted to arrange this trip so that we could fly out on Saturday 18th, we didn't have much time. Once again the pressure was on.

The following week was a nervous one – and not for the first time. As well as doing my normal university duties such as seeing students, lecturing and so on, I also spent several hours a day in the Madlab with Mark, Iain and Ben trying different currents at different frequencies. This would all be good for the scientific papers which would undoubtedly follow from our work. At the same time, Mark, Iain and Ben were setting up the internet demonstration, while I got on with booking our flights and accommodation.

I emailed Henning Schulzrinne, a professor at Columbia University in New York, to see if he would be willing to help us with a base at that end. He immediately emailed back in the affirmative and one of his researchers, Xiaotao Wu, communicated with Iain in order to get the internet link set up. Our plan was that the experiment would take place on Monday 20 May, mid-morning New York time and mid-afternoon Reading time. By the middle of the week things seemed to be going well. Sarah booked her flight to New York and said that another reporter would be at the Reading end when it all happened, to make sure that everything was above board.

On Thursday we had some bad news that put me very much on edge. When we started testing in the lab we discovered that now only five electrodes were working. This was getting critical. Would we have any electrodes left to do the internet link-up? Mark felt that it could simply be that the contacts on the terminal pad were dirty and needed cleaning, and we wondered what would happen if he gave them a quick clean – would we regain some of the lost electrodes? After cleaning, we discovered that we had lost another two. When cleaning the contacts Mark had had to bend the wires over at the point where they came out of my arm. Perhaps with so much bending back and forwards, two more wires had snapped? We could only guess, although it was probably the same reason we had lost the other con-nections. Whatever the case, we now had only three electrodes working. While it was true to say that in reality we only needed one electrode to work in order to carry out our experiments, at the rate we were losing the electrodes, Iain and I would arrive in New York to find that the whole implant was out of commission. There was no way to establish exactly what the problem was, and whatever we tried seemed to make matters worse. We just had to hope for the best. So early on the morning of Saturday 18th, Iain and I headed off to New York.

With this part of the experiment we wanted to achieve a direct, electronic connection between my nervous system in New York and the Madlab in Reading. Our hope was that the signals picked up from my nervous system when I moved my hand could be transmitted across the internet and out to the articulated hand situated in the lab, causing it to move in the same way as my own. If that was successful, we then wanted to send signals from the Madlab in Reading, across the internet and down on to my nervous system in New York, to stimulate my finger. We were hoping to achieve a bi-directional communications link between my brain in New York and the Madlab in Reading.

We took the gauntlet with us, fully fitted out with the radio/transmitter receiver board, as well as a lot of paperwork to explain what it was all about if we were stopped for inspection at an airport. In its metal case the gauntlet looked the strangest piece of technology imaginable and we were distinctly worried that we might have a considerable problem getting it on to the aircraft, especially as we were heading for New York. But we were amazed when we walked through the inspection at Heathrow with no problems at all. Neither of us was searched and they didn't even ask to look inside the gauntlet case. The same was true at the Newark end – we just sauntered through customs without a word. I had travelled with an implant in my arm, with a connector-pad attachment and case containing a very suspicious looking piece of technology, and nobody had commented. It made me rather dubious about security arrangements.

On Monday morning, Iain and I embarked on the two-and-a-half hour journey to Columbia University. When we arrived, we were greeted first by Henning himself, then by Xiaotao. After having conversed with then by email and telephone during the previous week, it was good to meet up with them face to face. It took us about an hour to get things set up and establish contact with Mark and Ben at the Reading end, but we were ready when Sarah arrived at 10.30a.m.

First we wanted to prove the link by incorporating the Kyberd articulated hand as we had done before, but this time making a connection via the internet. Through web cameras in both Reading and

New York we could clearly see the hand at the Reading end, while Mark and Ben had a good view of us in New York. We completed the link so that signals from my nervous system, via the implant and the gauntlet, were transmitted first to the computer in New York and from there, via the internet, out to the hand in Reading. When I moved my own hand, the articulated hand stuttered at first, not quite following my own movements. It would start to close and then open, without any input from me. We tried a few tests movements, from which Mark adjusted the hand so that it could operate correctly from the strength of my neural signals being picked up in Reading.

As soon as I got the thumbs up from Mark, I tried again. This time it worked like a dream. As I closed my hand, we could see the hand in Reading follow my own movements exactly, with a slight time delay due to the distance involved; when I opened my hand, the articulated hand followed suit. It felt great. I carried out some smaller movements and once again the articulated hand tracked my own movements accurately. I had successfully controlled a robot hand on the other side of the Atlantic by means of signals from my nervous system sent across the internet. I was on a high. We had accomplished our first aim, but we still had more to do.

When we had previously carried out the experiment in the Madlab, all we had shown was that an amputee could have an articulated hand fitted which they could control from their brain in the normal way. But what we had now achieved was much more significant – a cyborg power. We had shown how signals from my brain could be transmitted around the world, via the internet, to operate a piece of technology. Not only that, but with the visual feedback received, I could control the technology as desired. It really was a super-human power, meaning that, as a cyborg, your physical powers controlled directly from your brain are not restricted to your immediate body's capabilities. In essence, your cyborg body extends as far as you have an electronic connection. With the internet this means that your body extends, as a network, around the world.

Next we got things ready to work in the reverse direction. In order to make sure that I felt something, we decided to use a current of 130 micro amps, with 100 signals being sent per second. When Mark pressed the button in Reading we hoped that I would feel this as one distinct pull on my left index finger. When he pressed the button three times, with short intervals between, the hope was that I would feel it as three distinct pulses. Our idea was that I would sit facing away from the computer screen with my eyes closed. Sarah would then hold up a number to the web cam so that Mark could see what she had selected. He would then press the button that number of times and I would say how many sets of pulses I had received. With Henning, Xiaotao and Iain looking on at the New York end and Mark, closely watched by Nicola, another *Mail on Sunday* reporter, at the Reading end, Sarah wrote a number on a card and held it up. Mark indicated back to Sarah that he had received her request, and Sarah asked me if I was ready. I said I was, and wondered how many sets of pulses I was about to receive.

When the first pulses came through they made me jump and yelp. With no means of communication with Mark, they came as a bit of a shock, even though I knew what was about to happen. The first set was followed by three more, which I accepted without any bother. In total I had felt four sets of pulses, so I shouted out 'Four'. Sarah confirmed that this was the number she had written and I whooped with joy.

We went through the procedure again, just to make sure. Sarah held another number up at the web camera. Again the first set of pulses startled me and made me jump. This time it was only followed by one more set, so I shouted out 'Two'. Once more Sarah confirmed this as correct. Everything seemed to be working well.

As one final test Sarah suggested that her colleague in Reading should choose a number, so that there would be absolutely no chance whatsoever of me knowing what to expect. This time the first set of pulses really made me jump, as I simply wasn't ready for it. I had guessed that the total might amount to three or five, certainly something different from before. I was surprised when the total I felt was four once more. When I shouted out 'Four', I worried that maybe I'd missed one. But I needn't have worried, as this was quickly confirmed as the chosen total. The experiment had been a complete success: we had sent signals from Reading, across the internet and down on to my nervous system in

New York in order to move my finger, and this had been confirmed by not only Sarah, but also Henning and Xiaotao at Columbia. Although it's something of a cliché, I was definitely over the moon.

Our achievements had opened up a wealth of possibilities. In the future it would mean that by connections to the nervous system and ultimately the brain, technology could be operated and controlled via the internet from just about anywhere in the world, merely by thinking about it. Not only that, but it would be possible to control a person's movements and actions at a remote location, by selecting and sending signals across the internet from a computer. What we had achieved certainly broke new ground as far as the interface between humans and computers was concerned.

It was clear now that as a cyborg not only do your physical capabilities extend as far as the internet will take you, but so too do your powers of absorbing information. As a result, your perception of the world is completely different. You are not limited, as is the human body, to taking in information from your local vicinity via your eyes and ears; instead, information can be transmitted directly to your brain from anywhere in the world. A cyborg could, in the future, have one eye in Hong Kong, another in Sydney and another in Paris. A cyborg body could even extend to other planets.

At lunchtime, Sarah, Henning, Xiaotao and I went off to celebrate. On the one hand I felt delighted that we had got another successful demonstration under our belts, but at the same time I realized that we still had much more to do on our return to Reading. Once we had finished lunch, Iain and I picked up our luggage and raced back to Newark in order to catch a late afternoon flight back to Heathrow.

This time getting through inspection proved to be distinctly problematic. At the first X-ray check I was asked to open the metal case containing the gauntlet. Once I opened the case the officials went berserk and started shouting, calling over the supervisor. When he arrived I calmly tried to explain what it was all about and what we had been doing in New York. At the mention of my implant and my cyborg status, things got distinctly worse. Despite producing page after page of explanation I was asked to take my shoes off, take my belt off and stand in a star fashion, while the supervisor went to fetch his boss. A few moments later the big chief arrived and began a strict line of questioning. I remained in grovel mode, in the hope that that was the best action. It seemed to work. After several more minutes I was allowed to put my shoes on and proceed.

When Iain and I got to the gate to board our flight we were stopped again for a further inspection. This time the inquisition was not so severe. It transpired that the people at the first X-ray check had telephoned ahead of us to warn the airline what to expect, so clearance was given without many more problems. Inside I felt a lot more confident about the security procedures than I had done at Heathrow. We arrived back in the UK early next morning.

Over the next few days we worked hard to get everything ready for Sarah's next Reading visit on Thursday 23rd. One piece of good news was that, despite the trip to New York, we still appeared to have three electrodes fully functioning, and each one of these could be used to stimulate my finger. By Thursday morning we were just about ready.

We wanted to carry out three experiments that day. First, to link up my nervous system so that, via the implant and interface, my neural signals could be used to change the appearance of jewellery. Second, I wanted to try out extra-sensory input. This was something I was really excited about – an ultrasonic sense, a sixth sense, in addition to the five human senses. Third, we wanted to see if, by placing electrodes at particular points on the outside of my head, we could link the signals on the array with those monitored on my brain. We could, for example, try stimulating my nervous system via the array, and see what signals appeared in my brain.

When Sarah and the photographer arrived, we began by demonstrating Moi's jewellery in operation. The item that we demonstrated was a fashionable necklace that Moi had worked on with Iain's help. The necklace was dependent on the signals it received to change its colour from red to blue with all the colours in between. Moi's general idea was to link it with emotions so that it would change colour dependent on heart rate, and therefore reflect the mood of the wearer: red for calm, blue for excitement. The jewellery would thus come alive on the wearer's body, interacting with it in dramatic fashion.

But this piece was set up to operate in response to signals from my nervous system, and I didn't think that I would look too good wearing the jewellery. So Irena took an hour off work to model for me. In its steady state the necklace shone bright red, but as I squeezed Irena's hand, the necklace changed to blue in response to the signals on my nervous system. It was a dramatic effect and really suited Irena, particularly the blue! It was great fun as I released and then squeezed Irena's hand to see the jewellery change colour. I was delighted for Moi that her jewellery was working as well as looking good, but also that Irena was at long last part of the whole experiment.

For this experiment I was wearing the part of the gauntlet that held the interface unit. As I moved my hand, signals from my nervous system were transmitted to the computer via a radio transmitter on the interface unit. Here the signals were used to determine how much my hand was open or closed. Signals were then transmitted out to the necklace to dictate how much red or blue should be showing in response to the signals from my nervous system. In the future this technology could clearly be developed to give an instant indication of a person's state of mind. As long as neural signals could be recognized as related to a certain brain state – perhaps when the person was angry or sad – this could be reflected by an external indicator. For me, the indicator was the jewellery and its changing state was dependent on my motor signals.

Photos were taken of Irena and me, then Irena on her own, wearing the jewellery, while I changed its colour as I moved my hand from my seat at the workbench. Before Irena went back to work, I put on the full gauntlet in order to demonstrate how the system functioned as a whole. With the gauntlet on my arm in full operational mode, I not only felt like a cyborg, but distinctly looked the part.

Once Irena was on her way, I began to be connected up for some extra-sensory input. I put on a baseball cap that Iain had fitted with an ultrasonic transmitter and receiver. It looked as though I had a couple of antennae sticking out of my head. On the right antenna, the ultrasonic transmitter sent out a high-frequency sound signal such that when something came close by it reflected the signal back to the ultrasonic receiver on the left antenna. From there a signal was sent via the gauntlet to push a current down on to my nervous system, as a series of pulses. As an object or person came closer, so the number of pulses increased, and as the object moved away, so the pulses reduced until they stopped altogether. In that way I could, so the theory went, obtain a distinct idea as to whether something was close to me or not, in the same way a bat senses its environment.

Having an extra, non human, sense was one of the things that I had been looking forward to very much. But all sorts of questions lay in the back of my mind. What would it actually feel like? Would I be able to make use of it? Would my brain be able to deal with the signals or would it choose to ignore them? Some people I had spoken to suggested that it would probably take my brain several months to adapt. If that was true, this demonstration would turn out to be a waste of time. Yet we were prepared to give it a go. I put on a blindfold in order to cut out any visual input, and positioned the baseball cap on top of my head. I was ready to begin.

At first I stood still while Iain moved a large board in my direction. I felt the pulses increase and shouted that it was getting closer. As the pulses increased I shouted even more. Then the pulses subsided and I indicated how I felt. As the pulses increased again and subsided, so I shouted clearly what I was feeling. Sarah confirmed that I was able to judge what was going on very well.

To describe what I actually felt inside is almost impossible. There was no question of my brain taking three months or even three minutes to adapt: it was on to the new, sensory information straight away. I felt exhilarated and on a high. It was tremendous. To me this meant that if a blind person was fitted with this same technology *now*, their brain would tune to it and make use of the signals immediately. With the blindfold in place, my brain tuned into the signals that were appearing on my nervous system via my ultrasonic headgear. With my visual sense removed, my brain was happy to focus on the new stimulation it was receiving. There was no visual input to confuse my feelings. It felt absolutely incredible.

I moved around to see what it was like and shrieked when something seemed near. Sarah shouted that no one was coming close to me. I felt something must be wrong, how could my new-found sense play up already? As I raised my head the signals subsided, which I informed everyone of. Iain came up with the solution straightaway. When I was moving around I had tilted my head forward and had picked up reflections from the workbench immediately in front of me. As I raised my head so I lost the reflections. The ultrasonic sensors on my headgear were operating at head height, and providing a sweep of one to two metres ahead of me. So, with my head held normally, the workbench was well below my line of sense. In dropping my head, the bench had been detected. I moved my head up and down and confirmed Iain's analysis. Although I had gained a new sense, I needed to learn how to use it, how to direct it.

Positioning the sensors on my head meant that I could receive the incoming information on objects directly around me. To be truthful, though, it would have worked in a similar way if sensors had been positioned elsewhere on my body, on my back for example. That would have given me the sense of an object being close behind me. Even stranger than that though, we could have positioned the sensors elsewhere, in a room in New York for example, and I would have been able to sense when someone walked into the room.

With an extended cyborg body and an internet link, it would be possible for an ultrasonic sense to be remote from the normal human body. A cyborg can therefore sense the world anywhere the internet can take them. Not only that, but the sense can be of any type we want. We had shown ultrasonic input, but it could easily have been infrared, ultraviolet or X-ray instead. I didn't want my new sense to be removed, as it was tremendous fun, but I knew we still had much to do. It felt strange when the wires were disconnected and I lifted the blindfold from my eyes. Back to the limited world that humans sense, I thought.

For the final demonstration on the 23rd I had to undergo some slight preparation. Free of the headgear, I headed off to the hairdresser's with Sarah and the photographer. Once there my head was completely shaved. This was part of the experiment that I had not been looking forward to very much, yet when it happened it didn't feel so bad, just a trifle cold. As I sat in the chair at the hairdresser's watching my locks flutter to the floor, I not only thought about the experiments we would be able to try later on but also realized that this was most likely the last trial I would undergo for the whole project. It actually made me feel a little sad, and it was the first feeling I had had that the project would be coming to an end before long.

When we got back to the department I sat in a chair next to an EEG machine while Nicoletta, a PhD student, firstly put various gels at different points on my bald head, and then attached electrodes. I not only had wires coming out of my left arm, but I now had wires connected to my head. She switched on the machine and a couple of juddery traces appeared on the monitor. When she asked me to blink my eyes, the traces moved up and down at a much greater rate.

For Sarah it was merely a quick demonstration to show what our next plans were. For me it would mean being connected up in the same sort of way over the next couple of weeks, so that we could try to link together the signals Nicoletta obtained on the EEG machine, with those we were dealing with via the implant. Although it would take up some time it would be good from a scientific viewpoint to get some idea of how the extra-sensory signals affected what was going on in my brain, and how the signals emanating from my brain affected the signals that appeared in my arm to move my finger. It would provide lots of useful data for academic papers for sometime to come and was well worth having my head shaved for.

While the first set of experiments in April had shown how signals from the brain could be used to control robots, an articulated hand and the local environment, the second set of experiments had taken our work to an entirely different plane, which excited me immensely.

With the New York link-up we had shown how the cyborg body extends well beyond the bounds of a human body; that with an implant of the type that I had, signals to and from my brain could be transmitted across the internet around the world. We also showed that sensory input, of types not available to humans, can be picked up from around the world, rather than from the simple human-body perimeter. A cyborg body truly is a global one.

That afternoon I felt relaxed for the first time in a long while. We had completed a lot of demonstrations with a considerable amount of success. We still had the wheelchair control to finalize though and, most important of all, Irena needed to be involved. But unless something else cropped up, or something untoward happened, that would be the end of the experiment as a whole. I emailed Peter Teddy to suggest that in the next few weeks it would be appropriate for the implant to be extracted, and he emailed back straightaway to say that I should telephone him as soon as I was ready, and he would book an operating theatre. In the meantime, if we were to get things ready for Irena's involvement in the next couple of weeks we had an awful lot to do – the pressure was on once more.

CHAPTER 15

LOOKING BACK OVER the week just gone by, I was amazed by what we had managed to achieve: the internet link-up between Reading and New York, followed by extra-sensory input, not to mention interactive jewellery. It had been a tremendously exciting few days. I think Iain, Mark, Ben and I were all still on a high, but at the same time pretty exhausted, as we hadn't had any time off at all for quite a while. But time was passing all too quickly and we really needed to get on with the next phase. As it turned out, the next phase was thrust upon us before we had much time to think about it.

On Friday 24 May I received an email from Chris Skidmore, the chairman of the University Ethics Committee. They had given us the all-clear to go ahead with the experiment involving Irena. Remembering how close to the wire we had been with regard to ethics clearance for my own operation, it was a relief to get this application through in good time. Chris also said that although the committee had given clearance for the operation, whatever effect it might have on the subsequent relationship between Irena and myself was entirely up to us.

I immediately phoned Irena to tell her the good news. I assumed that because she had been nagging me to push forward with her part of the investigation, she would be overjoyed. This was certainly not the case. Instead she asked me if we had her operation booked in, and if we had the necessary equipment ready. Given that the extraction operation for my implant was scheduled for 13 June, less than three weeks away, we only had those three weeks in which to involve Irena. I had to admit that we still had a lot to do. Later on, Irena told me that when I mentioned the ethics approval to her, this was the point at which she suddenly realized that it was really happening and that she would finally be part of the experiment. After four years of speculation, she knew then that she would eventually feel for herself how much we could sense from each other's nervous systems.

I immediately went to see George at the Tilehurst Surgery to discuss the options. We talked about the possibility of the microneurography for Irena, in which needles would be pushed into her median nerve from the outside. George said that although he had never done it before, as long as we could supply the needles, he was happy to do it. When he asked when this might happen, and I replied that it had to be done before 13 June at the latest, he raised his eyebrows and gave me one of his incredulous stares.

It transpired that he, Jacqui and others from the surgery were leaving for a conference in Trinidad the next day, and wouldn't be back until Sunday 9 June. In addition, he had training days on the 11th and 12th, so it didn't seem realistically possible in the time we had available. However, after a little bit of negotiation it was agreed that there was a possibility that we would do something on 10 June. I had been expecting a bigger time window, and I think George would have liked some time to prepare but, given the pace we were working at, that simply wasn't possible. So we agreed that George would put the needle – or needles, we still weren't sure exactly how many – in place on the morning of the 10th and remove them at his last appointment at 6p.m. on the same day. On the one hand I felt very pleased, and somewhat relieved, that it was all booked in and the plans were firming up, but it meant that we only had one day on which to get everything done.

No matter what success we had achieved so far, Irena's role in the project was indeed key. My ultimate goal was clear and focused: to achieve thought communication between individuals. Everything to this point had only gone to strengthen my resolve in that direction. With Irena on board, through microneurography, my hope was that we would be able to achieve some basic form of communication from her nervous system to mine and then back the other way. I was tremendously excited at the thought, and anything we achieved over and above that really would be amazing.

When putting Irena's ethics approval application together, I had been assisted by Jennifer Cote from Frederick Haer & Co (FHC) in Bowdoinham, Maine, in the US. Jennifer had supplied me with a lot of information on the type of needles we could use, what sterilization procedures were required and what was involved in the surgery. I now set Mark on her trail again, so we could order the appropriate needles from FHC, as well as any necessary wires and related equipment. We had to be all set to go for it on 10 June, as we wouldn't have any spare time to waste, so it was important that we order the correct needles as soon as possible, to get them suitably sterilized in time. Different needle types required different sterilization, and our final choice would have to take into account the available time.

On Monday 27th I received a huge boost on the financial front. First, an email arrived from Analog Devices in Ireland to say that they would be able to provide some funding to help with the project. They had lined me up to give a cyborg presentation in November, and on the back of that were happy to make a contribution to the project as a whole. It wasn't enormous but I was grateful and knew that it would help. The second piece of good news came when Jim Wyatt popped in to go over the *Ultimate Real Robots* magazine royalties that were scheduled to come to the group and be invested in the project. Because of the success of the magazine, it looked as though the royalties would be such that they would provide enough to keep everything afloat over the next year when combined with the support from Fujitsu and Analog Devices. For every magazine sold, the group got a percentage. Not only was the magazine still selling at the rate of 250,000 copies per issue, but it was now scheduled to be launched in the US. It meant that I could relax a bit on the financial front, for the time being at least. Mark, Ben and Iain's jobs were secure.

In the morning post came the call for papers for an IEEE (Institute of Electrical & Electronic Engineers) workshop to be held in September in Berlin on Human–Robot Interaction. As it seemed ideal for our purposes, I mobilized Mark, Ben, Iain and Peter Kyberd and suggested that we submit a paper largely on what we had done for the demonstrations in April, controlling the articulated hand, the Diddybots, etc. Everyone accepted that we would have to produce academic papers on what we were doing at some time, and this workshop seemed to be perfect, although the time was short.

Later on a message came through from Peter Teddy saying that he would not be able to carry out the extraction operation on the 13th, as he was too booked up with other operations. However, he felt that the extraction was something that Amjad Shad could deal with, as it was Amjad who had had the practice in removing the array from the sheep's nerves.

That night I phoned Amjad to go over everything with him. He said he was happy to do the extraction, and felt confident about it, although the 13th would not be possible, as he would be attending a conference in Paris. He said that Tuesday 18th should be all right, as long as he could book an operating theatre. I was happy with this news, as it meant that we would have a little more time to take some more readings and get some final demonstrations done, particularly controlling the wheelchair from my nervous system. It also meant that if anything went wrong with Irena's microneurography on the 10th, we would have some time to try it again later in the week.

For the rest of the week Mark and I were camped down in the Madlab. Most of the time we were working on stimulating my nervous system, trying different current values, different signal frequencies, leaving gaps between signals – all kinds of different methods. We wanted to achieve 100 per cent accuracy in stimulation. I was still feeling the current running up the inside of my left index finger. Sometimes my finger suddenly jumped, which was a fantastic feeling. I also did more tests with Nicoletta using the EEG machine, attaching electrodes to the outside of my head. The aim of this work was to stimulate my finger via the array and pick up signals in my brain with the help of external electrodes. Unfortunately, with the equipment we were using, and the fact that my hair was beginning to grow back, this proved to be very difficult. So mainly it was just Mark and me, working late into the night. We continued in the lab over the long Jubilee holiday weekend. It was a good time, the university was quiet, there were no telephone calls and no interruptions – we just kept going, taking readings. Every so often we had to break when the end of my left index finger started throbbing. It was almost as if the charge running up my finger was accumulating at the tip, but maybe it was just my finger muscles tightening up.

On the afternoon of 4 June we were joined by Peter Kyberd and Suzi Halliday. Suzi had been with us a month earlier at the Gait Lab in Oxford, and wanted to try some more tests. She was from the Nuffield Orthopaedic Centre in Oxford, studying for a PhD. Suzi's aim was to try and stimulate my left index-finger muscles by applying a current directly to them so that we could measure, via the implant, the resultant signals heading back up to my brain. We were all interested to see what would happen, but for Suzi there was the possibility that the results might be helpful with her research into people with movement difficulties.

She injected a couple of electrodes into the muscles on the palm of my hand just to the bottom left of my index finger, and another pair to the bottom right. Through these she input a current into the muscles to move my finger first in one direction and then the other. We were able to record a fantastic range of signals through the array, the signals repeating themselves nicely as my finger was moved by the current, and we recorded a much better set of results than we had done when we were in Oxford.

Having a computer-controlled current injected into my finger, thus making it move, was tremendously exciting. My brain just seemed to accept, without question, that an external force was at work. At the point where the electrodes had been injected through the skin, it stung a lot as the current was injected, but I was interested to find out what would happen, so put up with the pain. As far as I was concerned, this work could easily help a lot of people in the future, so any trivial pain I experienced was well worth it. When we had finished, I had to pull the electrodes out myself. The first pair came out without a hitch, but the second pair didn't want to budge and it took a lot of manoeuvring before they popped out. Mark said that I cried like a baby. I think he was joking.

Once Suzi had gone we phoned Jennifer Cote in Maine. Mark had found out more about the microneurography needles for Irena, and we knew that as we had less than a week to go before we needed them at the surgery, we should have ordered them by yesterday at the latest. After much discussion we agreed on the needles required. We would use two needles, one with an electrode on the end, which George would push into Irena's median nerve, and the other to act as a reference, and be pushed under Irena's skin in the vicinity of the first. Attached to the end of each needle was a connecting wire with a banana clip on the end. Once the needles were in place, Irena would be plugged in – it was that simple.

There was an incredible variety of needles on FHC's books and Jennifer was very helpful in finalizing our choice, the electrode resistance being important, given the monitoring equipment that we already had. The needles we chose were very fine, less than half a millimetre in diameter, and just over three centimetres in length. They were made of a composite of platinum and iridium. Jennifer also advised us on sterilizing the needles. This process would be relatively straightforward in comparison with my array, merely involving putting them in an oven at 270°F (134°C) for about four minutes. We placed our order, and within an hour Jennifer had shipped them out to us by express delivery.

At home I brought Irena up to date with things. The surgery was booked, the needles were on their way across the Atlantic, but I still hadn't figured out where to get them sterilized. Irena and I talked about what would happen during her operation. She doesn't like needles at the best of times (does anyone?) and I knew that she was being incredibly brave to want to go ahead with it. We sat next to each other on the settee, holding hands and looking at each other. Irena said how nervous she was, and scared of the needle being pushed into her median nerve, but she knew that with some anaesthetic she would not feel too much pain. I told her that I simply couldn't express my feelings, but that I was so pleased that it looked as if it was all going ahead and that she would be involved. I also told her that she needn't worry, as everything would be perfectly okay and a lot of fun, but inside I felt so responsible for her. I knew that there were actually a lot of things that could go wrong, such as infection or applying too much current to her nerves, but I had to trust my own abilities, and those of George and everyone else involved, that we would get it right. Irena was worrying enough about it all anyway, and there was no need for me to add to her anxiety.

The next morning I phoned Lynn, the nurse standing in for Jacqui at the surgery. She had good news, informing me that they had the facilities in the surgery to carry out the necessary sterilization of the needles. We agreed that I would take the needles with me when I went for my weekly check-over on Thursday night, as long as they had arrived by then. Another worry out of the way.

That Wednesday Mark and I continued to work on our stimulation research. Fortunately the three remaining electrodes on the array were still holding out. We hoped they would do so for another few days at least, to enable us to complete all our demonstrations, particularly the link up with Irena that was scheduled for Monday. However, every time we sat down in the lab to start testing, it was tense. Would there be any electrodes still operative or would that be it, end of project? As soon as we had established that they were still working, we were able to relax a bit and get on with the day's work.

What we hoped to do on Monday was monitor signals on Irena's nervous system and detect when she was opening and closing her hand. These open/close movements could be sent via the internet to the stimulator unit on my gauntlet to either stimulate my nervous system or not. So, with Irena's hand open, I wouldn't receive any stimulating pulses, whereas with her hand closed I would. We then hoped to do everything in reverse, with me making the movements and Irena being stimulated. Although this would be a very basic form of communication, it would be the first direct, purely electronic communication from nervous system to nervous system. It was a hugely exciting concept and, should we be successful, the resulting implications for future communication between two people were immense.

When we took time out from testing, Iain and Mark worked on

getting things ready for Monday. Before we sent signals from nervous system to nervous system, we would need to check Irena's electrode to see if we could monitor and record signals when she moved her hand. For this we could use the Bionic Tech equipment that we had previously used to monitor my own movements. We would then try to stimulate Irena's nervous system to see what movement or feeling we might be able to bring about. For this we planned not only to use what we had already learned while stimulating my own nervous system, but also a new stimulator module that was specifically designed to link up with the needles we had bought from FHC at the same time. I wondered whether Irena would feel the same sensations as I did and what value of current we would need to inject in her case.

In the meantime Ben worked on getting the wheelchair ready for Tuesday 11th, as it was something that we still hadn't demonstrated. The plan was that I would sit in the chair and make it move around using the neural signals from my left arm, in the same way that I had controlled the Lego robot back in April. But Ben still needed to link up the signals that would be transmitted from the gauntlet in my arm to the control box on the wheelchair. Jocelyn Selim from *Discover* magazine in the US had contacted me, asking if she could write a story on what we were up to. We agreed that she would cover Monday's link up with Irena, then on Tuesday we would demonstrate the wheelchair, leaving anything else that we might want to do for later in the week. As with Sarah Oliver, who oversaw the earlier demonstrations, it was good, I felt, to have an independent observer to witness and report on what we were trying to achieve.

On Thursday 6th the package arrived from FHC and, apart from the fact that I had to pay an astronomical fee in tax, everything seemed to be in order. So, late that afternoon, I delivered the needles to Lynn at the surgery and she promised that they would be sterilized, ready for Monday.

For the rest of the Thursday and the whole of Friday we continued as we were, testing in the lab, preparing for the next week. If we had time later in the week, Mark wanted to see if we could get some feedback from Peter Kyberd's articulated hand. Up until now I had merely closed and opened this hand using signals from my nervous system, its movements copying those of my own. But I had not been able to 'feel' when the hand held something. By stimulating my nervous system, the aim was for me to feel it when the articulated hand gripped an object. On the fingertips of the hand were force sensors, so that as the hand pressed against an object, signals would be transmitted via the computer, down on to my nervous system. The stronger the force applied by the hand, the stronger the signals would be. Mark wanted to see if I could not only feel that the hand was gripping an object in this way, but also if I could attempt to apply just enough force to grip an object. This would, of course, be very useful if such a hand was to be used for amputees in the future. In general, though, things were looking good for Monday – you might say they were 'well in hand' – so I decided to let the guys have a weekend off for a change.

My own weekend involved quite a bit of book writing. I knew that if I wanted to get on with *I, Cyborg* so that it was completed as the project concluded, I had to knuckle down. We were now only a week away from drawing the experiments to a close, and just over a week from the extraction of the array. So I spent the time trying to put the latest events into words while they were still fresh in my mind. As a scientist it is easy to remember the demonstrations and the research results and to report on what happened, but it is very difficult to recall what it felt like, what the atmosphere was like, how people behaved. When undertaking an experiment, you have to concentrate so much on the central focus of what you are doing that you tend to overlook, or quickly forget, what is going on around the event.

But it was also very important to take time out to be with Irena. I could tell that she was getting increasingly nervous about Monday. For her, a day in the Madlab would be very different from her normal daily life in the administrative offices of the Legal Services Commission. When she had visited the lab before, apart from helping out with the interactive jewellery, it had merely been to have a look at what research was going on. Now she was to be directly involved. But before that could happen, she had to have two needles pushed into her left arm, and I think it was principally that event that played on her mind and worried her.

During the weekend we went shopping, went bowling, got ourselves an Indian takeaway and rented a video. But mostly in the time we were together, we talked. A lot of people had helped along the way with the project, but I did feel that quite a few had also been awkward, slowing things up and putting obstacles in our way. While the project had gone very well and it was amazing what we had achieved, Irena felt more strongly than I did that we could have gone even further if we hadn't had to deal with so much hassle. While she was certainly looking forward to Monday and hopefully getting the results we wanted, she was also disappointed that she hadn't been more involved.

Irena had really hoped that she would have an implant identical to the one that I still had in my arm, and it was difficult for her to accept that getting ethics approval, never mind finding a neurosurgeon to carry out the operation, had looked to be impossible. But things had shifted from our initial plans; even my own implant was somewhat different from our first ideas. She was also disappointed that it looked as though we wouldn't be able to transfer emotional signals to and from each other. But that was an area that would simply have to wait for the future. We had gone a little way in trying to understand some of the complexities of the signals we could detect on my own nervous system, but certainly had not reached the point where we could transmit a 'happy' signal from one person to another, for example.

Above all, Irena exhibited sheer excitement at being involved and taking part in the first nervous system to nervous system communication experiment. And just as in my case, the high, the adrenalin, maybe something inside us all that pushes us to look where no one has looked before, despite the dangers, was dominating the fact that she was scared stiff of having needles pushed into her arm on Monday morning. In one sense she was longing for Monday to come around as quickly as it could, but in another she was quite happy to wait.

When I was a child and having a bad time, my father would say, 'All these things will surely pass.' It is something I always remember when I am in the dentist's chair, or am bored stiff while listening to an uninspiring lecture. You just have to sit there and it will all be over before long. Unfortunately, as well as bad times passing, so too do good times, albeit in the latter case far too quickly. So it was that the weekend passed and we arrived at Monday with Irena in a shaky but up and at 'em state, rearing to go.

We woke at our normal time, around 6.15a.m., to find ourselves faced with a grey and murky morning, typical of what had been up to now a depressingly wet and windy June. When Irena is nervous, she tends to busy herself with all sorts of odd jobs around the house, such as tidying, vacuuming, washing up and so on. By the time we left that morning we must have had the cleanest house in Reading.

To start with we drove in to the Cybernetics Department to check that the final preparations had been made. Everything seemed to be in order: the equipment was ready, the wires and connectors were in place, and the computers were up and running. As well as the needles I had taken to the surgery to be sterilized, we had others, as back-up, in the department. I offered to show them to Irena so that she could see what they were like but, perhaps unsurprisingly, she said that she would rather wait until we got to the surgery. So, in a rerun of the trip to Oxford on 14 March, Irena and I headed off to the surgery in our car, with Mark in the back seat, camera in hand.

At that time in the morning, around 10a.m., the traffic is not too bad in Reading, so I was expecting the trip to take us twenty minutes or so. I tried to direct the conversation towards subjects other than the experiment, but Irena seemed more interested in talking about the project as a whole and in particular what was going to happen when we got back to the Madlab.

When we arrived at the surgery it was full of the usual collection of folk ready to unload their assortment of Monday-morning ailments on to their overburdened GP. The waiting room is quite light and airy, with yellow seats and a well-worn carpet, and we quickly found a corner of the room in which to sit. We didn't have to wait too long before George appeared to greet us. The three of us walked with him down the corridor to his room and once inside the conversation began in a fairly lighthearted fashion, mostly about his trip to the conference in Trinidad, from which he had only returned at the weekend. However, he had gone into the surgery on Sunday night to swot up on microneurography and it was not long before the conversation headed in that direction.

George had two pairs of needles on his desk that Lynn had ensured were sterilized. He would only need to use one pair, so the others were kept as a back-up. Mark and I made sure that George knew which was the electrode needle and which the reference. In fact, the electrode had a piece of white tape attached to the end, while the reference had some blue tape. Irena later told me that when she first saw the needles she wondered how she was going to cope with the pain. Would she manage to be brave and not scream too much in front of Kevin, Mark, Jacqui and George? At the time she looked stunned, and my heart went out to her.

George then proceeded to talk to Irena in a calm, reassuring way. He held her left hand and asked her to make an 'O' shape by linking the tip of her thumb and her second finger together. He said that in this way a tendon just below the wrist is tensed, which would make it easier for him to locate the median nerve. He then described to Irena how he would gently push the needle into place in her nerve and that she should expect to feel some tingling in her fingers. When that happened the electrode would be in place. He said that in the past he had had to inject patients experiencing certain problems directly into the nerve, so there was nothing for her to worry about. We were aware that George had really done his homework on the procedure and was well on top of the situation.

George then led the way along the corridor and down to the treatment room where Jacqui was waiting for us with a smiling face. It was the same room that George had used for my 1998 implant, with a window on one side and a treatment bed jutting out from the wall on the other. Apart from a computer in the corner, there is an array of cabinets around the room containing bandages and various pieces of equipment, such as forceps and scissors.

Irena lay down on the bed and, despite our attempts to lighten up the atmosphere with some chit-chat, you could see that she was anxious. After putting on surgical gloves, George cleaned Irena's arm just below her wrist, saying that he wouldn't use any anaesthetic because she would need to feel it when the electrode needle made contact with her nerve. I could sense an immediate feeling of panic within her. She – and I – had been expecting her to be given a little anaesthetic, on the surface of her skin at least. But she was wonderful about it and merely gritted her teeth.

George then took the first needle, with white tape attached, out of its sterilized pouch and proceeded to slowly but firmly push it through Irena's skin towards her median nerve. It wasn't as easy as we had imagined and he had to use quite a bit of force. Before long Irena said that she felt some tingling, but it didn't seem to be as strong as George had previously implied. We were not sure if a good contact with the median nerve had been made so, after a little discussion, George suggested that it might be best to push in another white-taped electrode needle, just to make sure. Irena gasped and bit her lip. But we all knew that, having come this far, it would be silly if we got back to the lab and found that the electrode wasn't making contact with the nerve.

So the second, back-up, electrode needle came out of its pouch and George had another go, this time a little nearer to Irena's wrist. The second needle didn't go in as easily as the first, and appeared to bend a little as George tried to locate it in position. He needed a pair of forceps to help him push it home. I could see that it was giving Irena a lot of pain, but she remained brave, shrieking on a couple of occasions when it was particularly painful. However, once again, while Irena said that she did feel something, it was not the sort of convincing tingling that George had suggested. But there were no more electrode needles so nothing more could be done. Very quickly George took out one of the needles with a piece of blue tape attached, and swiftly pushed it under Irena's skin a couple of inches further up her arm. Each needle had been pushed in at an acute angle, and to its full extent. All that remained above the surface on Irena's skin was the coloured tape, connecting wires and banana clips. Jacqui, who had been holding firmly on to Irena's hand for most of the operation, used micropore tape to stick the needles down and keep them in place. She then put a bandage around Irena's arm for general protection. Even though the process had only taken about fifteen minutes in total, Irena looked much relieved that it was all over.

We thanked George and Jacqui, said we would see them again at 6p.m. for the needles to be removed, and rushed off back to the university. On the way Irena seemed to be quite relaxed. The part of the experiment that she really hadn't been looking forward to at all was now over, and she was eager for us to get on with things. Her arm was still quite painful, so she took her second Neurofen of the morning, which seemed to damp down the pain a bit. In the car she talked about what had just happened and how she had been shocked when George said that he was not going to use anaesthetic of any kind.

As soon as we were back at the department I made us a cup of coffee and we settled down in the Madlab to get on with things straightaway. Jocelyn Selim was already there; she seemed quite young, in her mid-twenties, and appeared to be excited about it all, even though she wasn't quite sure what to expect. I had informed her by email what we were going to try to do, but nevertheless I gave her a quick overview of the set-up in the lab. Having taken many days finding out about the signals on my own nervous system we knew what to do, so when we connected one of Irena's electrodes to the Bionic Tech monitoring equipment, we had a good idea what to expect on the computer monitor when she moved her fingers. But would we see the same sort of signals? We were still not sure if either electrode was making good contact with Irena's nervous system.

We were all excited and tense, Irena perhaps most of all. Before, in the Madlab, she had witnessed the signals from my own nervous system, but like the rest of us, she knew that if we didn't see any signals at all, just noise, that that would be the end of our work for the day. If that was the case, there was a possibility that she would have to go through the whole needle-insertion routine back at the surgery later in the week so that we could have another attempt. Her eyes were glued fixedly to the computer monitor as we finalized the link-up, pushing connecting cables into place between Irena's electrode and the monitoring equipment.

Via the monitoring software, we first had to find out where Irena's electrode appeared on the screen. The software was set up to give us one hundred choices. It had taken quite a bit of time to find where information from the twenty electrodes in my own nerves appeared on the monitor, and with Irena we had to find only one from the hundred choices. I hunted around the software, using the computer mouse, clicking on each electrode option. For most we got no display at all, while for others large noise signals were displayed, showing that there was no connection. But on number eight we seemed to have a low-amplitude noise signal displayed. That looked to be the one, so I selected it using the mouse. Now came the big test: if it was the right choice, would we see anything on the screen when Irena moved her fingers? We looked at each other expectantly.

Irena waggled the fingers of her left hand and we could see instantly that we were on to a winner. The screen displayed the usual plethora of slow muscular signals looping over the top and bottom of the display, interspersed with the familiar, heartbeat-style, neural signals. It was all systems go and Irena beamed with delight. But our celebrations were mainly internal and muted – we had an experiment to get on with.

Mark helped me to fix the gauntlet, complete with interface unit, in place on my left arm and quickly tested out my side of things to make sure that when he pressed his little black button my nervous system would be stimulated via my left index finger. It was working well. All our efforts over the last few weeks meant that we had gone from being 70 to 80 per cent successful with stimulation to, near enough, 100 per cent.

Next, Iain made sure that we could clearly detect Irena's finger movements. The connection from her nervous system was therefore switched from the monitoring display to a PC. When she moved her fingers by closing her hand, the signals were detected. After a period where Iain adjusted the tolerances that were being measured by the computer, we reached the stage where, when Irena closed her hand, a green light flashed on to the screen, and when her hand was open, the light changed to red. So we now had signals travelling from Irena's brain, via her nervous system and the electrode, to the PC, which changed the light when she moved her hand. At another bench in the lab we were able to send a signal from a different PC through the stimulator unit, via the interface card on the gauntlet, down to the array, on to my nervous system and up to my brain. All that remained was to connect the two PCs together, via the internet, which Iain did immediately. We were ready to give it a try.

Everyone knew, Irena in particular, that for me this was the big one. Of all the demonstrations we had done and the testing we had carried out, this was the one experiment that I really wanted us to do. To send signals from one person's brain to another, via their nervous systems, via the internet, for the very first time, meant everything to me. For the first time signals would not be converted to sound waves or passed via touch, they would be electronic signals all the way, from brain to brain. If we could get this to work, I could see clearly how, in the future, we would be able to transmit signals directly from brain to brain and bring about some form of thought communication by way of brain implants. But would it work? How would my own nervous system respond to Irena's pulses? Would I be able to detect them accurately? No matter what successful demonstrations had gone before, this was the one that mattered. This was the experiment which I had put all my efforts into achieving. I pulled the blindfold over my eyes so I couldn't see what was going on, and said that I was ready. Irena held her hand open. The Madlab was utterly silent, the atmosphere tense and expectant.

I waited. It seemed to take an age. But then I felt it, a shot of current, a charge, running down the inside of my left index finger. A beautiful, sweet, deliciously sexy charge. I felt like I had never felt before. I jumped with surprise more than anything else and shouted, 'Yes!' After a few seconds it went again, another charge, just as sweet, just as clear. I shouted out again. Then again and once more. Each time I felt a pulse I shouted, 'Yes!' Even though I couldn't be sure whether Irena was moving her hand or not, I shouted to her to slow down, the pulses were coming through thick and fast and I guessed she was having fun. For some reason no one confirmed that everything was working as it should – for all I knew something might have gone wrong. Was Irena moving her hand each time I felt a pulse or not? I lifted my blindfold and turned around to face the others.

There they were, Irena seated, with Mark, Iain, Ben and Jocelyn standing behind her. Every one of them had a big grin on their face that stretched from ear to ear. I thought no one was going to tell me, they were still amazingly silent. Iain was the first to speak and he confirmed that each and every time Irena had closed her hand, the green light had shown on the PC screen and on every single occasion I had responded with a 'Yes'. This was beyond my wildest dreams. Beforehand I had thought that we might achieve 50 per cent or even 80 per cent success rate, but to get it right every time was absolutely wonderful. In addition, it transpired that at no time had I felt a pulse and shouted out when Irena had not closed her hand. There were no false calls.

We had done it, the first direct nervous system to nervous system link-up. I was thrilled, and wanted to run over to Irena and give her one almighty hug. But we both still had our nervous systems wired up to our respective computers on opposite sides of the lab. Irena teased me by closing and opening her hand three or four times. I didn't have to see her do it, I could feel it. We didn't have to hug, we didn't have to say anything to each other. We had a new way – our own way – of communicating now.

It wasn't that we wanted to get my finger to move in exactly the same way as Irena's, to be controlled from her brain rather than mine, but simply that we could send a signal from her brain, her nervous system, directly to mine – and we had achieved it. To copy a movement exactly would probably need many more electrodes, and would be something for the future. For us, at 2.14p.m. on 10 June 2002 in the Madlab at Reading University, we had achieved the first direct nervous system to nervous system communication. From this start point, I realized that it wouldn't take much to work out Morse-code style signalling between nervous systems to send any sort of message we wanted. But for us, what we had achieved was sufficient. Mark unplugged me and Iain disconnected Irena. As the guys started to connect us up for a link in the reverse direction, Irena and I sat and talked to Jocelyn about what had happened and how we felt. She had got herself a great story.

Irena told Jocelyn, 'It was great when Mark connected me up to the computer and soon I could see that when I moved my fingers, signals appeared on the monitor. Then on another computer a green light appeared when I closed my hand. It was me who controlled the light –

amazing! When I sent Kevin a message through the computer I felt privileged to be part of it. Although I felt pain all the time, particularly when I closed my hand, I was, at the same time, so excited that it was working.' Meanwhile, I was on a high, almost in a sort of drunken stupor, purely due to the success of the experiment. I knew that what we had just done might just change communications for good.

It didn't take very long before we were ready to take the next step. This time Irena was connected up to the stimulator we had purchased from FHC which, in turn, was linked by cable to the PC. We hadn't yet tried to send signals down on to Irena's nervous system, so we still had no idea what sort of current would be necessary, what she might feel – if anything – and where she would feel it. Would everything be roughly the same as it was for me, or would it be completely different? Mark turned the stimulator current way down low and pressed the button.

Perhaps, not surprisingly, Irena said she didn't feel anything. So Mark turned up the current slightly and tried again. Once more Irena gave a negative response. Using our own home-built stimulator, it had taken us days and even weeks to realize the right level of current and the type of signal we needed for me. In Irena's case we didn't have that sort of time, as the needles would be removed at 6p.m. Mark turned the current up once more, and Irena said, 'Yes!' It was actually a little less current than was needed for stimulating my own nervous system – in Irena's case about 60 micro amps – but it was enough.

Iain switched the triggering mechanism from the button that Mark had been pressing so that the PC's signals would do the triggering. Once again I sat down on the opposite side of the lab, still wearing the gauntlet. Mark checked that when I moved my fingers the PC indicated that the movement was recognized. As usual it took some more twiddling with the tolerances in the software to ensure that the PC didn't give any false indications. Every day was a little bit different. Each day my nervous system seemed to exhibit slightly different signals. But then, once more, Irena and I were directly linked up to our respective computers, although this time everything was in reverse. Iain set up the internet connection between the computers and we were ready to go for it again.

As we waited to see if we could successfully reverse the experiment, the tension built in the lab once more. Although I knew we had been successful communicating in one direction, and that there was no apparent reason why we couldn't do the same the other way, I was still nervous. Everything was quiet once more as Irena and I concentrated on what we were doing. Irena had to feel the stimulation when I moved my fingers. Unlike me, she hadn't had weeks of practice, and I worried that she might not recognize the signals.

As Irena pulled the blindfold over her eyes, she indicated that she was ready. I waited a few seconds and then moved my fingers. Irena remained silent. I tried again, with the same result. Mark said that it might work better if he turned the current up a little more, which he did, another 5 micro amps. Although Irena was not aware of it, I moved my fingers again.

This time Irena immediately said, 'Yes', she had felt it. I moved my fingers again and once more Irena said, 'Yes'. I waited for quite a few seconds to make sure Irena was not picking up any false signals, then moved my fingers once more. Instantly she said, 'Yes'. I repeated the action several times, on each occasion leaving a different time space between movements, just to break up any rhythm. I think Irena may have missed one occasion, but that was all – otherwise everything had gone perfectly. It was unbelievable. In my wildest dreams I could not have conceived that it would all work so well. We had successfully demonstrated sending signals from my nervous system, across the internet, to Irena's nervous system. Irena pulled the blindfold from over her eyes and stared at me, wearing the most wonderful smile that I have ever seen. I gazed back at her with probably the silliest grin imaginable. I was speechless. 'But who needs to speak when you can communicate in the way we just have,' I thought to myself.

From the tense, expectant atmosphere earlier, I think we were all inwardly jubilant, but there was actually, if anything, quite a solemn air. It felt very strange. My stomach tingled. You believe something is technically possible yet at the same time it is awesome. Some people laugh at you and say you're being ridiculous. But you work towards it year after year with a team who believe strongly, like you do, and then the goal is reached. And rather than shout, cheer and jump around, you sit there smiling but not knowing what to say or even what to think.

Mark snapped us out of it by saying that he wanted to do a bit more testing with Irena while she was still wired up. Irena was very happy with this, so she and Mark started off with some more stimulation tests. Ben, who had generally been rushing around helping Iain and Mark make the links all day, helped me disconnect from the computer and took the gauntlet off my left arm.

About 5.15p.m. I dragged Irena away from Mark's testing and we drove back to the surgery, accompanied by Jocelyn in the back seat. George and Jacqui greeted us straightaway and once more Irena lay on the bed in the treatment room looking much more relaxed than she had been earlier in the day. It only took a few seconds for George to take the bandage off Irena's arm, remove the electrodes and put a plaster over the entry sites. He told Irena that she might experience a later reaction, and that if her lower arm showed any signs of infection she was to return immediately. And that was it. We drove Jocelyn back to her bed and breakfast near the centre of Reading and returned home.

On the way back, I bought Irena a big bunch of flowers, and we stopped off for some food: tonight was not a night for cooking ourselves. Over a glass or two of wine, Irena told me how surprised she had been earlier in the day when George had said that he was not going to use anaesthetic. But for her the worst part was when George tried to push in the second electrode. It had affected her much more than I could have imagined. She said that at the time she felt she couldn't bear it, that she was going to be sick or to faint. But she had hidden her emotions and inner feelings very well.

It had been a truly momentous day. Beforehand I had worried that the microneurography wouldn't work, that we wouldn't obtain a good contact with Irena's median nerve or, with so much to do, that something would go wrong. Yet we had achieved it: bi-directional communication between our nervous systems. It was true that we had only done the basics, but that was enough. I thought back to Alexander Graham Bell's experiment in 1876. How did this one rank with that, I wondered?

We compared notes on how we felt the stimulation, and we decided that George must have pushed the needles into a different part of Irena's median nerve from the place in which my array was. Irena said that when stimulated, it felt like lightening running from her palm up the inside of her second finger, not her index finger, as in my case. It sounded not too dissimilar from my own experience, she merely felt it on a different finger. She was delighted though that her wrist and hand appeared to be fine, with no immediate adverse reaction, swelling or pain. We talked about how only a year earlier, our marriage had looked to be on the rocks. Yet here we were, closer than ever before, having experienced something that no couple before us had experienced.

It is rare for a husband and wife jointly to take part in a scientific experiment. Yet that was exactly what we had done. The experiment and all the trials, tribulations and delays to get there bound us together in a very special way. It felt as if it was us against the world. Things had changed a lot between us. We told each other everything. We even seemed to know what the other was thinking. It was scary.

The next day Irena went off to her usual job in the Legal Services Commission. For me it was back to the Madlab for my last few days with the implant. There were still a couple of things that we wanted to do, but generally a feeling of 'after the party' was rife. We still hoped to demonstrate how I could control the wheelchair from my nervous system, and Ben had got everything ready. However, when making a final check, Iain blew up a chip in the chair's control box just before we were ready to go for it. Mark had to order a replacement controller but was told that it wouldn't arrive for a couple of days. We were slightly disappointed that we couldn't do that experiment immediately and, all in all, Tuesday became something of a low-key day following the excitement of the day before.

Wednesday the 12th kicked off with a telephone message from Lisa at the Radcliffe Infirmary, who said that my extraction operation was definitely on for Tuesday 18th, less than one week away. I was to arrive by lunchtime and wasn't to eat or drink beforehand. I felt very pleased that we were not facing a delay but, while I looked forward to the extraction, for the first time I felt sad that it was going to end. It had been a tremendously exciting three months, and in a way I didn't want it to come to a close. Yet at the same time I was by now pretty much exhausted.

That afternoon we successfully stimulated my nervous system by taking feedback from the articulated hand. What I mean by this is that as I closed the hand on an object – a glasses case – signals were passed from force sensors in the hand's fingertips, back to the PC and from there down on to my nervous system. With my eyes closed and the blindfold on, I knew when the articulated hand was gripping an object, not because I could see it, but because I could feel the force it was applying – on my own hand. The hand probably gripped the object a little more than it needed to, but that didn't matter too much. It worked. Two months ago achieving such a result would have been a revelation, but now Mark and I merely took it in our stride.

On the 14th I realized that it was now exactly three months since the array had been implanted. A sort of anniversary. Coincidentally, I received a telephone call from the 'Think Tank' in Birmingham to ask if they could display the implant when the Queen visited for their grand opening on 2 July. They were delighted that it would be possible in terms of timing and, even more so, when I agreed to it. I emailed Amjad and Peter to tell them, and got an immediate response from Peter, saying, 'Does that mean I am now by Royal Appointment Implanter to HM the Queen?'

The replacement wheelchair control box arrived in the morning post and just after 1p.m. we took the wheelchair out to the front of the Cybernetics building in order to do the demonstration. Ben had rigged up a little box on the right armrest of the wheelchair. The box contained four blue LEDs (Light-Emitting Diodes), only one of which was lit at any one time. They corresponded to the forwards, backwards, left and right controls for the wheelchair. Ben had arranged it so that each LED was lit for a second or so, then the next one, and so on. With my gauntlet in place the signals from my nervous system were being transmitted to a radio receiver on the chair that was linked to the control box. All I had to do was close my hand at a particular time and the chair would respond to whichever command I had selected. I waited until the 'forwards' LED was lit and closed my hand. The chair moved forwards.

I spent the next half hour driving the chair around. At first it was a little difficult – I closed my hand in an attempt to turn left, missed my timing and turned right. But it didn't take me long to get the hang of it. After a while I was driving the chair around under the control of signals from my nervous system. I wouldn't go so far as to say I was like a true professional, but I did manage to feel reasonably confident. Mark videoed the whole proceedings, Iain took some still photographs, Jocelyn interviewed us all and Ben said he felt that it was one of the best demonstrations we had done. It clearly meant that, with a suitably-placed implant in their brain, a paraplegic should be able to drive themselves around in a wheelchair, merely by thinking about it. Not for the first time I was absolutely delighted.

Once again we had successfully demonstrated how signals from the nervous system could be used to operate technology in a relatively straightforward way. A detailed analysis and understanding of the signals monitored and used was not necessary; a wheelchair could be driven around with the simple hand-open/hand-closed movement. What was important was the entire cybernetic system – the wheelchair and human combined. It would be nice to try out this particular experiment on someone who could immediately benefit from it, someone with very limited movement or control.

After that, Friday seemed to be something of a downer. It felt like the time in a soccer stadium after an exciting match has just taken place, when everyone has gone home. There it stands, empty, with just the litter to be cleared up before you can go home yourself. I went with Jocelyn to Battle Hospital in Reading to get some X-rays taken of my left arm. When I saw the pictures I was amazed at how much wire was actually there. No wonder I had been able to pick up radio signals. It was good to see that the array still seemed to be in place and that none of the electrode pins appeared to have broken off.

At lunchtime I sat by myself in my office and reflected on what had happened since the last set of demonstrations for the *Mail on Sunday*. The hours and hours Mark and I had spent in the Madlab trying to stimulate my nervous system seemed to have paid dividends.

We were now obtaining a 100 per cent success rate – every time a signal was applied, I felt it. But maybe it was simply that my brain had learnt to recognize the signals more accurately? Whatever the case, it was useful to be able to employ the technique to get feedback from the fingertips of the articulated hand, so that I could feel the force the hand was applying. The wheelchair demonstration was certainly very visual and a clear indication of what was possible with the technology now, as well as what might be possible in the future – perhaps driving a car around in the same way?

But there was no question in my own mind: by far the biggest event not only of the last few weeks, but of the whole experiment, was the nervous system to nervous system link-up between Irena and me. If I had to pick out one moment, one instance, from the whole experiment when I felt shivers running up my spine, then that moment was when I felt the first signals on my nervous system in response to Irena moving her fingers. When that happened, I knew instantly that thought communication was within our grasp.

That afternoon we said goodbye to Jocelyn, who was heading back to New York, our story taking shape on her laptop. Mark and I did some final stimulation testing as the three old faithful electrodes were still working. But it was difficult to get motivated any more: we had gone as far as we could go. All that really remained was for me to look towards Tuesday and a trip back to the Radcliffe Infirmary for the implant to be extracted.

CHAPTER 16

OVER THE WEEKEND of 15 and 16 June I had a chance to think over all that had gone before, in particular the period since my implant operation on 14 March. The array had now been in place for over three months and all was still well. Even though seventeen of the twenty electrodes had stopped working, three had survived and they had been enough. With one month to go I had thought that the implant would not hold out this long, but since then I had been a little bit more careful in what I did with my left arm. We had been lucky. With no signs of infection or implant rejection, it seemed that the same technology could easily be used in a more general way, not only to help those with a nervous-system problem, but also to enable extra activities. For long-term implantation, though, it is probably the case that the technology needs to be stronger and more robust to withstand the rigours of permanent interaction with a human body.

We had undertaken all the demonstrations we had originally set out to do, and they had worked. Perhaps the only thing missing was a Braille nervous-system reader. But I was aware that, in reality, when we stimulated the nervous system that was exactly what we were doing; the only difference would have been to send signals on to the nervous system in a predefined sequence so that I might recognize specific letters. But I felt that with the link-up between Irena and me we had, in fact, gone much further.

I was still surprised by the comments of some critics when the array was implanted, in particular the statement that this 'leads us nowhere'. Given all we had learned about the capabilities of the technology and its interaction with the human body, and everything we had demonstrated, it seemed amazing that anyone could hold such negative, shortsighted views. I had been particularly interested in how my body adapted to the arrival of the implant and certainly, from the very start, I regarded the array and wires as being a part of me. Having it extracted, I knew, would be like losing part of my body, almost an amputation.

One of the most interesting investigations was when I received my ultrasonic extra sense. It didn't take months, or even days, for my brain to adapt and adjust to the addition of a new sense. I was happy with it from the beginning and I quickly learned how to make use of it. What to do with the rest of my body when the new sense was in place, particularly my head, probably would take a little longer to learn. However, given our results, I couldn't see why a person who was blind couldn't be given such a sense now.

There was no question that with an extra, different sense in place, my perception of the world around me had changed. With a blindfold on, my visual sense was impaired. But with my new-found ultrasonic sense I could detect objects when they were nearby, although I didn't know, in the usual way, what they were. However, that was not important to me. All that I was aware of, all that I could perceive and make sense of, was something close by.

One area we hadn't managed to get too far on was the recording and replaying of nervous-system signals associated with emotions. It was easy to produce signals related to shock or excitement, for example, but picking out signals related to emotions from everything else that was happening on the nervous system was, for the moment, a challenge to be faced in the future. Maybe we would get somewhere in analysing the data we had recorded. More likely though, further studies would be necessary.

A deeper understanding of pain and the possibility of recording signals linked with having too much to drink would also have to wait. I remain convinced that, electronically, it will be possible to record such signals and play related signals back on to the nervous system, but such experiments will have to be put off for the time being. One problem appears to be that emotions don't tend to happen as single occurrences: one thing sparks off another. By measuring at a single point on the nervous system, all that can be witnessed is a combination of what's taking place. The signals need to be understood more deeply, and possibly broken down into their constituent parts.

At one time I had thought that the array would remain implanted for a few weeks, maybe a couple of months at most. In the three months it had actually been in place, and for some time before, the project took over not only my own life but also Irena's. It was therefore fantastic that we were both part of the culmination of the project, the point at which signals were passed directly between our nervous systems. On reflection it is still difficult for me to express my feelings of that time. It's probably the same feeling a soccer player gets when he has just won the World Cup – sheer excitement coupled with thoughts that you have done it, that it is already history and in your past. This had been the most phenomenal experience of my life.

Linking technology with the nervous system, as we had done, was one thing. The way ahead clearly points to brain implants. Irena said to me, 'But that is dangerous if you don't need them, if you don't have a problem that they can help with.' Yet we faced such dangers, to a much lesser extent, when we both had electrodes pushed into our nervous systems.

This really is the crux of the whole moral and ethical dilemma. Using implants to help a person with a disability is one thing, but using them to upgrade a perfectly healthy individual is something else. Yet clearly we have the technology to do that now. As a result of the experiments carried out I have no doubts in my own mind that, by direct brain implants, it will be possible to upgrade the intellectual capabilities of humans, by turning them into cyborgs. Extra memory, clip-on maths abilities and multi-dimensional processing would all appear to be there for the taking, as indeed are numerous extra-sensory powers. Not just ultrasonic, but infrared, X-ray and more. However, thought communication is the biggest – yet most likely – step of all. It is certainly the direction in which I want my own research to head in the future.

In the last few months, scientifically, I had travelled a long way. Before my latest implant I had had ideas about what might be possible and what might not. Many of these – such as controlling robot vehicles directly from the human nervous system – were no longer mere ideas, but had actually taken place during the project. In addition to this, some of my visions for the future had received supporting evidence, or a step along the way had been made – such as the internet link-up between Irena and myself – which has the potential to lead towards thought communication. So I can now reassess my view of the future in light of the conclusions drawn from the project.

In the short term – the next ten years – it is evident that the medical world will benefit enormously from the form of implanted technology we employed, linking to the nervous system and brain. There is no question that for those with a break in the nervous system it should be possible, with more research, to first control body functions that presently cannot be controlled, and second, to hand back control of those functions to the individual. In this latter case it may well mean that the nervous system is re-routed, or that a bridge is made over the break, using implant technology on either side of the break.

But what we have done is, in many ways, more far-reaching. It was evident from our results that an individual with an implant in their nervous system can control their environment and the technology around them. With brain implants, it would appear to be possible for this to happen in a well-defined way in the next few years. It is more a matter of whether society will accept it, rather than whether it is technically possible.

However, it would appear that the range of uses for implant technology within medicine is much broader. Because of the way electronic signals can be used to change the electro-chemical balance of the human brain, it is possible that numerous medical problems could be tackled in this way. E-medicine is definitely an exciting field that lies immediately ahead of us. Will it be possible to remove a headache, not by taking an aspirin, but by inserting an electronic signal? We need to find out.

Some of the demonstrations we carried out will have an immediate impact on the medical world in terms of helping those with a relevant problem. At the same time, they raise many ethical questions if treatment is given to those who do not have a problem. Extrasensory input is a prime example. In the next decade it should be possible for people to be given a number of senses that they do not have now. One conclusion that I would draw from our own experiments is that the brain is ready and willing to take in such information. It is happy to adapt when a new opportunity comes along.

Remote control is another double-edged issue. It would be good to allow those who are bedridden to remotely control their environment, just by thinking about it, but what about driving our cars by thought signals alone, or flying an aeroplane? With thought signals, the pilot wouldn't even need to be inside the plane. Perhaps more importantly, by linking up the brain in this way, it would be possible for others to remotely control an individual's actions, will and desires. In some instances it might be regarded as a good thing to remotely control someone else's brain, but the idea that it might be our own brain being controlled is quite a different matter.

Looking further into the future, *In the Mind of the Machine* expressed my worry that machines would become more intelligent than humans and thus take control. However, when a cyborg is formed by linking human and machine intelligence a symbiotic state is arrived at, a compromise in which humans are upgraded. With the interlinking of human and machine brains, even in a relatively limited way, it should be possible, within the next fifteen years, to upgrade memory, improve mathematical capabilities and increase considerably one's knowledge base. When linked to the network, a cyborg has the potential for an intelligence way beyond that of a stand-alone human.

Indeed, this is the key to the future. Cyborgs have the potential to be tremendously powerful both mentally and physically, principally because their bodies are not limited to a single autonomous entity, as are humans. Creating cyborgs cannot be regarded in any other way than as a discontinuity, a non-linearity, in evolution. It is one of those things that happens every so often that, in an evolutionary sense, completely changes the order of things.

What is the next step for me? That's easy to answer. Following on from the success of transmitting signals directly between the nervous systems of Irena and I, it is clear that we will be able not only to control technology merely by thinking about it, but to communicate with each other by thought signals alone. A technological telepathy, if you like. The next fifteen to twenty years will certainly see me trying to bring that about. Where will the best link-up with the brain be? What complexity of implant, or implants, do we need? How rich will thought communication become? These are some of the questions that I want to tackle in the coming years. Not to see whether thought communication is possible, but rather to find out how best to bring it about. Cyborgs with extra memory and networked physical capabilities are indeed an enormous step on from humanity as we know it.

The big question now faced by humanity is how do we deal with the possibility of superhumans? Using the technology to help those with disabilities is obviously a good thing in itself, but if the same technology enables superhuman abilities, how should we react? Should we try to stop it, something which I feel, in practical terms, is not possible? Should we simply go for it, perhaps allowing commercial concerns to drive things forward, and profit through new needs and desires? Or should developments be policed or marshalled by governments through international collaborative agreements? These are all important questions which need answering.

I started writing this book on 1 January 2001 and it is now 15 June 2002. In that time I have learned a lot, opening up, I dare to suggest, a number of doors along the way. I have experienced life as a cyborg. It is good. It is fun. It is immensely powerful and goes way beyond the bounded existence of humanity.

In three days' time I will make another trip to the Radcliffe Infirmary to have my implant removed. My days as a cyborg are, for the moment, numbered. On Tuesday 18 June, it will be back to life as a human again.

I wonder how long it will be before it's possible for me to be reinstated as a cyborg? Already I'm looking forward to that time. As someone once said, 'I'll be back'.

CHAPTER 17

Not to be read before 1 January 2050

Dateline: 1 January 2050

THOSE WHO PREDICTED that intelligent machines, robots if you like, would inherit the earth from humans didn't get it quite right. But those who predicted that humans would stay in control have certainly been proved wrong. The earth is dominated by cyborgs – upgraded human/machine combines that have managed to harness the new-found super intelligence of machines and use it for their own ends.

The cyborgs were formed not by direct physical enhancements, such as powerful arms and legs, but by mental hook-ups. Their brains are linked, by radio, directly with the global computer network. They can tap into it, call on its intellectual power, its memory, merely by thinking to it. In return, the global network calls on its cyborg nodes for information or to carry out a task. The network operates as an entire system. An individual cyborg is almost worthless without its radio link to the network, and without its cyborg nodes the network is relatively powerless. Yes, the network can control some fairly stupid machines, such as military fighter planes or supermarket trolleys, but it cannot have a direct effect on humans without the assistance of cyborgs.

A happy balance has therefore evolved whereby cyborgs and intelligent machines work together in harmony, both needing each other. The cyborgs can communicate with one another, via the network, by thought signals alone and, if the network has problems, the cyborgs can revert to their former human way of signalling called speech; although as time goes by this is becoming less useful. As the cyborgs learn to use thought communication more, so they forget how to speak – speech is a dying art form. That said, a few cyborgs interested in human anthropology do still practise speech, but more for its novelty value than for any other reason.

So humans were able to take on board intelligent machines and make use of them, but in doing so the very fabric of humanity itself had to change. And this led to a number of unexpected side effects. With super-intelligent brains, cyborgs have used their ability to think in hundreds of dimensions, to come up with a completely new Theory of the Universe. New forms of energy conversion were discovered. Now that the nature of light is better understood, it has become possible to obtain unparalleled energy supplies by direct light-to-heat conversion. Distant planets and galaxies are being visited since it was discovered that travelling faster than the speed of light was a trivial exercise. It is now possible to buy a cheap day-return to the Milky Way, depending on how one defines a day.

The average food intake of a typical cyborg is much lower than that of a human. Once it was realized that the physical aspects of the body were not needed as much as before, it was a case of channelling more energy resources to the brain area. It was something the humans simply didn't cotton on to. In the late twentieth century, as their lives became more technologically orientated, so they became, on average, more obese. For cyborgs, overeating isn't a problem, as the intelligent network ensures that cyborg brains only desire to eat sufficient amounts of the right types of food.

Even this has thrown up surprising results however. While cereals were historically considered to be good for the human's physical condition, different foods were found to be more conducive to mental processing. While orange juice was regularly taken, perhaps, unsurprisingly, meat products, especially bacon, were also clear winners. Other short-term pluses, such as peanuts, were combined with stimulant inputs such as coffee. However, it was found that the effects of caffeine stimulation were much more easily brought about by electronic, rather than chemical, stimulation of the mental processes.

It is interesting that many of the technological inventions introduced by humans in the twentieth century have become obsolete by 2050, their functions having been taken over by the intelligent network. So, no need for telephones: all communication is via the network, brain to brain. No need for television or videos, as visual stories and games are simply downloaded, as required, to the individual's brain.

Much of this came about gradually. Mobile phones took on board text and then visual communication. Separate networks ceased to exist. As brain implants became popularized and socially accepted, so mobile phones were effectively positioned inside, rather than outside, an individual's head. As this transition occurred, so the need for speech dissolved into thin air.

Policing also took on a new form. When a cyborg is about to commit a crime, the network is aware that they are thinking about doing it, before they do it. The only crimes are therefore those carried out by mutant cyborgs with malfunctioning brains and, of course, those members of the human subspecies still living a wild, uncivilized existence, much as all humans did at the beginning of this century.

By combining the result of the genome project with cyborg technological upgrades, a complete transformation of the world of medicine occurred. Indeed this was one of the main driving forces that led to humans wishing to be upgraded with implants in order to become cyborgs. For the purposes of procreation, gene mapping provided a good analysis as to who would be a perfect genetic partner. Not surprisingly, when it was realized that any offspring from such relationships had, statistically speaking, a much higher chance of being very successful in life, so genetic dating agencies came into being.

However, it wasn't long before each individual, at birth, could be given a life-route map. This indicated, under normal expectations, what that individual should avoid in all senses – food, habits, activities and so on – in order to increase their life expectancy significantly. It also pointed clearly to what they needed more of, especially with regard to dietary and vitamin supplements.

The most amazing transition occurred, however, when it was realized that the human brain does not have to make its own decisions about food and activities. In fact it had been found that the human brain was particularly bad at doing this. With a genetic indicator clearly stating 'No chocolate cake', it was found in many cases that such instructions were being overridden, even though the human felt emotionally distraught in so doing.

The result of this was the trademarked 'Slimplant'. The Slimplant chip, implanted into a secret part of the brain, was able to deal with all dietary and activity matters. Essentially it gave clear instructions as to what each person should eat. With its radio-computer link, each Slimplant was connected to the network, which enabled real-time downloading of genetic instructions and feedback information on the very latest body-state conditions of an individual. Slimplant was an instant hit with all weight-watchers as it provided the ultimate answer. Obesity in those who were given Slimplant was wiped out overnight. It wasn't a case of crash dieting, however, but rather one of good, regular, dietary habits. Before long Slimplant was such a part of everyday life that, as much more powerful implants were developed, Slimplant became a regular subset, a standard feature.

Implants allowed many body functions to be monitored in real-time, including heart rate, blood pressure and temperature. By 2030 these values had been linked into the 'Genetwork', the trademark medical network designed for interactive body stimulation and monitoring to enable longer life. Initially those who were linked up, via an implant, to the Genetwork were, on average, able to boast a life expectancy more than thirty years longer than the average human. This meant that many daily physical activities became routine, the heart being pushed by the appropriate amount for each individual.

Recently though, a range of brain implants has become available in which many standard requirements such as the Slimplant and Genetwork connection are all part of an overall implant package. This package also includes a communication port for thought input/output and a port for eliciting stimulation and excitement.

This latter role came about partly with the introduction of e-medicine, in particular using electronic signals to remove the effects of pain. However, as had previously been the case with chimpanzees, it was found to be relatively easy to download a selection of electronic signals to elicit pleasure in an individual cyborg. A timeout is used for safety purposes, depending on the age of the individual, their gender, race and previous experience. The most frequently downloaded packages can in fact be traced back to virtual reality, where they originated as 'virtual sex'. Around 2025 it was discovered that by stimulating the brain in a specific way, not only could sexual pleasure be brought about, but that it was relatively easy to link this with other thoughts communicated to an individual. So it was pretty straightforward for an individual to fully believe that they were obtaining extreme sexual pleasure with the person of their choice. As you might imagine, having an implant to allow for this rapidly became very popular.

It was quite funny how simply looking into the future was so frightening to some. Back at the time of the Millennium, numerous folk indicated that linking their nervous system to a network would result in a loss of individuality and an erosion of privacy. Not only that, but some saw as a distinct negative the idea that the network would be able to interact with, and even monitor, each nervous system. Many referred to a machine Big Brother.

But as with many technological advances, people only opt for them if they feel they are either gaining something significant or that they will be left behind if they don't choose to have them. In particular, the medical, communication and entertainment possibilities rapidly caused Big Brother fears to be overcome. People accepted a reduction of their individuality with great pleasure, quite simply because what they gained was enormous. Not only that, but an initial trickle quickly switched to a stampede, leaving only a minority who wished to remain purely 'human'.

With the arrival of the internet and the subsequent digital identities, just what an individual was became blurred. It was realized that one physical individual could be many individuals on the internet, could take on different personalities, could have partial identities and, most important of all, could quite easily take on board a part-human part-machine identity – indeed it seemed to be a natural thing to do. So for many they just drifted into cyborg life. The pressure of the technological world, and the desire to remain a player in it, was simply too great. Becoming a cyborg happened as a part of nature.

Overall, life for cyborg's in 2050, as you are no doubt aware, is very good. In a sense all cyborgs act as a collective because of their network connection. As a part of the network, as a node on it, they have value, they are someone. It is sensible therefore to do things that are good for the network as a whole. Looked at in another way, every cyborg has an intelligence, that is part-human, part-machine. The machine side of this is a collective intelligence, shared by other cyborgs. It is therefore in all cyborgs interests to value their machine part.

As a result, cyborgs have morals, values and ethics which relate to life as a cyborg. Machine intelligence is valued, the network is valued. The route to becoming a cyborg is still through human birth and hence human babies are valued – the best of these being allowed to become cyborgs. Those who are not upgraded, however, remain as something of a subspecies in adulthood.

For a while an argument ensued among geneticists: when a cyborg mother and father produced a cyborg baby, would this baby be more ready, genetically, to become a cyborg than a baby born of mere human parents? Some DNA theorists felt this would not be the case. Practice proved them wrong, however. The habits of cyborg parents clearly influenced the brain make-up of their babies. Over a very short space of time, therefore, babies were being born to cyborg parents whose body make-up, in particular their brain, was much more in tune with becoming a cyborg. As a result, a new society divide quickly sprang up. Cyborg parents gave birth to babies who became cyborgs. Humans gave birth to babies who remained human.

Due to the rapid nature of brain development in the early years of life, it was found best to wire up cyborg babies very shortly after birth. In this way, as their brain developed, it readily got used to its ability to off-load problems to a network computer and to most of its memory being in a computer. At an early age, cyborg babies learned to sense the world in about a dozen different ways, conceive ideas in many dimensions and communicate just by thinking to each other.

Memory and mathematical capabilities of the biological part of cyborg brains rapidly diminished, as did those sections of the brain associated with speech and human-language understanding. Instead the biological-brain part soon developed in the area now associated with thought communication. Initially this communication was very basic, being nothing more than old-fashioned telegraphy. But quite soon abstract, multidimensional ideas were being shared, in parallel, between cyborg brains. Quite clearly cyborgs rapidly became intellectually far more capable and far more powerful than humans.

So cyborgs you might say, alongside intelligent machines, effectively run the world in 2050. And just as predicted by many, humans have a relatively poor lifestyle, and are treated very much like a lesser animal, which essentially is what they are. In fact it could be said that humans have more in common with chimpanzees and cows than they do with cyborgs, all being purely biologically based. All the major decisions, all the manage- ment and organizational issues, even everyday life, are controlled by cyborgs. After all, cyborgs are more intellectually capable and far more powerful than humans, so why should they ever listen to the trivial animal noises that humans make? In general, the main function of a human is to work, as slave-like labour, for cyborgs. Some cyborgs are understanding – after all they evolved from humans just a short time ago. However, many are cruel. In the same way that humans generally used to mistreat creatures less intelligent than themselves, many cyborgs now mistreat humans.

It is funny when looking back through history to realise that when humans were running the earth, while many of them appeared to understand what evolution meant, some of the not-so intelligent among them did not; that, at some time in the future, humans would be surpassed. In particular, some retained the completely illogical belief that humans would 'always' remain in control.

However, quite a number of the world's most eminent scientists pointed to the dangers that lurked with the increasing amount of intelligence exhibited by machines. In the year that I was born, 1954, Norbert Wiener, a father of cybernetics, argued that electronic components were thinking machines capable of taking over many human decision-making processes. He cautioned humans not to be stupid enough to let machines become their masters, which, even as long ago as 1954, he saw as a distinct possibility.

Meanwhile Warren McCulloch, one of the pioneers in the field of artificial neural networks said, 'Man to my mind is about the nastiest, most destructive of all the animals. I don't see any reason, if he can evolve machines that can have more fun than he himself can, why they shouldn't take over, enslave us, quite happily.'

Towards the end of the last millennium some scientists, including myself, furiously waved flags of warning about the impending dangers of humans bringing about machines with a mind of their own; their own agenda and their own moral values. As the new century dawned, so others came on board in increasing numbers. Early on Bill Joy, chief scientist at leading computer company Sun Microsystems, laid his cards firmly on the table by warning of the impending threat of creating machines with superior intellectual capabilities.

The following year Steven Hawking, perhaps the most highly regarded theoretical scientist in the world, and the holder of the same chair as Isaac Newton at Cambridge University, followed suit and even went one step further when he said, 'In contrast with our intellect, computers double their performance every 18 months, so the danger is real that they could develop intelligence and take over the world.' He added, 'We must develop as quickly as possible technologies that make possible a direct connection between brain and computer, so that artificial brains contribute to human intelligence rather than opposing it.' He was, of course, referring to the creation of cyborgs.

Now, in 2050, as we look back to the start of the century, we can see that numerous senior scientists had, even by that time, clearly pointed to the demise of the human race at the hands of intelligent machines. Not only that but several, including Steven Hawking, had indicated that the cyborg route – upgrading the human brain with technology – was the necessary route ahead for humans. But having indicated such strong support, creating cyborgs also raised enormous ethical questions.

On the one hand there were the generally acceptable positive reasons for the introduction of implant technology to help those with a disability. Before my own implant operation in March 2002 we looked at the possibilities of alternative senses for blind people, pain removal for the long suffering and even electronic medicine. However, purely within the area of spinal-cord injuries, a whole range of possibilities existed whereby such technology could, it was felt, be of benefit. Here I feel it is worthwhile copying verbatim an email from Brian Gardner of Stoke Mandeville Hospital, forwarded to me on 1 March 2002. This is, need I tell you, a highly confidential document and under no circumstances should it be divulged to another party. He wrote:

> The human brain and spinal cord are linking structures that can be changed through stimulation. All the disabilities that spinal cord injured patients have arise from disordered nerve function. Potential benefits of the use of implant technology include, amongst others:
> 1. Re-education of the brain and spinal cord-precise and varied stimulation patterns can be applied to central and peripheral nervous tissue.
> 2. Prevention of spinal deformity.
> 3. Treatment of intractable neurogenic and other pain.
> 4. Assisting bladder emptying.
> 5. Improving bowel function.
> 6. Treatment of spasticity.
> 7. Improvement of respiratory function – assisting coughing and breathing.
> 8. Reduction of cardiovascular maleffects.
> 9. Prevention of pressure sores – for example by providing sensory feedback from denervated areas.
> 10. Improvement and restoration of sexual function.
> 11. Improved mobility.

12. Improved capability in transfers and activities of daily living, especially through improved hand, upper limb and truncal control.

When I first read this email I was in a period of depression because the 2002 operation had been delayed. But this served to spur me on and inspire me with a wave of motivation. If what I was about to do could help bring about some of these medical solutions, then what was the problem if I was delayed by a week or two?

But just as all these potential medical positives were seen in a favourable ethical light, so the idea of taking the human form and upgrading it to realize enhanced capabilities had both its ethical supporters and opposers. The supporters either felt it was necessary, due to the increasing power of intelligent machines, or quite simply felt, why not? For the opposers, there was the reality that, with part-human, part-machine brains, so cyborgs would have cyborg morals, and ethics, rather than having human morals and ethics. Whereas this would be fine for cyborgs, the opposers saw clearly that this would present a problem for those who remained human – either by choice or because the opportunity to upgrade did not present itself.

For me, at the beginning of this century, the picture was clear. If people wanted to remain human then that was up to them, no one should force them. But an evolving divide was occurring. In choosing to remain human such individuals decided to become part of a subspecies.

Looking back from 2050 we can now see that life as a cyborg is something we take for granted. It is hard for us to imagine the filth and squalor in which humans lived in the first few years of this century. It is difficult to conceive the medical problems that humans took for granted and accepted as part of everyday life. It is almost impossible to picture how humans of that time were limited in their outlook on the world.

Try to imagine if you will – and this may be difficult I know – having to communicate with one another, not by thought as we do now, but by speech. Try to picture space around you not as the multidimensional entity that we now understand, but as a three-dimensional image. It is clear to see how, with such limitations, humans regarded the speed of light as an upper limit! Try also to think about only being able to view the world around you in terms of a human's five senses. We must be truly grateful to those cyborg pioneers of the early part of this century who helped to create the intellectual, cultural, clean and medically efficient cyborg society in which we live today.

It was this picture of a future life as a cyborg that spurred me on, that drove me forward to carry out the implant experiments. And I was not disappointed by the results. I was both shocked and amazed by the results. But there again, in the summer of 2002, even I was not aware of exactly how events would run. All I knew was that when I was asked if I wanted to risk the unknown existence of cyborg life or to stay in the comfortable, but obsolete, existence of a human, my answer was exactly the same as it is now, forty-eight years later:

'I want to be a cyborg.'

BIBLIOGRAPHY

Aleksander, I., *Impossible Minds*, Imperial College Press, 1996.

Aleksander, I., *How to Build a Mind*, Weidenfeld, 2000.

Ampère A.-M., *Essai sur la philosophie des sciences, ou exposition analytique d'une classification naturelle de toutes les connaissances humaines*, 2 vols., Bachelier, Paris, 1843.

Bateson, M. C., *Our own metaphor: A personal account of a conference on the effects of conscious purpose on human adaptation*, Smithsonian, 1991.

Berkeley, G., *Three Dialogues Between Hylas and Philonous*, ed. R. M. Adams, Hackett, Indianapolis, 1979.

Branner, A., Stein, R. B. and Normann, E. A., 'Selective Stimulation of a Cat Sciatic Nerve Using an Array of Varying-length Micro electrodes', *Journal of Neurophysiology*, vol. 54, no. 4, 2001, pp. 1585–94.

Brooks, R. A., *Robot*, Allen Lane the Penguin Press, 2002.

Bundy, A., 'Letter to New Scientist', *New Scientist*, 18 September 1995.

Butlin, C. with Warwick, K., Chapman, S. and Watson, C., *Rise of the Robots*, Channel 4 Television Publishing, 2000.

Chapin, J. K. et al., 'Real time control of a robot arm using simultaneously recorded neurons in the motor cortex', *Nature Neuroscience*, vol. 2, 1999, pp. 664–70.

Chapman, J., 'Monkey Masterminds', *Daily Mail*, 16 November 2000, p. 23.

Chase, V. D., 'Seeing is Believing', *MIT Technology Review*, May/June 1999.

Clark, A., *Natural Born Cyborgs*, Oxford University Press, 2002.

Cochrane, P., *Tips for the Time Traveller*, Orion Business Books, 1997.

Crichton, M., *The Terminal Man*, Vintage, 1994.

Delgado, J. M. R. et al., 'Intercerebral radio stimulation and recording in completely free patients', *Journal of Nervous and Mental Disease*, vol. 147, 1968, pp. 329–40.

Delgado, J. M. R., *Physical Control of the mind: toward a psychocivilized society*, Harper & Row, New York, 1969.

Dotson, R. M., 'Clinical Neurophysiology Laboratory Tests to Assess the Nociceptive Systems in Humans', *Journal of Clinical Neurophysiology*, vol. 14, no. 1, 1997, pp. 32–45.

Dreyfus, H. J. and Dreyfus, S. E., 'Making a mind versus modelling the brain: Artificial Intelligence back at Branch point', in *The Philosophy of Artificial Intelligence*, ed. M. A. Boden, Oxford University Press, 1990.

Dyson, E., *Release 2.0: A design for living in the digital age*, Viking, 1997.

Dyson, G., *Darwin among the machines*, Allen Lane, 1997.

Fukuyama, F., *Our Posthuman Future*, Profile Books, 2002.

Fullick, P., *Physics*, Heinemann, 2000.

Geary, J., *The Body Electric: An anatomy of the new bionic senses*, Weidenfeld, 2002.

Gibson, W., *Neuromancer*, Ace Books, New York, 1984.

Gifford, C., *Robot*, Dorling Kindersley, 1998.

Gifford, C., *Media*, Dorling Kindersley, 1999.

Graham-Rowe, D., 'Half fish, half robot', *New Scientist*, 10 June 2000.

Grand, S., *Creation*, Orion, 2001.

Greengard, S., 'Head Start', *Wired*, vol. 5, no. 2, 1997.

Griffiths, S. (ed.), *Predictions*, Oxford University Press, 1999.

Grusky, S. T., *Silicon Sunset*, InfoNet Press, 1998.

Guiness Book of Records, Guiness Publishing Ltd, 1999.

Guiness Book of Records, Guiness Publishing Ltd, 2002, p. 178.

Haraway, D., 'A Manifesto for Cyborgs: Science, Technology and Socialist Feminism in the 1980s', *Socialist Review*, vol. 80, 1985, pp. 65–108.

Hayles, M. K., *How we became Posthuman*, University of Chicago Press, 1999.

Joy, W., 'Why the future doesn't need us', *Wired*, vol. 8, no. 4, 2000.

Karny, M., Warwick, K. and Kurkova, V. (eds.), *Dealing with complexity: a neural networks approach*, Springer, 1998.

Kennedy, P. R., Bakay, R. A. E., Moore, M. M., Adams, K. and Goldwaithe, J., 'Direct control of a computer from the human central nervous system', *IEEE Transactions on Rehabilitation Engineering*, vol. 8, no. 2, 2000, pp. 198–202.